EXPERIENCE–BASED LEARNING:

How to Make the Community Your Classroom

EXPERIENCE-BASED LEARNING:

How to Make the Community Your Classroom

Larry McClure
Sue Carol Cook
Virginia Thompson

Foreword by:
David Hampson
Chief of Career Exploration Division
Education and Work Group
National Institute of Education

Rex Hagans, Director
Education and Work Program

 Northwest Regional Educational Laboratory
710 S.W. Second Avenue
Portland, Oregon 97204

Marcia Douglas, editor

July 1977

Published by the Northwest Regional Educational Laboratory, a private nonprofit corporation. The work upon which this publication is based was performed pursuant to a contract with the National Institute of Education, Department of Health, Education and Welfare. The opinions expressed in this publication do not necessarily reflect the position or policy of the National Institute of Education, and no official endorsement by that agency should be inferred.

This publication is not printed at the expense of the Federal Government.

ISBN   0-89354-600-3

Library of Congress Catalog Card Number: 76-58219

Printed and bound in the United States of America

CONTENTS

FOREWORD

Experience-based learning combines the best elements of academic class-room learning with the test of learning by doing. It broadens the base of the classroom to make the whole community the learning environment. It places young people—at a critical stage in their personal development—in the real world alongside adults ready to treat them as peers.

Concern about the practical purposes of American education has been a constant theme since the founding of the Republic. Ben Franklin's Academy, the Morrill Act forming land grant colleges and the Smith-Hughes Act of 1917 were all indicators of this concern for pragmatic, useful education.

In recent years a number of blue ribbon panels have looked at the relation-ships of education and work. The Panel on Youth of the President's Science Advisory Committee, the National Commission on the Reform of Secondary Education and the 1971 White House Conference on Youth are but a few of those who have raised serious questions about what we are presently doing in schools.

Each of these distinguished groups has suggested that our high schools are too far removed from the adult world. They note that young people are not widely offered good developmental opportunities in the area of career decision making, and they make a number of recommendations on how the gap between education and work can be bridged.

Experience-based learning was originated several years ago to create such a bridge and help students acquire not only essential academic learning and basic skills but also lifelong learning skills and the ability to cope with new and changing situations. Originally described as Experience-Based Career Education, the techniques discussed in this book have been rigorously devel-oped and evaluated by professional educators who were fully aware of the faddish, bandwagon nature of many innovations in education. They were particularly concerned that experience-based learning stand the test of external examination. Consequently, the results of this developmental work combine the best aspects of academic and work-related education in an experiential setting.

The successful blending of academic studies with sound work experience requires a structure. Experience-based learning combines four major capabili-ties too often presented as discrete segments: (1) community involvement,

(2) individualized instruction, (3) guidance and (4) new roles for staff as managers of learning. These four components are integral to the community-centered delivery system and personalized nature of experience-based learning.

As you consider using the learning strategies described in this book, take a special look at the interactions among community people, school staff and students. These qualities perhaps more than anything else mark the success the National Institute of Education has documented in the six years of development of Experience-Based Career Education as an alternative secondary school program.

As you become familiar with these concepts I think you will agree they represent a direction for American education that will increasingly come into focus over the next few years. Experience-based learning will take its place as one of the increasing number of exciting and viable alternatives for the transition of our youth from school to work, from adolescence to adulthood.

David Hampson, Chief
Career Exploration Division
Education and Work Group
National Institute of Education
Washington, D.C.

ACKNOWLEDGMENTS

Experience-based learning is more than a dream, even though it started that way in 1971. The ideas we share in this book were actually given life by hundreds of students, parents, staff and community volunteers who are still actively involved today in an alternative way of designing curriculum and delivering instruction.

The real credit should go to the school districts and communities that were pacesetters in the techniques described here. First and foremost we wish to thank the community of Tigard, Oregon, where the original model, called Community Experiences for Career Education, Inc.—(CE)$_2$, began in 1972. Experience-based learning was given substance and reality through the tireless efforts of a dedicated (CE)$_2$ board of directors and staff, working cooperatively with the Tigard Public Schools and countless community resource people. Many other districts have since adopted the concepts pioneered in Tigard. Special recognition is given to the early adopters—Hillsboro (Oregon) Union High School District; Kennewick (Washington) Public Schools; Colville (Washington) Public Schools; Kodiak (Alaska) Public Schools; and Billings (Montana) Public Schools, all of which have generously provided us with sources of information and examples of student work for inclusion in this book.

We are proud to acknowledge the U.S. Office of Education and the National Institute of Education, where support for the developing, testing and implementation of experience-based learning has been strong. We are also grateful to the many individuals at the Northwest Regional Educational Laboratory who devoted their support and talent to the preparation of these materials.

Larry McClure
Sue Cook
Virginia Thompson

INTRODUCTION:

A MILLION WAYS
TO MAKE LEARNING REAL

> What is needed is greater diversity in
> formal education which reflects the
> actual diversity of the learning
> situations and the variety of
> experience that living in today's world
> demands.
> —*National Panel on High School
> and Adolescent Education*[1]

Remember a TV show that opened with the words, "There are a million stories in the Naked City, and this is one of them..."? We believe there are at least that many learning opportunities beyond your classroom walls, each one offering young people the chance to become actively involved in the process of education.

This book is intended to show you how off-campus learning opportunities can be opened up for students—whether you live in a metropolitan center, small city or isolated town. The procedures were developed and tested by teachers who have broadened their concept of what education is by using the community as their classroom.

What is experience-based learning? Consider the case of Sandy Ortega as an example of experience-based learning. For Sandy, the only things that really count are airplanes and the high adventure of helping people get from one place to another in the shortest possible time. How would you as Sandy's teacher capture this natural interest and turn it into productive learning? There are many alternatives:

- Excuse Sandy to visit the school library for help in locating good reading.

- Give Sandy credit for watching and reporting on a TV special on flight.
- Suggest a total class project on transportation with Sandy in charge of the airways group.
- Check out a film for Sandy on careers in the commercial airlines.
- Invite a local airline ticket agent to speak to the entire class.
- Arrange a group field trip to the airport and tour a jetliner.
- Send Sandy off campus with a prearranged learning contract or project in hand.

Each of these activities has merit and can be a valid learning experience for the right student at the right time. Yet this book is based on the premise that the *last* option—the student's personal experience in the community—can be the *best* way for many young people to learn.

Teachers know, of course, that experience-based learning doesn't just happen. It requires carefully structured activities using community resource people and their working environments as not only the setting for student learning but also the content. Although experience-based learning means that students must take a more active role in designing and carrying out their own education—gradually moving from dependence on textbooks toward more self-direction—it also requires teacher commitment. Each community's potential for providing successful learning experiences will be realized in direct proportion to the imagination, time and energy teachers apply in helping students plan individual learning activities.

There is growing support for integrating experience-based learning into education and there are many ways that experience-based learning can be accomplished. We are introducing you to *one* approach or series of activities that has been verified by five years of day-to-day use in a program developed by the National Institute of Education and the Northwest Regional Educational Laboratory.

The experience-based learning procedures described in this book are adapted from a comprehensive program called Experience-Based Career Education. The Northwest Regional Educational Laboratory and three other institutions[2] are now providing assistance to local education agencies interested in adopting this career focused, alternative program. If a full-time, community-based program is a possible next step in your school or district, we urge you to look into Experience-Based Career Education. On the other hand, if a gradual introduction to "the community as classroom" seems more workable, the experience-based learning techniques described in this book should be of real help.

This guidebook will answer six important questions:

- **How is experience-based learning different?**

  Chapter 1 defines experience-based learning, how it got started and ways you can use it with your students. Excerpts from the chapter may be particularly useful in helping you make a case for moving young people outside the school walls.

- **How do you structure experience-based learning?**

Chapter 2 suggests four tested techniques that can be used separately or in combination to help students take advantage of community resources and learn through experience:
1. *Writing a journal* is a process to help young people see how all experiences can have educational value.
2. Use of volunteer resource people to certify that students have acquired certain basic *survival skills for a changing world* helps schools tap the expertise of the community and gives young people face-to-face encounters with interested, concerned adults.
3. Enabling students to spend several hours on a *community site exploration* can open up totally new career vistas and self-awareness, as well as giving the students valuable practice in critical thinking as they complete specified exploration activities.
4. Carefully planned *learning projects* can be developed from the daily activities of adults at community sites and related to students' individual interests and needs. These site-related projects are the heart of a full-blown experiential learning program.

- **How can you link community resources with student projects?**

Chapter 3 suggests ways to analyze off-campus resources for the learning potential they can provide.

- **How do you write student projects?**

Chapter 4 describes a step-by-step procedure for planning project activities based on learning opportunities in the community and writing these activities into learning agreements among students, staff and community resource people.

- **How do you locate resource people and involve them in experience-based learning?**

Chapter 5 will help you locate appropriate community sites and prepare resource people for their roles in experience-based learning.

- **How do you manage the process?**

Chapter 6 offers suggestions for administering experience-based activities in which students are following individual schedules in the community.

FOOTNOTES

[1]National Panel on High School and Adolescent Education, *The Education of Adolescents* (Washington, D.C.: U.S. Department of Health, Education and Welfare, 1976), p. 8.

[2]Appalachia Educational Laboratory, Charleston, West Virginia; Far West Laboratory for Educational Research and Development, San Francisco, California; Research for Better Schools, Philadelphia, Pennsylvania.

1

DEFINING
EXPERIENCE-BASED LEARNING

> ...students can learn about their community
> and about humanity only outside the
> classroom. In the classroom they can, with
> the help of their teachers and peers, examine,
> analyze, even celebrate what they've
> discovered and compare their findings with
> those of others; but they must have the world
> outside the classroom as the primary
> motivation for learning, and at the heart and
> soul of what they learn.
>
> —*Foxfire 2*[1]

SEVEN CHARACTERISTICS

If you were to talk to students involved in experience-based learning programs today, you would find them growing in seven important ways:

1. Learning how to learn
2. Learning about life
3. Learning about careers
4. Learning about themselves
5. Learning to be responsible
6. Learning about others
7. Learning by doing

While these seven characteristics are certainly not new to education, they have been given greater emphasis in the experiential activities you are about to consider.

Learning How to Learn

> Never have I seen our daughter put so much of herself into school work, seen her so involved with math, science, government and her rights as a citizen.
>
> —*Parent*

> We personally feel that it's a new and wonderful alternative...where you get all the 3 Rs and a practical application of what you're learning in a work-related experience. A real boon to the student who has a good mind but needs more than an 8 a.m. to 2 p.m. classroom situation.
>
> —*Parent*

> It's the first time I've really looked forward to school. By the end of the year I will have done more work than in my two previous years combined.
>
> —*Student*

Experience-based learning emphasizes everyone's need for lifelong practice in the basic tools of learning—reading, writing, speaking, analyzing, asking questions, computing, finding resources, solving problems. These process skills help the learner become self-reliant and confident to pursue independent goals: in short, equipped to enter a life of continued growth and learning.

Students in experience-based learning begin to see how knowledge is integrated when applied in the real world. Since subjects such as reading, human relations, speech, mathematics, physics, geography and psychology are not separate domains for the design engineer planning a new hospital complex, neither should they be for the high school student. While students in experience-based learning engage regularly in actual tasks that apply learned skills in a realistic, integrated fashion, they are also encouraged to analyze these tasks to see the common applications of various basic skills.

Students in experience-based activities learn how to apply fundamental principles and, perhaps most important, where to find more information when they need it. This ability to find what they need gives young people a feeling of competence and is an essential skill for lifelong learning.

Experience-based learning emphasizes *processes*. For example, students are required to learn and practice the process of scientific investigation, but they may choose the areas in which they apply scientific methods. A student may select plant biology, astronomy, geography or even some area not usually associated with the content area of science and then use scientific methods of investigation to probe specific issues of interest or concern. Similarly, students learn a critical thinking method of problem solving and apply it to special problems they want to solve. By practicing processes such as scientific inquiry and critical thinking, they not only acquire lifelong learning skills but also begin to understand what these processes really mean.

Learning About Life

> I wish you could see students' faces light
> up when I ask them if they enjoy the
> program. It almost makes me sad when they
> tell me they are getting turned on to
> learning for the first time. They seem
> to be discovering that our generation
> isn't so bad either, which is only fair
> since we are discovering the same about
> them.
>
> —*Resource Person*

Experience-based learning puts students in touch with everyday experiences and a variety of people. Students get a firsthand view of the ways people cope with their surroundings and apply what they learn to the daily requirements of living—from solving problems to keeping physically and mentally fit.

Survival in today's complex world means more than just earning a living. Students need to know how to use their earning power wisely, get along with other people, exercise their rights as citizens, appreciate the rich cultural heritage of humanity, use leisure time and adapt to change. These are some of the life skills that will make adulthood more satisfying.

Learning About Careers

> Students get a keen insight into the inner
> workings of a business. It's not just a
> tour of the building, it's a personal
> involvement for the student.
>
> —*Resource Person*

> ...at the hospital, I was able to work with
> the children and give them baths. I kept
> the medicine room in order and made sure
> they had supplies. I saw how nurses
> performed their duties. At the Open Door
> Clinic, I learned how to fill out
> examination forms. I took blood pressure
> and learned the names of the instruments.
> All of this has given me opportunities I
> really needed and wanted.
>
> —*Student*

Career development, in its broadest sense, means "what do I do with my life?" Decisions in this area raise other questions: How much education do I need? What dealings will I have with other people? What satisfactions do I want from my work? What skills can I develop? What level of income do I hope to have? How do I change careers?

Students involved in community experiences learn that the timing of career decisions may differ from person to person. They will know this by experience, not just from a file of occupational information but from rubbing shoulders with a variety of people who have made career decisions in many different ways and with varying degrees of satisfaction. By encountering a number of careers, even in one job cluster, students will recognize the need for adaptability and flexibility in coping with future changes both within themselves and in the working world.

Students in experience-based learning are constantly matching facts about themselves with the reality of career choices: Do I want to spend seven years in college to be a lawyer? Do I know enough about plane geometry to do drafting? How much can I accomplish by visiting another community site?

Learning About Themselves

> With no peer pressures, the students can
> really get involved in a serious learning
> situation in which they see concrete results.
> This feeling of success is a first for many of
> them. The focus is on helping them to
> succeed, not on meeting unrealistic class
> standards.
>
> —*Resource Person*

Self-confidence is difficult to teach from a textbook. Experience-based learning tries to place students in situations that help them understand themselves, gaining confidence from their strengths and understanding their weaknesses as they grow in their abilities to absorb new experiences and to change.

Students involved in experience-based learning are challenged to reach out and take hold of many new types of learning resources. They begin to use a wide range of information about themselves from standardized measures, informal assessments and face-to-face interaction with staff and resource people. Students discover that they are not treated like children. They also discover that guidance is available at every turn to help them expand their horizons and potential as they move toward adulthood.

Learning to Be Responsible

> We feel it is really important to build positive, trusting relationships with students. This gives students confidence in you and forms a good basis for negotiation as time goes on. Students can accept firmer treatment regarding requirements if they basically believe in you and themselves.
>
> *—Teacher*

> We like the flexibility and freedom and the idea that the students are responsible for completing their work by certain dates although it's up to them to work out their daily schedules. We feel that is especially important if they plan on college.
>
> *—Parent*

Experience-based learning places responsibility for learning directly with individual students. They get practice in planning, making decisions and negotiating and evaluating their own tailor-made learning plans with immediate help from professional staff. Requirements and deadlines are specified and scheduling assistance is provided as an aid to students as they plan reasonable targets for accomplishing program work.

Students and staff define the limits and consequences of student behavior, and students are held accountable for their actions. Students learn to meet expectations, whether their own set of interests, needs and wants; graduation requirements; or particular site regulations.

Learning About Others

> With John's new interest in learning, he is meeting and talking with new people about new ideas and has found they are genuinely interested in what he has to say. The more he learns, the more he wants to know; the more he sees what he needs to know, the more confident he feels in the adult world.
>
> *—Teacher*

Experience-based learning makes the community the classroom; for example, an optometrist may explain lens refraction as part of a student's project, a bank official may certify a student's competency in certain credit transactions and a union official may discuss labor problems with a student group. In the process of sharing information, community resource people also provide models for some basic human skills that young people want and need.

Students using the community as their classroom become acquainted with a greater variety of adults than their counterparts in regular programs. Even though professional staff still play a strong role in the learning activities of experience-based education, these activities give the students plenty of room to learn from interacting with community resource people, as well as their peers. Resource people say they learn a lot, too—about their jobs and about young people, including positive qualities they may not have recognized before.

Learning by Doing

> Experience-based learning is great because students learn by doing, not just by reading about how something is done.
>
> —*Parent*

> This has given our son a real desire to learn—not just handing in an assignment on Thursday for a test on Friday, but gaining insight into what he needs to know to attain his own goals.
>
> —*Parent*

Students learn the skills expected of all high school graduates by *using* those skills in real situations. Rather than simply learning theories in the classroom, each student applies those theories to career-related problem solving.

Experience-based learning capitalizes on all sensory experiences: seeing the face of a client in the public defender's office, hearing the roar of a catalytic furnace, feeling the smoothness of a carefully ground lens, smelling the results of a laboratory test, tasting the quality of a chocolate eclair. Such firsthand experiences provide the framework for student explorations and projects undertaken at community learning sites.

The synthesis of experiences into a systematic learning plan is the curriculum in experience-based learning. Outcomes are generally measured by performance. Grades are de-emphasized in favor of records that reflect actual accomplishments.

WHY THESE CHARACTERISTICS ARE IMPORTANT

To demonstrate how experience-based learning techniques can extend and increase student involvement and interest in education, let's consider again the case of Sandy Ortega, mentioned in the Introduction. Remember that Sandy is interested in commercial flying and its growing influence on society. Imagine you are Sandy's teacher, following a traditional approach to education:

1. You plan a class unit on transportation, including air travel.
2. You bring pictures from the library to illustrate a discussion of the evolution of air transportation.
3. You show an action-oriented film on the air freight industry, which emphasizes how passenger jets can be converted to carry cargo at night.
4. You assign an essay on "Our Shrinking World."
5. Then Sandy tells you about visiting the airport to pick up an aunt and watching the crews prepare aircraft and load passengers.
6. For the entire class's benefit, you ask Sandy to interpret a map of the terminal that was available at the airport information desk.
7. You give a quiz on air transportation trends.
8. The rest of the class moves on to rail and trucking units while Sandy is still interested in airlines.
9. You and Sandy talk about the possibility of advanced study in particular areas of interest.
10. Sandy signs up for a roundtable session on careers in the airlines at the school's annual "Plan Your Future Day."

Sandy's motivation level in relation to these activities might look like Fig. 1-1:

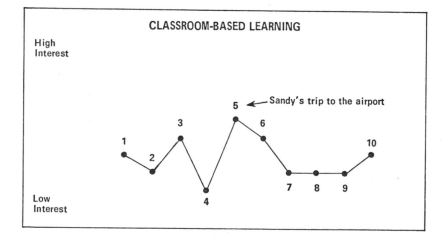

Figure 1-1. Sandy's motivation level in school.

At this point, you decide to try some experience-based learning techniques to see if there isn't a better way to turn Sandy's interest into something productive:

1. You call the airline office to arrange for Sandy to explore some specific jobs—airline pilot, flight attendant and so forth. That looks difficult to do right away, but somebody mentions that many travel agents are former airline employees. So you call a travel bureau.

2. Other teachers and the principal agree that Sandy can be excused to explore the travel bureau for a day and a half.

3. At your suggestion as part of the exploration, Sandy's parents arrange a $5 flight over the city through a local charter service to give Sandy a taste of flying.

4. Sandy completes a record of the exploration activities and discusses the experience with you. Based on Sandy's exploration and talks with former airline employees, you and Sandy discuss a variety of careers available in the air transportation business, including passenger agent and traffic controller.

5. Another exploration is set up, this time with the airlines so Sandy can find out firsthand about passenger scheduling and air terminal operations.

Sandy's motivation level for these activities might look like Fig. 1-2:

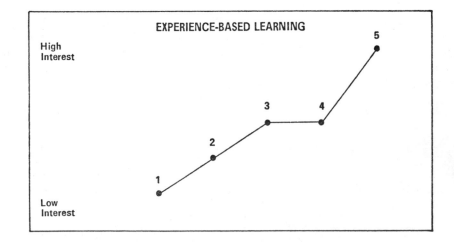

Figure 1-2. Sandy's motivation level out in the community.

At this point Sandy may want to know more about a specific occupation —traffic controller, for example. You could then plan a more in-depth learning activity for Sandy—a student project structured around the skills and knowledge needed by traffic controllers. This would be one more way of using the community as a learning resource.

A RESPECTED TRADITION

Experience-based learning acknowledges two things: (1) textbooks cannot contain all there is to be learned today and (2) real events have high motivational value for learning. The authors of *Foxfire 2* put it this way:

> ...more rewarding and significant things happen to kids outside the classroom: falling in love, climbing a mountain, rapping for hours with an adult who is loved or respected, building a house, seeing a part of the world never seen before, coming to some deep personal empathy with a kid from another background and culture, or genuinely understanding some serious community or national problem.[2]

If Maslow could observe experience-based learning activities today, he would be amazed at how his visions for education proposed in *Psychology of Science* have moved from theory to practice:

> My thesis is that experiential knowledge is prior to verbal-conceptual knowledge but that they are hierarchically integrated and need each other. No human being dare specialize too much in either kind of knowing. The two kinds of knowledge are necessary to each other and under good circumstances can be and should be intimately integrated with each other.[3]

Dewey, too, would be pleased to see the way students today are learning through direct community involvement. In *Experience and Education,* he warned that subject matter should never be kept in watertight compartments and isolated from the actual conditions of life.

The *Foxfire 2* authors add that off-campus experiences motivate students—

> ...to want to be able to write correctly and forcefully, or want to know history, or want to understand the complexities of nature and man through biology, botany, psychology, anthropology or physics. But we too often ignore these events, seeing them as "irrelevant" or "froth." Until they are acknowledged as important and relevant to the student's existence, all (the student) does inside (the classroom) walls is doomed to seem meaningless and without reason. What we must realize is that the walls of those buildings we imprison kids in now must come crashing down, and the world must be their classroom, the classroom a reflection of their world. The two must work as one.[4]

Phi Delta Kappa's *The New Secondary Education* underscores the need for experience-based learning and raises the critical issue of planning as an essential part of this kind of learning:

> All the analyses of a Shakespearean play in a book cannot replace the experience of attending a fine production, nor can ground training reconstruct the experience of actual solo flight. But just any experience will not do. Just as there are strategies of formal learning, so there are strategies of experience. The basic relevant qualities are appropriateness, intensity and preparation.[5]

That last point is important. Just because students have interesting experiences is no assurance these experiences are educationally valid.

No one should ever say teaching will be any easier because of experience-based learning. Enlisting and maintaining community volunteers and individualizing some of the learning experiences take a lot of time, and teachers' work days are already full. If you become interested in trying some of the processes described in this book, we suggest two major ways of gaining the necessary time and flexibility:

1. Find another teacher who wants to try experience-based learning with you and pool your classes. This gives you some flexibility in varying the groupings of your students and allows one of you to do the necessary community work to line up resource people and supervise student learning activities in the community.

2. Involve students actively in planning learning activities and locating learning resources. As you prepare for your classes, get in the habit of asking yourself, "Could the students be doing this planning?" Involving the students in this kind of curriculum planning and teaching can be an excellent learning experience for them.

Those who use experience-based learning techniques daily agree that it opens entirely new horizons for students and faculty alike. Yet, as the orchestrator of *Foxfire's* version of experience-based learning observes, teachers' responsibilities are often much greater than in conventional programs: "For one thing, it demands that you be ready for the unpredictable, for each (student's) experiences out there are going to differ, as will their responses to them."[6]

Experience-based learning requires the skills of enlightened educators and volunteers from community sites. It also asks students to take a more active role in the design and synthesis of their own education, gradually moving away from dependence on textbooks and grades toward self-directed learning and demonstrated performance. But the benefits of experience-based learning more than compensate for the efforts required to plan and carry out such programs. Not only do the facilities, equipment, materials and expertise available in the community far exceed those a school can reasonably provide, but students will gain a reality base for learning that will serve them the rest of their lives.

MAKING ROOM IN YOUR CURRICULUM

Experience-based learning can be incorporated into existing school programs in a variety of ways, including combining field experiences with course work or with extracurricular activities. Gradually moving students into the community is often preferable to an abrupt change from the traditional structure. Here are some ways experience-based programs are being integrated.

Traditional Required Courses

Teachers in courses like science, English, history, mathematics, health or physical education often release students for independent field work to supplement or replace ongoing classroom activities. The experience-based learning activities described in this book are ready-made tools that will fit even the most traditional course outlines.

Elective Courses

Under titles like "alternative futures" or "community internships," more and more schools are offering new elective courses that specialize in using off-campus resources. In these courses, students may be involved in such activities as recording the cultural history of their community by writing and publishing their own magazine or examining how water resources affect our habitat. Experience-based learning strategies can be used to enhance the built-in flexibility these elective activities offer.

Minicourses

Many districts offer three- or four-week minicourse options to balance regular semester or quarter course work. Students in these courses get short doses of hands-on experience in areas of special interest. Much of this can and should occur in the field, providing another way to introduce experience-based learning.

Occupational Exploration Classes

Thanks to federal, state and local initiatives in career development, junior and senior high youth often have opportunities for career explorations in the community accompanied by classroom preparation and followup. Experience-based learning strategies can help staff plan these explorations with students and ensure the best possible educational outcomes.

Independent Learning Opportunities

In schools that foster independent learning, students can be encouraged to keep written journals and share them regularly with staff correspondents. This process can help students develop feelings of trust in the adults with whom they correspond. It can also help students become more skilled in self-reflection. The community certification process which is becoming popular in competency-based programs can also be offered as a supplement to the regular school curriculum. Such a process might be coordinated from a central library or satellite resource center. Individualized projects planned to meet specified curriculum objectives can give students a firm guide for research and learning while still allowing plenty of room for flexibility. (These processes—journal writing, community certification and individualized projects —are described more fully in Chap. 2.)

Extracurricular Activities

School organizations like Thespians, Future Farmers of America, Distributive Education Clubs of America and Quill and Scroll as well as activities like Junior Achievement and Exploring are ideally patterned for experience-based learning, particularly when regular school credit can be given if students and teachers justify it in advance.

Schools Without Walls

Many districts have made it possible for groups of students to shift their studies from the classroom to community locations where the facilities and expertise already exist. However, these school-without-walls programs do not always provide opportunities for community resource people and students to negotiate learning activities together—an important element in experience-based learning. Experience-based learning strategies also provide for the integration of different subjects and help students expand their career interests.

Vocational Education

If cooperative work experience or other vocational education programs are offered in your school, experience-based learning techniques can be added as introductory or supplementary activities to help students take full advantage of the community exposure they will receive.

Magnet Schools

Some cities are developing magnet schools which offer students the opportunity to choose a program that meets their individual needs and interests. Each of these magnet schools might incorporate some experience-based learning options or one campus might be devoted entirely to the use of community resources as the primary vehicle for instruction. In either case, faculty would become facilitators of individualized student learning plans, using the vast resources of the community and its many natural instructors as the learning base.

Free Schools

Alternative schools sometimes fail because of poorly designed learning strategies, shaky accountability structures, inadequate attention to public relations and too little orientation for staff, students and parents. The experience-based learning techniques discussed in this book can help alternative schools avoid some of these difficulties while still nurturing the independent learning so valuable to students.

Open Concept Schools

The free flow of ideas that can occur when students are no longer physically confined within classroom walls still requires channels to regulate the flow of activities. Experience-based learning techniques capitalize on the interdisciplinary nature of community life but still provide some structure to the learning, including monitoring and documenting student performance.

Schools Within Schools

Even though there may be a common roof over students' heads or one large campus to call home, some districts are advocating a series of options for young people within a single institution. In such a setting, experience-based learning might be offered as a complete alternative—a school within the school emphasizing community studies, integrated curriculum and the application of basic skills.

Flexibly Scheduled Schools

As secondary schools try out new ways of organizing the daily schedule into variable time units, they often seek new curriculum patterns to give students increased responsibility for managing time. The materials and procedures offered by experience-based learning are most effective when students are required to plan time and resources carefully. In fact, the optimum use of community resources *requires* flexible scheduling so students can be on community sites at the convenience of the resource people and for amounts of time dictated by the learning activities themselves.

Continuation Schools

For students who have difficulties attending regular school, some districts offer special programs geared to individual needs—often available at night, enabling students to hold regular jobs by day. Experience-based learning can be used to provide direct ties between classroom theories and practical experience without relying on outdated textbooks and lectures.

Programs for Gifted and Talented

Experience-based learning strategies offer unique ways to enhance the curriculum for gifted students. They can give these students a reality base for their learning and put them in touch with community experts in a variety of fields. Experience-based learning also gives gifted and talented students the means to pursue their own interests and abilities as far as they can, yet still be within a structured sequence of learning activities that can be documented for future reference.

Senior Year Options

For students who complete graduation requirements early yet still want to maintain school ties, experience-based learning provides a mechanism for extending their educational programs along entirely new dimensions, perhaps with emphasis on independent study opportunities.

WHAT YOU WILL GAIN

Experience-based learning can bring to you and your students a new excitement about what education is, how it should occur and where it can happen. Experience-based learning—

1. Stresses the acquisition of *process skills* to equip an individual to be a lifelong learner.
2. Specifies what *learning objectives* must be met at community sites, then provides ways to monitor the achievements of each objective rather than expecting that students will learn simply by being off-campus.
3. Offers a *variety* of activities to choose from in planning learning rather than only a few options as the student tries to fulfill school requirements.
4. Provides *staff assistance* to students as they plan, evaluate and consider the implications of what they read, see and do rather than having common expectations for all students with very little time

for individual negotiation and follow-through.

5. Derives *curriculum objectives* in a carefully structured way to make sure credit will be equivalent to regular school requirements rather than considering the community site work as incidental to the standard curriculum and not of full educational value.

6. Focuses on what *adults* do and how they can actually teach young people rather than casting adults merely as tour guides.

7. Provides *opportunities* for students to make important choices as they are ready for them rather than assuming that all life choices will be made sometime in the future.

8. Helps students understand how each community site experience *relates* to other experiences rather than considering a site experience as an end in itself.

9. Asks students to *direct* their own learning after agreeing that the proposed activities are worth doing rather than telling students what they are supposed to learn, when and how.

10. Examines every *community site* for the curriculum content it offers rather than imposing a traditional curriculum structure on the sites.

11. Responds to the *individual needs* of each learner rather than offering standardized fare for all students to follow.

However you choose to adapt experience-based learning techniques, the ideas that follow should be helpful. Consider the four basic techniques outlined in Chapter 2—student journals, community certification of survival skills, community explorations and student projects—to see what might fit your situation. Perhaps you and your colleagues are already doing similar things with students. If so, maybe we can add to what you have already developed. If not, we offer ideas for you to try. Experience-based learning will serve your students for the rest of their lives.

FOOTNOTES

[1]Eliot Wigginton, ed., *Foxfire 2* (Garden City, New York: Anchor Books, Anchor/Doubleday, 1973), p. 5.

[2]*Foxfire 2*, p. 126.

[3]Abraham H. Maslow, *Psychology of Science* (New York: Harper & Row, Inc., 1966), pp. 46-47, 49.

[4]*Foxfire 2*, p. 126.

[5]Maurice Gibbons, *The New Secondary Education* (Bloomington, Indiana: Phi Delta Kappa, Inc., 1976), p. 54.

[6]*Foxfire 2*, p. 5.

2

STRUCTURING
EXPERIENCE-BASED LEARNING

> Learning is still incomplete until a third
> dimension has been added to concrete
> experience and formal study. This
> dimension, often omitted in school though
> essential to mastery, is productive
> activity: applying experience and studies
> in an activity yielding a product of worth
> to the student—an idea, a song, a building,
> a critique, a garden, a pilot's license, or
> a service.
> —*The New Secondary Education*[1]

The transition of youth from comfortable classrooms into the world as an educational resource is not always easy. Consequently, you may want to introduce off-campus experiences in stages to build school district and student confidence in this new style of teaching and learning. Students accustomed to class schedules, tests at the end of every unit and other kinds of traditional structure may need a gradual introduction to the new responsibility that experiental learning requires.

There are at least four important components of experience-based learning you might try: student journals, community certification of survival skills, community explorations and student projects. These activities are being used together or as individual strategies in many school districts today. They can be infused into ongoing instructional programs or combined into a total alternative to classroom instruction.

STUDENT JOURNALS

As more and more schools recognize the value of students going out into the community for many of their learning experiences, having students keep a personal journal can become a valuable tool for regular communication between staff and students. The journal can serve as a kind of two-way diary, allowing staff and students to keep in touch with each other on a regular basis over an extended period of time. Each student should write to a regular correspondent—a teacher, counselor or other adult who can help the student gain perspective and learn more about the art of communicating.

What Students Write About and Why

A journal is one of the best ways to help students begin a lifetime of learning using everyday happenings as the starting point. Journal writing is generally used in community-based programs because it encourages students to reflect on the meaning of their experiences. It works well in classroom settings, too, for the same reason. The process is helpful if you believe young people can learn about *themselves* from activities as diverse as watching television, reading magazines, talking with friends, visiting with a grandparent or playing soccer.

Practitioners of experience-based learning believe there is something to be learned in almost any activity if students gain skills in tying their experiences together. That's where feedback from a concerned adult—a correspondent—comes in. The journal is not only a record of experience but a guidance tool, enabling staff and student together to compare the student's changing opinions, interests, attitudes and values over a period of time. While the journal approach cannot substitute for other teaching/learning modes, it can point out how learning is a total process requiring all our senses.

Helping Students Write Journals

A journal writing guide can be used to orient students to the process and can serve as a reference through the year. Such a guide should identify the journal's basic purposes, give examples of student writing and state program or class requirements for completing journals. Figure 2-1 is a sample page from such a guide. This sample indicates the kind of information that can help students gain introspection about the events in their lives.

Review journal writing guidelines with students and read facsimile entries to help students understand the kinds of entries they can write. (See Fig. 2-2, page 24, as an example of journal writing guidelines.)

Exercises to help students start writing are helpful orientation activities—for example, free association games, make-believe letters or jotting down ideal characteristics of a journal correspondent. One way to help those

Getting Down To Writing

Remember, what is important is to share ideas, work out your thoughts or create. The journal is not so much a point-by-point description of your daily activities as how you think and feel about them. For example, don't just limit yourself to saying:

I overslept this morning and missed my bus so I was late to school. Mr. Lyon chewed me out because I missed my appointment with that metal sculptor we'd arranged for me to interview. It was just an all around rotten day, but tonight Jan and I went out for pizza and talked til midnight so I feel better about life tonight. But I'm sleepy. So that's it for tonight.

You see? You already know what you did. Put the events of your life in a context of thinking and feeling, evaluate them a little bit. Did the experience change you, affect you in some way or give you a special insight? How do you feel about the situation? What do you think about it? What effects do you predict the experience will have on your future actions? Learn from what you write. The journal will inform you only to the degree that you inform it. Discover what is interesting to you by writing it down. Concentrate on your reactions, your observations and your judgments about what's happening to you.

Figure 2-1. Helping students know what to write in their journals. (From *Student Guide to Writing a Journal*. Portland, Oregon: Northwest Regional Educational Laboratory, 1977, p. 3.)

students who freeze before writing might be to ask them first to use a tape recorder to talk to their correspondent and then simply transcribe what they've said.

The actual format of student journals can vary. Many programs ask students to keep their journals on regular notebook paper in a three-ring binder. In other instances, a stenographer's pad with lines down the middle of each page serves as a handy way to separate student and correspondent comments. No matter how students decide to organize their entries, it is important that journals have continuity and be more than just a collection of separate sheets of paper.

Setting Expectations

When adopting the journal strategy, you should establish requirements that can be reasonably met by students and correspondents alike. Some programs or classes using the journal strategy ask students to make daily entries; others ask for weekly entries. The choice may hinge on how much time you have to read and respond to the journals. If you adopt the journal process described here, consider staff work loads and how many journals can be given full attention on a weekly basis.

More important than the *amount* of journal writing is the issue of *what* the students write. Even though it sounds vague, some staff correspondents have found it useful to specify merely that students must write about "something that really matters to them." If they feel students are writing superficially, then they discuss this reaction with students in order to help them start using the journal as it is intended. Success of the journal hinges on students learning to communicate thoughts and feelings over an extended period of time.

Identifying Correspondents

Try involving several staff in the journal technique. Giving students a chance to write to an adult with whom they feel comfortable is important in experience-based learning. Involving other teachers also facilitates the journal's use as an integrating tool, particularly if those teachers are responsible for different subject areas.

Staff soon discover that journals offer an unusual vehicle for building their own awareness and sensitivity. Correspondents must be committed to the purposes of the journal and be willing to put some effort into making them work. Building trust relationships is not an automatic activity; staff and students both must take time and energy to write, respond to and follow through on journal entries. Also, they must feel positive enough about the journal to be honest about themselves and their feelings. While special training is certainly not necessary, some interpersonal skills (for example, feedback strategies like paraphrasing and describing one's own feelings) are often used by successful correspondents.

Responding to Student Journals

Encourage students to stretch their imaginations in their journal writing. You want them to learn to express accurately the things that are happening to them and their important feelings. Keep in mind, however, that correspondents should not be directing students but rather helping them to be themselves. Weigh the timing and appropriateness of suggestions carefully to avoid sermonizing. One well-chosen question can often be worth 1,000 words of advice.

Students will be writing about themselves in relation to community and school experiences. They should think about *integrating experiences, self-awareness and career development*. The following are issues and questions in these three areas that you as a correspondent might stress as you respond to students and encourage them in the journal writing process. (Your responses can be conveyed both in writing and in discussion with the student.)

Integrating experiences. An important part of experience-based learning is helping young people gain the ability to perceive relationships among interests, abilities and things they are doing now, both in school and out of school. Following are some typical notations that might help students increase their ability to integrate experiences:

- What did that experience mean to you? Could you do something about it if you had more skills? What skills?

- You don't seem to like the precision your mathematics teacher asks from you, yet you are interested in studying social sciences in college. That field calls for careful attention to details (research and statistics, for example). Perhaps you should think more closely about why you rebel against being precise.

- I gather you don't like the reading you do in literature class, yet you are full of stories about your life that make great reading for me. Why do you think you don't like to read stories but do like to tell them?

- Have you noticed how well you seem to handle situations with people? Have you thought about ways to polish your personal skills? What do you suppose you could do with these skills in the future?

- You have great dreams but you hop all around when it's time to make choices about classes. Why is that?

- You like carpentry with your neighbor but you can't stand it in your shop course. Think you just like working with your neighbor no matter what?

Self-awareness. You can help students be open and direct in their journals by being equally straightforward in your responses. The simplest way to encourage self-awareness is to be honestly critical of things you find hard to believe and share personal experiences which illustrate your own growth in self-understanding and honesty.

Helping others learn to look inward is an art. You must be willing to go on hunches; poke a little and see what happens. But be careful. You are not a psychotherapist; you are simply trying to give realistic feedback. In short, everything done with the journal should in some way help students increase their skills of self-reflection.

Example:

> *That was quite a journal entry, Anne. If it was an accurate picture of your week, I'm concerned. I get the feeling nothing interests you, that you'd rather be somewhere else doing something else. Do you really feel that way? What can we do together to improve the situation? Next time would you tell me about the work you've been doing and the people you know who could help you get more interested in what you're doing? I really want to know you better but I need your help.*

Avoid responses like "OK," "doing fine," or "keep it up" but try instead to focus on something specific in the entry itself: "Your words are telling me one thing but the experiences you describe suggest there's more. Didn't that person's actions bother you at all?" Pick up on apparently casual comments and lead the exchange into more subtle kinds of observation.

Career development. If you believe that everything we do in our lives can have career-related overtones, then you will want to help students think through their personal interests and lifestyle preferences as these factors relate to work environments. Help them see how their present experiences already require them to make important daily choices and that events, activities and environments they are encountering have direct impact on the quality and content of their lives, now and in the future.

Watch out for your own biases, though, including responses that imply any kind of sex stereotyping. You may be responding in ways that indicate a difference in career possibilities for females or males and not even know it. Avoid channeling students into careers; instead urge them to consider a variety of possibilities and to develop the habits of self-analysis and critical thinking necessary to match themselves with career options. Questions like these may help students get started on systematic career development:

- What are you interested in doing? What kinds of jobs seem to fit your skills now (or skills you could develop)? Do you know anyone already doing those kinds of things? Someone you know or read about?

- What do you think might happen to your other interests if you spent a lot of time working at that particular one? If you took a job like that what would it mean to your free time? Do you see yourself raising a family? Could you raise a family if you had that lifestyle? Would you want your kids to pursue those kinds of dreams?

- Do you like having free time? What do you think you'd do if you had all the free time in the world?

- You sound as if you don't like people telling you what to do. What if you were working? Does it make a difference if you're getting paid to do what someone tells you?

- I gather you like working with animals. Do you want to do that for a living? What kinds of jobs do you think you could get? Would they satisfy your other interests? Do you think you could cope with the same routine every day? Have you thought about wildlife management? Or being a veterinarian? Let's talk about these possibilities sometime.

Effective journal responses. Be careful about using journal entries as a basis for teaching writing or grammar. If red-penciling grammatical mistakes or making writing assignments becomes the top priority, journals lose their effectiveness as a way to keep in touch with students and for students to keep in touch with themselves. That is not to say journals cannot be used to improve a student's writing skills; in fact, students will often request such feedback on their journals, particularly if they are having difficulty saying something that's important to them.

Correspondents can point out weaknesses in writing indirectly through comments such as, "I can really sympathize with what you are trying to say but I'm not sure that I completely understand what you wrote here," thereby laying the groundwork for a talk about writing skills based on the student's perception of a real need. By encouraging students to put some effort into being accurate about what they are saying, correspondents can help students take pride in their ideas and opinions.

Remember, the regular activity of formulating, organizing and expressing ideas builds self-understanding as well as communication abilities. It is a means of organizing feelings and thoughts that might otherwise remain vague and formless. You don't have to be trained as a writing instructor to encourage students to do this. What is important is that the correspondent respond to the student's expressed intent and meaning rather than judge written style or content.

Example:

> *I am a little bewildered by your last journal entry. I tried to piece together the drawings and the words and I have seen the model you are building, but I need more help understanding what you mean. How about writing it out for me another way? Or bring in your plans sometime and explain them to me. We could tape-record your explanation, then let you hear the difference between your writing and speaking.*

Discussing Journal Entries in Person

Personal conferences are one way to keep track of the journal process. Students' problems with journals can range from laziness to hesitations about

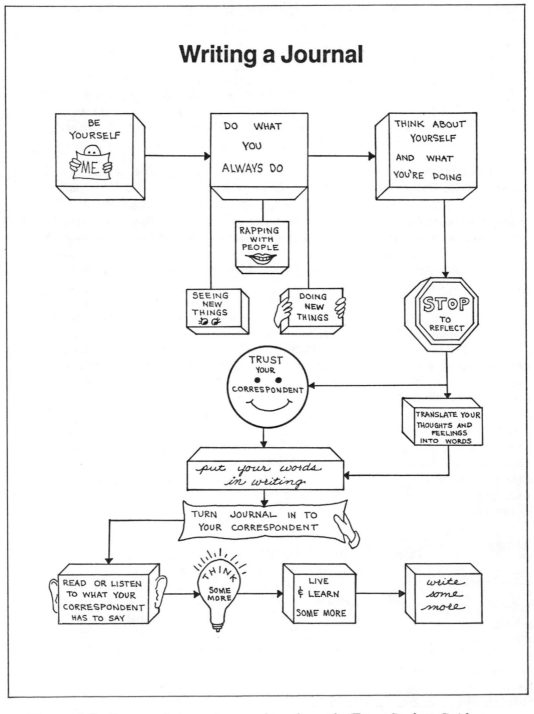

Figure 2-2. Steps to help students write a journal. (From *Student Guide to Writing a Journal*, p. 16.)

self-expression in any form. Difficulties will not be limited strictly to students, either, and staff members must be honest enough to recognize when their own attitude toward the journal or a particular student is causing the trouble. Sit-down conferences can help staff become better acquainted with students and initiate productive counseling interactions. While conferences should not take the place of written comments, they should definitely be considered as part of the journal process.

Meetings with students about their journals may take several forms. Most often, student and correspondent will simply stop for a few minutes and talk about an item of particular interest, enlarging on comments that have been written on the entry. On occasion, entries will suggest a serious personal problem or reveal a talent or capability which the student may have taken for granted. The correspondent or the student may then want to schedule a meeting for more discussion.

Conferences need not be long and do not have to happen on a regular basis. In fact, conferences can be as simple as stopping in the hall for a few minutes to talk with the student and add that extra dimension of face-to-face interaction to the journal relationship. Correspondents should avoid becoming pen pals who never see their students on a personal level.

If a student has been forgetting to make journal entries, a meeting between the student and correspondent can give the two a chance to talk about what's been happening. Such a meeting can be positive, particularly if the correspondent doesn't look backwards but instead says to the student, "Let's count this conference as make-up for the entries you've missed. We spent a lot of time going over some pretty important issues and that's what journals are all about." If you feel the student should make up past entries, try asking the student to do an hour or two of monologue on a tape recorder instead of actually writing entries. Or, suggest that the student write a paper about something personally important. If writing itself is a problem, suggest that this time the student try expressing something nonverbally—through a drawing or photograph, for instance.

Ensuring Confidentiality

Correspondents should not share the contents of journal entries either by showing an entry or discussing it with others unless the student agrees beforehand. This helps the student feel more confident about dealing with adults on a trust basis. In a sense journals are privileged communications and should not be used to assess student behavior or point out wrongdoing.

Information about a student's personal life is always a delicate issue. On one hand, such information can be valuable in guiding a student's personal development. On the other hand, misuse of personal information can cause the student to lose respect for the correspondent and even experience serious setbacks in self-confidence.

Changing Correspondents

A decision to change correspondents should not be left completely up to the student. It is not easy for a young person to say, "I don't like you, I can't open up with you; I want another correspondent." Correspondents must be sensitive enough to recognize when a student is having trouble and introduce the subject in a nonthreatening fashion. The conversation can begin as simply as, "I don't feel that we are getting anywhere in your journal. Want to talk about it?"

Example:

> *Dick, I'm trying to figure out what you really meant in your last journal entry. Your tone sounded joking, but I think you may be serious. Would you rather write your journal to Mr. Gentry? Tell me what's bothering you. We can make some changes if you want.*

Frequent changes will prevent the development of consistent interaction between the student and one correspondent, and that interaction is important to the journal process. Correspondents should first try to work with students to focus on and deal with whatever problems they may be having and suggest changing correspondents as a last resort.

COMMUNITY CERTIFICATION OF SURVIVAL SKILLS

Survival skills are defined in experience-based learning as everyday coping skills needed in adulthood (see Fig. 2-3 for examples). Schools may have units of study relating to some of these skills (electoral process, first aid and physical health, for example), yet the practicalities of other skills may be left for young adults to discover through trial and error (insurance, budgeting or credit). By requiring students to demonstrate that they can do fundamental tasks related to these skills before they are actually needed, schools can systematically break these skills down into manageable units of learning or competencies. Mastering the competencies will make it easier for individuals to become independent, self-reliant and self-confident.

Certainly the idea of demonstrating competence in the skills of daily living is nothing new. Scouting, for instance, has long awarded various merit badges for demonstrating the mastery of skills to experts in the community. Some states are now setting minimum competencies for graduation that are measured by performance.

In the experience-based learning approach described here, competencies are not meant to be courses of study but instead are short-term, highly concentrated, individualized experiences. Students must demonstrate their competence to adults in the community with expertise in selected skills. For example, bank officers or credit union officials may serve as competency certifiers. This use of community resources gives a valuable reality check to

COMPETENCY	SUGGESTED CERTIFIERS
1. Transact business on credit	bank official, credit union manager, finance company representative
2. Maintain a checking account	bank official
3. Provide adequate insurance	insurance agent
4. File state and/or federal taxes	tax official
5. Budget time and money	home economist
6. Maintain physical health and use leisure time effectively	PE teacher, recreation leader
7. Respond to fire, police and health emergencies	fire and police officials
8. Participate in the electoral process	city recorder, state and local officials
9. Understand local government	local government officials
10. Explain personal legal rights	attorney, consumer protection official
11. Make appropriate use of public agencies	city or county clerk, other government officials, League of Women Voters, Common Cause
12. Apply for employment	any employer
13. Operate and maintain an automobile	Motor vehicle examiner, police officer, mechanic, driver training instructor

Figure 2-3. Sample competencies and community certifiers used in experience-based learning programs.

each student's proficiency on stated tasks. While a student could just as well work from a textbook to compute interest on a loan, we believe retention is improved if the student has to ask a loan officer at a finance company to sign off on the accuracy of the computations.

This competency-based approach helps students acquire confidence in their ability to handle situations and obtain services. They learn, for instance, that public authorities can help in specific ways and that difficulties occurring with one individual or agency can often be resolved by recourse elsewhere. These are valuable lessons that help young people face adulthood—practical knowledge that comes from actually performing a task or solving a problem. Parents like the idea, too, particularly if they see the coping skills as a way for young people to avoid needless mistakes.

Identifying the Competencies Your Students Should Achieve

Ideally, you should involve some adult community representatives in identifying the survival skills considered essential to adult life in your locale. This allows for regional differences (from boating safety on the Great Lakes to using public transit systems in large cities) while acknowledging that there are some survival skills needed by all adults (filing tax forms, responding to emergencies and so forth). This community identification of essential skills is the first step in adopting an experience-based approach to competency certification.

Try also to give your students an active role in the entire competency planning and selection process. This not only gives them a stake in the outcome but also gives them valuable experience in interacting cooperatively with adults. You and your students can work together to assemble a selection committee (for example, students, parents, teachers and workers from the community). Adults on the committee should represent diverse work roles, values and lifestyles so that a real cross section of opinion is obtained.

There are two major advantages to soliciting the involvement of adult volunteers during the early planning of the competencies. First of all, their insight is crucial if your set of competencies is to fit local needs. In addition, you will gain a group of community supporters who acquire a stake in your school, program and students through their hard work. Figure 2-3 lists 13 competencies that have been identified by some experience-based learning programs. This list can be used as the basis for your community discussions. The forms used to help students complete specific tasks for each of the 13 competencies in Fig. 2-3 have been compiled in a workbook titled *Student Competencies Guide: Survival Skills for a Changing World* (see Appendix C). This student workbook can either be modified or used as is to guide students through the process of community certification of the specified activities.

With the selection committee's assistance, determine how many competencies students should be asked to complete and select those your community group thinks are essential. Decide also what performance criteria are necessary for students to show they can do the stated tasks for each competency.

Be prepared to discuss questions like whether the competencies should prepare young people for present conditions or should anticipate adult survival needs five to ten years hence. If your community population is highly mobile, it may be desirable to consider skills that people would need in other localities. An example of this would be a rural community where a high percentage of young people regularly leave the area after graduation.

Explaining the Competencies to Students

After the competencies for your community are identified, you should describe the competencies and certification procedures in a format students can use. Many experience-based learning programs follow a workbook format to convey this information to students. Figure 2-4 is a sample for one competency, "Understanding the basic structure and function of local government."

Students should understand two important things about competency certification. First, following through on certification is their own responsibility, including:

Understand The Basic Structure And Function Of Local Government

WHAT YOU DO

☐ Show an understanding of the job, duties, obligations and authority of elected and appointed officials.

☐ Explain ways in which you can hold an official accountable.

☐ Show an understanding of the effects of lobbying practices by interest groups and individuals.

HOW YOU DO IT--SPECIFIC ACTIVITIES

1. Observe the legislative and executive functions of local government in operation by attending a city council meeting.

2. Select a person from each of the legislative and executive branches of local government and explain that person's role and responsibilities to the satisfaction of that official.

3. Select an issue in which lobbying efforts were clearly involved and explain the effects of the lobbying efforts to the satisfaction of a professional special interest lobbyist.

4. Explain, to the satisfaction of your certifier, a variety of ways that you can hold officials accountable, including re-election, recall and direct pressure.

RESOURCES

A. Certifier:

B. Materials: See resources list in the back of this workbook. You *must* study the materials before meeting with a representative from the legislative and executive branches. Certifiers for this competency will probably want to meet with groups of students.

Figure 2-4. Sample competency outline. (From *Student Competencies Guide*. Portland, Oregon: Northwest Regional Educational Laboratory, 1977, p. 24.)

1. Scheduling target dates and meeting with certifiers
2. Obtaining necessary resources to prepare for certification
3. Arranging for transportation to the places of certification, if necessary
4. Maintaining contact with staff regarding planned completion dates, resource needs and any changes in schedule

Second, the content of individual competencies should not be negotiable unless the planning group decides to establish a process for such negotiation. By definition, the competencies are considered essential skills that all students should acquire. Flexibility and individualization may be allowed in the certification procedures (in scheduling, use of resources and choosing which certifiers to use) but not in the criteria to be met.

Each competency requires the student to assess present abilities and take the necessary actions to achieve proficiency. Students may already possess some of the necessary skills and can move through some competencies quite rapidly (owning and maintaining an automobile or bicycle, for example). Other competencies may be more involved, requiring the student to contact several public agencies for specific purposes.

Whatever the procedures involved for completing each competency, students will be following some basic steps in the process, and these steps will be repeated for each competency. Figure 2-5 illustrates those basic steps for community certification.

Additional points for students to remember include the following:
1. Their performance on the competencies will be evaluated by working adults in the community who are experienced in their field, and students should feel free to ask them any questions.
2. Schedules should be followed closely. It is extremely difficult to finish a number of competencies at one time; it is also unreasonable to expect that certifiers will be able to see students at a moment's notice.
3. It is the students' responsibility to make and keep appointments with certifiers. If they are unable to keep an appointment because of some emergency, they must call the certifier to make new arrangements.
4. Whenever appropriate, group meetings can be arranged for several students, and transportation shared.

Identifying People to Serve as Certifiers

Chapter 5 discusses how to recruit and orient community people to serve as resources or instructors for experience-based learning. The competency certifier's role differs from the resource person's role in that certifiers agree simply to verify when students have learned a particular piece of information your community thinks is important and can demonstrate proficiency in tasks related to that information.

Certifiers may prefer to come to the school to provide instruction and sign off on student proficiency; it is preferable, however, to have students earn

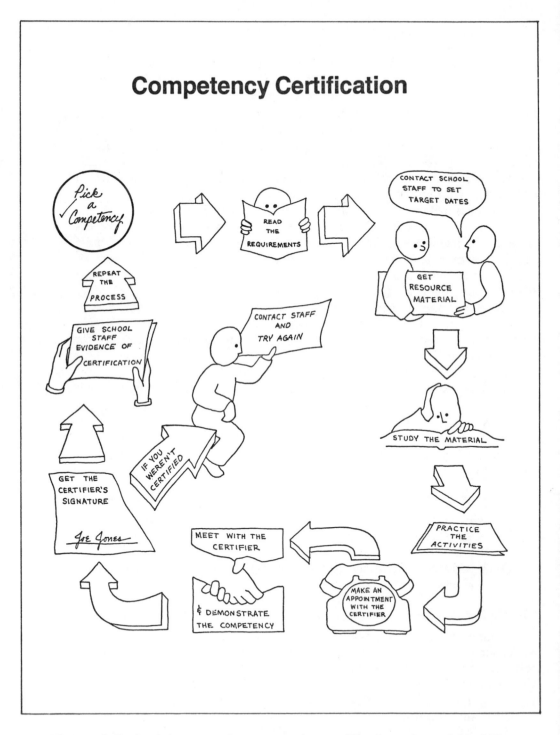

Figure 2-5. Student steps for community certification of survival skills. (From *Student Competencies Guide*, p. 3.)

certification by going directly to the community site and working with the certifier for a short period of time, usually no more than an hour. Remember, too, that school staff might also serve as certifiers for some competencies; a school nurse might certify first aid skills, for example, or the cafeteria manager certify knowledge of nutrition. In any case, make sure your certifiers are willing and qualified to help students acquire the identified skills and that they have a clear idea of what's expected of them.

Providing Resources for Students

Students should have access to a central file of certifiers so they can note names, titles, phone numbers and scheduling information in their competency guides. This file should be organized by competency, with a clear indication of which activities require certifier signatures. Figure 2-6 illustrates one way to prepare reference cards on each competency. These sample file cards list certifiers and suggest ways to contact them for each activity.

Students will also need access to a resource file of materials to help them prepare for certification. Staff, certifiers and students should all co-operate in collecting items for the file. Materials such as first aid manuals, tax information and consumer literature are often available at no charge. Your school librarian can be a real help, too, perhaps by keeping the files up to date and available as needed.

Staff may wish to ask students to gather resources for each competency as part of their orientation to the community. This can be particularly helpful if staff time for such tasks is limited. Resources should be screened, however, for usefulness and relevancy.

COMPETENCY 9 Local Government (cont'd)

Activities 3 & 4

Certifiers: Mrs. Susan Shaw   COMMON CAUSE (Lobbying Group)
                                 313 Burke Building
                                 City   334-4079

PLEASE READ THE MATERIALS ON COMMON CAUSE BEFORE
REQUESTING CERTIFICATION ON ACTIVITIES 3 AND 4.
CHECK WITH SCHOOL STAFF BEFORE MAKING YOUR
APPOINTMENT.

COMPETENCY 9 Local Government (cont'd)

Activity 2

Certifiers: Mr. Wayne Clark
                 City Administrator   778-4302
             Mr. Wilbur Booth
                 Mayor, City Hall   778-6021
             Mr. Robert Olson
                 Councilman
                 16309 N.W. State Street
                 City   778-9178

Procedures:
        1. Read City Municipal Code, "City Administrator"
            section. Check shelf for additional assigned

COMPETENCY 9 Understanding the Basic Structure & Function
             of Local Government

PLEASE SEE SCHOOL STAFF BEFORE MAKING AN APPOINTMENT WITH
CERTIFIERS

Activity 1

Procedures:
        1. Attend one City Council Meeting (2nd & 4th
            Mondays, Wilson Jr. High, 7:30 p.m.)
                a. Agenda may be obtained from school staff
                    the day of the meeting. Pick two issues
                    to follow.
                b. Pick up worksheets from school staff to be
                    filled out at the Council meeting. (Take
                    both the agenda and worksheet to meeting.)
        2. Certifier for Council Meeting: Mrs. Doris Hamilton
                                            City Recorder

PLEASE CHECK WITH MRS. HAMILTON AT LEAST 15 MINUTES
BEFORE MEETING BEGINS RE: YOUR CERTIFICATION

Figure 2-6. Sample reference cards directing students to the certifiers for one competency.

It should also be noted that not all materials need to be collected in a central location. Other materials available in the community (at a certifier's place of business, the local library and so forth) are also useful to students in preparing for competency certification. One way to guide students to such resources is to append a list of suggested agencies and materials to the student competencies workbook.

Recording Certification

Including a competency certification form at the end of the student workbook is one way to provide for certifier signatures. Certifiers sign this form for students when competency skills have been demonstrated satisfactorily. Staff also need a procedure for noting certification signatures in their own records as a back-up system.

Keeping the Wheels Turning

Regular staff contact with certifiers is necessary to keep you up to date on how the certification process is working and to help you resolve any difficulties.

Not only do you need to provide for initial orientation of certifiers and regular contact with them, but you should also plan for a review of the content, process, resources and requirements of your competency program after it has been in use for awhile. Since competencies and certification procedures are designed to match the needs of a local community and the expectations of adulthood, the whole process should be discussed regularly with certifiers for any needed revisions. If it is not feasible to assemble the certifiers, use a questionnaire to collect their responses and recommendations.

COMMUNITY EXPLORATIONS

The student's first real test as an experience-based learner is an actual community site exploration. Explorations are also a serious test for you if you are implementing them within a traditional school structure. Preparing community sites, scheduling student explorations and monitoring students in these community-based activities requires flexibility of time and movement. You will need a thorough understanding of school policy, as well as administrative sanction for the students' community-based activities. You may also need to share planning and monitoring activities with another teacher or teachers who can pool classes with you. Perhaps you could work out an arrangement with a person in your school who already oversees community-based activities, such as cooperative work experience. Or someone from a community volunteer group or a graduate student might help you implement exploration activities.

Using careers as the focal point, students set out on site visits that require at least several hours and sometimes several days to complete. They keep their eyes open to what's happening at the site, ask a lot of questions, gather reading materials and samples and try out certain activities. In short, they get the feeling of what it would be like to do that kind of work for a living—the good and bad, the ups and downs. Site issues and work values are often examined, too, including environmental issues.

The purpose of community exploration is to help young people practice critical thinking in evaluating their onsite experiences. Using a step-by-step process, each community exploration helps students learn about a specific job, relating that learning to their interests and abilities. By moving from site to site and completing several explorations, students meet a variety of people and experience many different work environments and lifestyles.

Explorations are intended to help students in the following ways:

1. Meet adults and see how they interact in the course of a normal workday
2. Learn about particular occupations while refining their career selection skills by—
   • Investigating the personal and educational/training prerequisites of specific jobs
   • Examining how psychological, social and environmental factors affect working conditions and job satisfaction
   • Comparing personal characteristics and values with those perceived at various work sites
3. Confidently use interviewing and critical thinking/observation techniques to gather information and draw conclusions
4. Gain a better understanding of the relationship between learning and earning a living
5. Acquire a sampling of how writing, speaking, listening and mathematics relate to specific jobs
6. Learn to find their way around the community more easily

7. Use new data gained during explorations to adjust their individual goals and learning plans, particularly in terms of future exploration site choices and in-depth projects

The exploration process is *not* intended to provide entry-level job skills for students, although students should experience some hands-on learning about specific skills in order to assess their aptitudes for that work. The primary concern of explorations is that students practice decision-making and information-processing skills they will need and use for the rest of their lives.

Explorations usually last from three to five days, preferably with students onsite from three to five hours each day. Exact schedules are, of course, worked out within school schedules and at the convenience of each resource person. How many career explorations students complete depends on schedules, transportation options and the number of community sites available in relation to the number of students using sites. Some experience-based learning programs ask students to complete at least five explorations a year. On the other hand, students usually want to do many more as they discover the opportunities of community learning.

Recruiting Sites for Community Explorations

Chapter 5 outlines procedures for establishing a network of community sites for experience-based learning activities, but a few points are worth mentioning in relation to community explorations.

The people you contact at prospective exploration sites will need to know the kinds of learning experiences students are expected to have during community explorations and what their role will be. For example:

1. Each exploration usually lasts approximately 15 hours.
2. Students will be investigating a job, not training for it.
3. Students will complete specified exploration activities. (Show resource people samples.)
4. The resource person will assist school staff in evaluating student performance at the site.
5. A teacher will be available to advise or assist the resource person.

After general agreement is reached about placement conditions, try to record some basic information about the site to help students choose where to go and also to identify resources and basic skills students will be able to use at that site in completing their exploration activities.

Many experience-based learning programs have found it useful to have a prepared Site Information form that can be completed by a teacher or student and resource person together or by the resource person alone. This Site Information form is completed for each learning station (a particular job or department) being made available to students at each community site.

Figure 2-7 illustrates the kind of information form that some experience-based programs have tested in conjunction with the community exploration process. (Copies of this form are available; see Appendix C.)

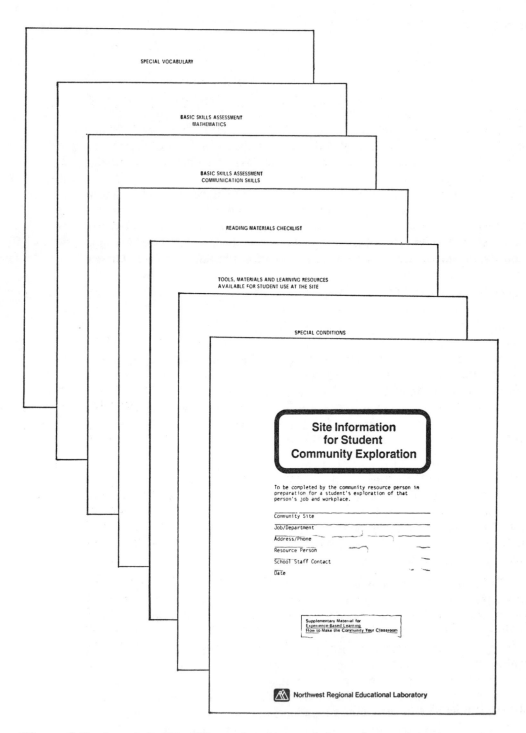

SPECIAL VOCABULARY

BASIC SKILLS ASSESSMENT
MATHEMATICS

BASIC SKILLS ASSESSMENT
COMMUNICATION SKILLS

READING MATERIALS CHECKLIST

TOOLS, MATERIALS AND LEARNING RESOURCES
AVAILABLE FOR STUDENT USE AT THE SITE

SPECIAL CONDITIONS

**Site Information
for Student
Community Exploration**

To be completed by the community resource person in
preparation for a student's exploration of that
person's job and workplace.

Community Site

Job/Department

Address/Phone

Resource Person

School Staff Contact

Date

Supplementary Material for
Experience-Based Learning
How to Make the Community Your Classroom

Northwest Regional Educational Laboratory

Figure 2-7. A sample Site Information form to help students select sites and complete their exploration activities.

Guiding Students Through Explorations

Community exploration should be a self-directed process for students, and experience-based learning programs have found that a prepared exploration guide is a useful way to help students carry out their onsite activities. The guide or record should be designed so that procedures for completing it are self-explanatory. Following are some of the things an exploration guide can instruct students to do:

1. Interview the resource person and record the interview either in writing or on tape.
2. Answer questions listed in the guide based on site observations and personal interests and aptitudes.
3. Take photographs or draw sketches and write descriptions of site scenes—services, products, equipment, people.
4. Obtain and read site-related literature (catalogs, brochures, training manuals, reports, etc.).
5. Complete basic skills tasks required for the job being explored (reading and written communication, math).
6. Write an evaluation of the site experience.
7. Ask the resource person to evaluate the exploration record and certify that performance has been satisfactory.
8. Write a thank-you letter to the resource person.
9. Turn in the exploration record to school staff for evaluation; if it is unsatisfactory or incomplete, continue working on it until accepted by staff as satisfactory.
10. Have a conference with staff to talk about the completed exploration and get ready to select a new site to explore.

In sum, the exploration record requires students to make observations, collect useful information, use the information to perform tasks and analyze the tasks in relation to personal values and goals. This process encourages young people to sort out their various (and possibly conflicting) values and abilities as these relate to career preferences. It also gives the students a better understanding of the site and themselves.

What can an exploration record look like? Figures 2-8 through 2-12 illustrate sample completed exploration activities for one student investigating a Legal Aid site. These are just a few selected pages from the *Student Record of Community Exploration* used by many experience-based learning programs (see Appendix C). Students complete one record book for each site they explore.

Choosing the First Exploration Site

Exploration begins with assessment or awareness activities that help the student match personal interests and needs with sites that look compatible.

Getting Started on Your Exploration

Community Site _____ *Legal Aid* _____

Resource Person _____ *Jane Gilmore* _____

Address _____ *5th and Main* _____ Telephone *681-0321*

What type of job are you about to explore? __ *Investigative assistant* __

> **Before you explore this site** and job, describe what you expect, based on information from career tests you have taken or knowledge you already possess.

Why did you choose this job to explore? ____ *Might be interested in going*

___ *into some kind of law work someday or another career where*

___ *people's problems are solved. I've heard it's not easy,*

___ *though, so I want to talk with people in this profession.*

_____

_____

What do you think this exploration will be like? __ *I saw some other explorations*

___ *done here and it looks interesting. Not like on TV at all.*

___ *Lots of work goes on behind the scenes.*

_____

_____

_____

Fill in the dates and hours you have agreed to be at the job site.

Week of	Monday	Tuesday	Wednesday	Thursday	Friday
April 8	2-4	2-4	10-12 Court		
April 15				8:15 - 11:30	8:15 - 11:30

Figure 2-8. Sample student entry at the beginning of a site exploration. (From *Student Record of Community Exploration*. Portland, Oregon: Northwest Regional Educational Laboratory, 1977, p. 3.)

Examine Your Job Interests and Aptitudes

One way to match or mismatch yourself with a job is to compare the job with things you enjoy doing, are capable of doing or would like to learn. In the following activities, analyze the skills and tasks required by the job you are exploring and compare them with your own preferences and abilities.

	Give an example from the job site	Do you like to do this?	Can you do it?
Working With Things			
Precision work	*Checking information*	*yes*	*yes*
Operating equipment			
Handling materials			
Working With Information			
Interpreting facts	*Following up client story*	*yes*	*yes*
Organizing and using information	*Writing case study*	*yes*	*need practice*
Copying, sorting and putting things together	*Building case file*	*yes*	*I'm learning*
Working with numbers or words	*Writing case study; checking facts*	*yes*	*yes*
Working With People			
Counseling	*Interviewing client*	*yes*	*yes*
Discussing and bargaining	*Consulting staff – legal counsel*	*yes*	*I'm learning*
Supervising			
Selling			
Teaching	*Helping clients understand their rights*	*yes*	*need practice*

Figure 2-9. As the exploration continues, the student looks at personal qualities in relation to job tasks. (From *Student Record of Community Exploration*, p. 8.)

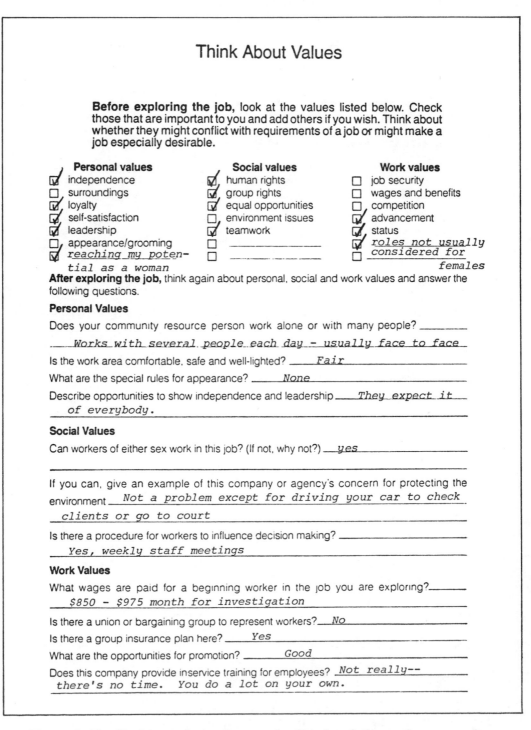

Think About Values

Before exploring the job, look at the values listed below. Check those that are important to you and add others if you wish. Think about whether they might conflict with requirements of a job or might make a job especially desirable.

Personal values
- ☑ independence
- ☐ surroundings
- ☑ loyalty
- ☑ self-satisfaction
- ☑ leadership
- ☐ appearance/grooming
- ☑ *reaching my potential as a woman*

Social values
- ☑ human rights
- ☑ group rights
- ☑ equal opportunities
- ☐ environment issues
- ☑ teamwork
- ☐ _____
- ☐ _____

Work values
- ☐ job security
- ☐ wages and benefits
- ☐ competition
- ☑ advancement
- ☑ status
- ☑ *roles not usually considered for females*
- ☐

After exploring the job, think again about personal, social and work values and answer the following questions.

Personal Values

Does your community resource person work alone or with many people? _____
___ *Works with several people each day – usually face to face*

Is the work area comfortable, safe and well-lighted? ____ *Fair* _____

What are the special rules for appearance? ____ *None* _____

Describe opportunities to show independence and leadership ___ *They expect it* ___
of everybody. _____

Social Values

Can workers of either sex work in this job? (If not, why not?) ___ *yes* _____
_____

If you can, give an example of this company or agency's concern for protecting the
environment ___ *Not a problem except for driving your car to check*
clients or go to court _____

Is there a procedure for workers to influence decision making? _____
Yes, weekly staff meetings _____

Work Values

What wages are paid for a beginning worker in the job you are exploring?_____
$850 – $975 month for investigation _____

Is there a union or bargaining group to represent workers?___ *No* _____

Is there a group insurance plan here? ____ *Yes* _____

What are the opportunities for promotion? _____ *Good* _____

Does this company provide inservice training for employees? *Not really--*
there's no time. You do a lot on your own. _____

Figure 2-10. Student analysis of personal values in relation to the community site. (From *Student Record of Community Exploration*, p. 11.)

Mathematics Skills Required by This Job

See the Site Information form for this site. On page 7 of that form the resource person has described five actual job tasks requiring mathematics skills.

Copy those five tasks below and verify with your resource person that they are still necessary tasks for the job you are exploring. (If any of them are not, ask your resource person to write another task for you.)

Try to perform **all five** tasks. The purpose is for you to discover some of the real requirements of this job in the area of mathematics skills. You may be unable to perform one or more of the tasks, but trying them will give you a better idea of what this job requires.

Have your resource person sign the form. The resource person's signature certifies that you **tried to** perform the tasks and whether or not you had difficulties.

1. _Keep record of time spent on each case_

☑ Performed satisfactorily   ☐ Performed with difficulty   ☐ Can't do

2. _Check computations on consumer fraud case on supermarket pricing_

☑ Performed satisfactorily   ☐ Performed with difficulty   ☐ Can't do

3. _Help client in bankruptcy case compute interest on purchases_

☐ Performed satisfactorily   ☑ Performed with difficulty   ☐ Can't do

4. _Submit monthly staff report for expense accounts_

☐ Performed satisfactorily   ☑ Performed with difficulty   ☐ Can't do

5. _Help client file appeal on negligent driving charge (alleged error in computing distance from stop sign)_

☑ Performed satisfactorily   ☐ Performed with difficulty   ☐ Can't do

Jane Gilmore
Community resource person

April 11, 1976
Date

Figure 2-11. Math-related activities the student can perform at the site. (From *Student Record of Community Exploration*, p. 13.)

Comments and Evaluations

Student: Write one or two statements about this community exploration summing up your reaction to it, particularly how it matches up with your career expectations.

While I know there are some real problems with our justice system in America, for the most part it works if people are shown how to exercise their rights and responsibilities. I have seen some sad situations and some dedicated people. I have also seen some happy faces. There are lots of lawyers today and more looking for jobs. But if you're good, you can make it. There are other ways you can apply legal training, too.

I want to keep looking at this possibility.

     Gloria Sorenson 4-19-76
      Signature   Date

Community Resource Person: Describe briefly your reactions to this exploration and your evaluation of the student's performance.

Gloria did a fine job on her exploration here and I think she should keep going on her personal quest for a possible career in this area. Call me for some more ideas.

Gloria Sorenson   has completed this   *Jane Gilmore* *April 22 '76*
Exploration Record to my satisfaction.   Signature   Date

School Staff: Write your evaluation of this exploration and how it has affected the student's self-awareness and career planning.

Let's get together with Mr. Updyke and Ms. White to examine next steps, Gloria. You have made a great start here with some thoughtful experiences.

How about doing a project in this area next?

      Ted Alexander 4-28-76
      Signature   Date

Figure 2-12. Concluding evaluations of the exploration by the student, resource person and school staff person. (From *Student Record of Community Exploration*, p. 14.)

There are several kinds of career interest inventories available to schools to help students in this site selection process; ask your school guidance and counseling staff for suggestions. It's a good idea to try the assessment out on yourself and other teachers before using it with students to make sure it actually elicits the information students will need. Also be sure that assessment instruments are free of sex role bias and stereotyping and encourage students to consider a wide range of possible occupational choices.

If students can complete initial career assessment activities before starting explorations, school staff will have an idea of the kinds and number of community sites students want and can make sure there are enough sites available to match anticipated student needs. Career assessments should then be repeated through the year to keep data current as students' attitudes change.

To help them select exploration sites, students should have access to descriptive career data. Remind students that valuable information resources include written career literature, fiction and nonfiction books, magazines, newspapers, audiovisual materials and people. In addition, a cumulative file of exploration records completed by other students can provide background for site choices. There should also be individual folders on sites that have agreed to participate with your school. These folders, with Site Information forms, staff notes and site-related literature, should be available for student reference.

Near the site file you might post a map of the community with pins identifying participating sites. The map can help students gain a sense of the community they will be exploring and also helps you both plan transportation. Ask students to assist in preparing such a map as an orientation activity.

In the beginning, you should not expect to see all students following a logical process of deduction to arrive at clearly reasoned site choices. The influence of television programs, the careers of relatives, peer group choices, popular opinion and cultural values all have a strong effect on student choices. As students complete a few explorations, however, their reasons for site selection should become more defined.

Talk to students about their interests and help them recognize biases and assumptions that may be conditioning their self-perceptions. Help them articulate some kind of rationale for their choices but, at the same time, avoid challenging their reasons too much. The exploration process itself will help students examine the many influences that motivate career planning.

Defining Student Rights and Responsibilities

Students are expected to conform to site regulations and the basic policies at each site regarding behavior. Some work places may require specific dress or grooming, for example, or prohibit smoking. Generally, it is very effective to have students learn these requirements and policies directly from their resource people, rather than providing too much information to students in advance. Part of the value of explorations for students is learning firsthand why sites have certain restrictions, benefits and so forth.

In addition to observing site rules and regulations, students can be held responsible for the following activities during community explorations:

1. Taking the lead in deciding which sites to explore
2. Planning the schedules they will follow at the site with resource people and school staff
3. Arranging for transportation to the site
4. Completing exploration records for each site and turning them in when signed by the resource person
5. Attending followup evaluation sessions with school staff

Generally, students participating in experience-based learning have the right to renegotiate activities and objectives as their experiences lead them to revise goals and reinterpret their learning needs. However, since explorations last such a short period of time students are strongly encouraged to complete all explorations, even if the site they are exploring does not turn out to be what they expected. If a student does find it necessary to drop a site, ask the student to provide a rationale for this decision. If an exploration is being terminated, it is also advisable to have the student personally call the resource person to explain.

It is important to remember that the exploration is a short-term, low risk venture for students and resource people alike. Encourage everyone to be frank with each other and to recognize that the student is truly exploring or investigating. Students and resource people should not feel inhibited about expressing opinions freely and honestly examining the appropriateness or suitability of particular careers for individual students.

Making Arrangements With Resource People

The exploration process places a lot of responsibility on the student for making and following through on decisions. All students are expected to meet new adults and situations, but the burden of initial site arrangements can pose too early a challenge for some students. It might be wise for you as the student's teacher or adviser to make the *first* telephone call to arrange an exploration. You will not only pave the way for the student to make subsequent contacts, but you can discover immediately if there are any snags in arrangements. Your contact with resource people helps assure these volunteers that the school has sanctioned the student's community-based learning experiences. It also lets them know whom to call if they need assistance and gives you an opportunity to discuss program expectations for students.

The advantage of spending full days onsite. Ideally students should spend at least one entire day at their sites to gain a complete picture of the many intangible as well as tangible characteristics of a given job. Whole days (school days of at least three to five hours) spent with a resource person enable the student to see typical ups and downs, staff meetings and so forth. This gives the student a chance to feel the pressures, conflicts and tensions that go with the work, as well as some of the benefits that come from working intensively with others including comradeship, the subtle balance necessary for team cooperation, and success in solving problems.

Some jobs have daily routines requiring different skills in the morning than in the afternoon—another reason for having students onsite for full days. For example, if a student accompanies a grocery distributor during the early morning phase of the job but leaves after deliveries are made, the various bookkeeping and organizational chores that keep the business going will be invisible to the student. If it is not feasible to schedule students for full-day explorations, a good compromise could be to arrange to have one day of each exploration correspond to the full work day and the rest of the exploration worked into the school schedule.

What the student does at the site. Students and resource people are basically free to work out the best methods for exploring each site. The first day is usually spent touring the workplace, meeting employees and receiving a general orientation. On subsequent days the student's time should be divided between observing the resource person's daily routine and working on the program's required exploration activities. Keep in mind that the emphasis of community explorations is on observation, although the student can become involved in actual job tasks if appropriate and agreeable to the resource person. (See Chapter 6, page 178, for more on the legal aspects of community exploration activities.)

In addition to observing the resource person and other employees at the site, the student should obtain and read site-related literature (brochures, training manuals, policy statements, materials used to orient new employees and so forth). Whenever possible, copies of such literature should be filed with the completed exploration record for future reference by other students.

Opportunities for keeping busy during an exploration vary from site to site. Students might attend staff meetings, training sessions and other group activities that help them see how people relate to one another on the job. They can go along on delivery runs or errands and, if it's useful, observe the work of several different employees around the site. Rotating among various work stations can help students see the component parts of the work process and understand the importance of communication.

Part of the school's responsibility is to help community volunteers identify ways their particular site can be explored profitably without cutting too deeply into work time. You can reassure resource people by reviewing the exploration process with them and showing samples of exploration activities the students will complete. You can also point out that allowing students to follow them through their daily routines is an effective way of minimizing the time they have to spend away from their work.

A final point to keep in mind is that there are ultimately no failures in explorations: students can learn as much from their mistakes as from their successes. Of course, adults should be sensitive to students' difficulties and try to help them deal positively with problems. At the same time, however, students have a right to discover their own limits and learn to recognize when psychological or physical limitations are real barriers to achieving a desired goal.

Reviewing the Student's Exploration Activities

An exploration record should have places for both the resource person and school staff person monitoring the exploration to write evaluations of the student's work and sign their names certifying that the activities have been completed to their satisfaction. There should also be space for the student to sum up reactions to the exploration. To avoid extra site visits, students should complete exploration records and obtain needed comments and signatures during their last day onsite.

Staff will then evaluate the student's work for completeness and level of performance. Has the student been thorough in completing all parts of the exploration process? Does the student's work measure up to demonstrated potential capabilities? The record should be further evaluated, along with the entire exploration, during a debriefing between staff and student. Following that meeting the student is given credit for the completed exploration and the record is filed. (Completed exploration records are often useful to other students in selecting sites they want to visit.)

Debriefing the Exploration

Followup conferences to review site experiences may be scheduled either with individuals or small groups of students. Even though staff will have evaluated each student's completed exploration record in writing, the debriefing conference is important in helping to avoid the danger of site explorations becoming too repetitious. Discussion of each exploration helps the student decide where to go next and why, bringing the exploration process full circle to a reconsideration of educational goals and lifestyle aspirations.

As the culminating learning activity of the exploration, this conference helps students consider how the knowledge and skills gained during exploration can be applied to future information gathering and decision making. Through careful questions during the meeting you can help students sharpen their skills in observation and analysis and guide them toward activities that increase their understanding of themselves, careers and community issues.

You might ask students the following kinds of questions:

- Was a given incident typical of that job or merely unique to that site or person? If you can't answer, how can you find out?
- Have other students encountered similar situations at the site? At other sites? How have they dealt with the situations?
- What have you learned from this experience? How can you now apply what you've learned in new situations?
- Are there things you wish you had done differently? What are they?
- If you were a resource person, what are some things you would do to help a student feel comfortable at the site? How could you help a student learn important things about the job?

Followup conferences also help students analyze any contradictions between what they think interests them and their reactions to a particular exploration. You may have discussions like these:

- In your exploration record you say that you would like to operate heavy construction equipment, but on the career assessment you said you don't like to sit for long periods. Do you think sitting in the fork lift for long periods would be difficult for you?
- During orientation you wrote that you wanted to train for a career that paid a high salary and had a lot of responsibility. But on this exploration you did barely enough work to get by. How do you think an employer will feel if you only make a minimal effort?
- You said you would like to take a mechanical drawing course and liked to design furniture or buildings, but you didn't take much care with the floor plan you drew of your site. Can you explain this?

Choosing Subsequent Exploration Sites

Community exploration is a continuous process, with each site exploration leading to another in a logical sequence (see Fig. 2-13). After exploring their first sites students will begin to build the experiential base for more carefully reasoned decisions about careers. Initial enthusiasm may have been dampened or enhanced, or personal contacts with community resource people may have led to new insights.

It is important for staff to help students see the value of continued examination of their interests and possible alternatives. The followup conference at the end of each exploration gives staff the opportunity to help students make this kind of examination. It also is a good time for the student to select the next exploration site. Following are a few questions you might ask the student concerning site choices:

- Why do you want that site?
- What is its relation to the other sites you've explored?
- Do you have any special activities you'd like to do there?
- What have you heard about the site from other students?
- How does it relate to what you think you want to do with yourself after high school?
- Do you know the kind of work it involves? Have you ever done anything like that before?

STUDENT PROJECTS

In-depth learning projects for students represent one way to make full use of the community as an educational resource and are the keystone in experience-based learning. Projects enable students to follow through on their explorations of community sites by returning for longer and more intensive learning experiences. Project activities relate to academic learning, skill development (interpersonal and job-related skills as well as basic skills) and the individual student's personal, learning, lifestyle and career objectives. If you have an independent study program in your school, you are familiar with this type of learning situation. Perhaps some of the ideas that follow could be incorporated into an existing program or serve as a basis for developing a new one.

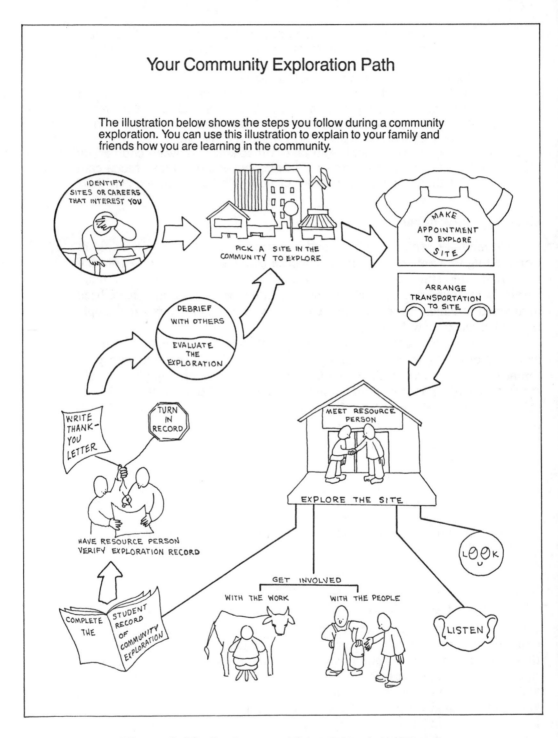

Figure 2-13. Student steps for community exploration.
(From *Student Record of Community Exploration*, p. 1.)

Basically, the project is a format or method for designing learning activities that are—

- Problem centered (beginning with a question or issue for which the student must seek a solution)
- Related to each other in topic or theme
- Connected in a logical sequence
- Interdisciplinary (combining learning in more than one skill or subject area)

For the individual student, projects provide an effective way of using self-assessment and diagnostic data for educational planning. They also provide a structure to help staff monitor and support individual learning experiences and a standardized format for students to use while pursuing individualized and self-directed learning activities in the community.

When built from the exploration process, projects help students explore and refine personal interests while increasing their proficiency in the performance of basic skills (reading, writing, communications). The project format helps students relate their site experiences to other learning activities. Projects also help students acquire and practice such learning skills as critical thinking/problem solving, negotiation with peers and adults, self-assessment, goal setting and planning, use of resources (both human and material), scheduling and use of time, and accountability to self and to school expectations.

Distinguishing Projects from Explorations

On explorations, students examine many sites in their community and begin to make choices about careers that appeal to them, the lifestyles they want to experience and the kinds of learning they need to achieve their goals. Although students on explorations have extensive interaction with resource people, the primary emphasis is still on observation and career possibilities.

Projects, on the other hand, represent a different level of site involvement for students and are structured over longer periods of time than explorations. Although project activities may or may not be related to career decision making, they require students to make the transition from *observing* to *doing*. Through these activities, students become firsthand participants in the human and work processes associated with particular sites and occupations.

In short, it is through site-related projects that students fully encounter the experiential aspect of learning. They select and carry out specific activities, perform realistic tasks alongside working adults and follow up by reflecting on the results of their actions.

Learning How to Plan and Write Projects

The key thing to remember about projects is that they correlate each student's personal and educational needs with the reality of learning opportunities in the community. Project planning gives you the opportunity to help students see how subject matter is used in everyday situations. You and each student together look at the potential learning opportunities of a given community site and select specific activities for the student to pursue in relation to a project topic or theme. You use what the student has learned from previous explorations as part of the project design. You build basic skill activities into the project, based on the student's assessed learning needs. As the student completes the project, you involve resource people in assessing what the student has learned and suggesting possible next steps.

All of these considerations are critical to well-planned student projects. Because the real payoff in experience-based learning is in developing these individually negotiated projects with students, Chapters 3 and 4 explain more fully the project planning and writing steps summarized above. Chapter 3 takes a detailed look at how a site's learning potential can be fully analyzed in relation to academic subjects, basic skills and work tasks, and how "starter projects" can be developed to acquaint students with the whole experience-based learning process. Chapter 4 explains how site analysis can be translated into specific learning objectives and then into projects developed individually with each student. In addition, Appendix A contains 25 sample projects as examples of learning activities that have been successfully planned with students in actual experience-based learning programs.

STUDENT SUPPORT AND FOLLOWUP

Scheduling

To help students meet their time commitments in experience-based learning activities, staff should make sure each student has a clear idea of all scheduled activities and has written dates and deadlines on a planning calendar. If there is a time conflict or if students and staff agree that a new opportunity warrants taking a day away from the middle of an exploration or a student project, the student should immediately contact the resource person, discuss the conflict and try to negotiate a change in schedule. Both staff and students should try to avoid sudden changes in midstream, however, or interruptions that stretch an exploration or project out unnecessarily.

Attendance

When a student misses a day at a community site or arrives late several times in a row without good reason, the resource person should contact school staff about the problem. Staff can then schedule an immediate conference with the student to discuss the problem and hopefully come up with a solution. Poor attendance can cause the resource person to lose valuable work time as well as confidence in your school's ability to monitor community-based learning.

Behavior and Performance

Student behavior during onsite experiences is ideally handled by the resource person, with school help and advice available as needed. Students need to learn that they are in the adult world and are expected to act in accordance with site regulations. The resource person should be frank in explaining requirements. A student who is habitually late or who is not fulfilling other obligations at the site needs to hear about this directly from the resource person, as well as praise for things done well. If resource people feel uncomfortable dealing with student behavior, however, they should not hesitate to call on school staff to handle the situation.

If a student does not meet a resource person's expectations in completing exploration or project activities requiring site certification, the resource person should withhold a satisfactory evaluation and clarify expectations with the student. The student then has the choice of doing additional work or not receiving credit. You, too, have the same responsibility to evaluate students' onsite work and require that students do a good job on the various activities.

Always encourage resource people to call the school staff if any special difficulty arises. Especially with students or resource people new to this type of learning, school staff should try to follow up the first day of a student's placement with a personal visit to the site to make sure things are working well. This is also an option you can exercise if you have any reservations about a particular student/resource person combination.

Student Performance Review

A Student Performance Review by the resource person is an invaluable way of giving the student feedback in standard categories of job-holding behaviors during the completion of project activities. Figure 2-14 illustrates a sample form used for this purpose in a number of programs that are totally experience-based. The form is used to record a student's attendance and punctuality, attitudes, responses to the learning process and onsite perform- ance. It lets staff know how a student is doing at the site in these areas and is a good vehicle for initiating career guidance. School staff and the resource person can both counsel the student about the important role these factors play in helping a person hold a current job or acquire another.

Student Evaluation of Learning Site

The Student Evaluation of Learning Site process parallels the Student Performance Review. While the resource person evaluates the student, the student in turn gives feedback about the resource person and site experience (see Figure 2-15 for sample form). The resource person and the student should then meet and share each other's evaluations.

STUDENT PERFORMANCE REVIEW

Student   _Kelly Robbins_   Date _4-7-77_
Resource Person   _Jan MacKay_
Site   _County Realty_

	Needs to improve	Improving	Satisfactory	Commendable	Excellent	Not applicable
ATTENDANCE/PUNCTUALITY						
Reports to community site on time		✓				
Adheres to established schedule			✓			

Comment:

	Needs to improve	Improving	Satisfactory	Commendable	Excellent	Not applicable
ATTITUDE						
Understands and accepts responsibility					✓	
Observes site rules					✓	
Shows interest and enthusiasm					✓	
Courteous, cooperative					✓	
Good team worker			✓			
Judgment					✓	
Poise, self-confidence				✓		
Demonstrates appropriate dress/grooming			✓			
Concerned for equipment/property					✓	

Comment:

	Needs to improve	Improving	Satisfactory	Commendable	Excellent	Not applicable
LEARNING PROCESS						
Uses initiative, seeks opportunities to learn					✓	
Takes responsibility for own learning					✓	
Quality of assigned projects				✓		
Asks questions of appropriate person				✓		
Uses learning resources at community site				✓		

Comment:

	Needs to improve	Improving	Satisfactory	Commendable	Excellent	Not applicable
PERFORMANCE						
Begins assigned tasks promptly			✓			
Seeks feedback concerning performance		✓				
Accepts feedback information		✓				
Uses criticism constructively			✓			
Completes tasks assigned			✓			
Progressively requires less supervision			✓			

Comment:

ADDITIONAL COMMENTS: *Kelly is a natural for this work. At first he felt he knew it all, but he's learning there are still things to be learned.*

Jan MacKay
Resource Person

Figure 2-14. Sample form for resource person evaluation of student's onsite performance.

```
STUDENT EVALUATION OF LEARNING SITE

Student ____Kelly Robbins_____ Date __4-7-77__
Resource Person ____Jan MacKay_____
Site ____County Realty_____
                                                          Yes
                                                            No
                                                              Does Not Apply

RESOURCE PERSON DEMONSTRATES AN UNDERSTANDING OF ROLE BY:
Orienting student to work of the company            ✓
Introducing student to other people                 ✓
Orienting student to facilities                     ✓
Clarifying expectations of dress/grooming           ✓
Defining rules and punctuality                      ✓

Comment:

RESOURCE PERSON PROVIDES A PRODUCTIVE LEARNING ENVIRONMENT BY:
Being interested in development of student and program  ✓
Being willing to take time to help                      ✓
Encouraging independent work on assigned tasks          ✓
Understanding why student is there                      ✓
Giving feedback on performance                          ✓
Encouraging new and meaningful experiences              ✓
Supplying company information and materials             ✓

Comment:

ARE YOU:
Satisfied with your present learning site?          ✓
Gaining valuable learning experiences?              ✓
Clear on your performance review?                   ✓

Comment:




ADDITIONAL COMMENTS:  Jan is a great person to be with!  She really knows
    real estate and can teach it, too!

                              Kelly Robbins
                                 Student
```

Figure 2-15. Sample student evaluation of the resource person's effectiveness.

Skill Development Record

Development of specific job skills is almost inevitable during student use of a site, sometimes even during explorations. It can be extremely useful to the student to document what skills have been learned, and you may want to use a Skill Development Record for this purpose (see Figure 2-16 for sample form).

SKILL DEVELOPMENT RECORD

Student _____ *Kelly Robbins*

Site _____ *County Realty*

DIRECTIONS: 1. Ask your resource person to take a few minutes to discuss with you the skills you will be acquiring at the site. List them below and note target dates for completion.

2. Ask your resource person how well you should be able to do each task and note under TASKS/SKILLS. For example:

   a. Number of units per (hours, days, minutes)
   b. Percent of accuracy required
   c. Able to initiate and complete without supervision

3. Have your resource person record the extent of your participation:

   a. You have <u>observed</u> the task
   b. You have <u>practiced</u> the task
   c. You have <u>performed</u> the task

4. When you think you can do a task as well as the resource person says you should, have him/her check you on the task and fill in the last two columns.

TASKS/SKILLS	EXTENT OF PARTICIPATION	TARGET DATE	COMPLETED	RP INITIAL
Secure and read title printout	*Performed*	*3-15*	*3-18*	*J.M.*
Research property background	*Performed*	*4-1*	*3-27*	*J.M.*
Write real estate listing without supervision	*Practiced*	*4-1*	*4-5*	*J.M.*
Determine income property value with 100% accuracy	*Practiced*	*4-1*	*4-1*	*J.M.*
Write earnest money receipt without supervision	*Practiced*	*4-5*	*4-5*	*J.M.*

Figure 2-16. Sample record of skills learned at community site.

On arriving at the site, the student and resource person agree on the skills to be learned. The student writes these skills and performance expectations on the record sheet along with target dates for mastering them and begins either observing employees or actually practicing the skills.

Project activities can also be tied in with skills identified on the Skill Development Record. However, project activities are primarily oriented toward integrating site experiences with more comprehensive learning objectives (see Chapter 4).

When completing the form, the resource person notes whether the student has observed, practiced or performed each skill, with performance judged on the basis of whether or not the student can do the skill at a level suitable for employment.

FOOTNOTE

[1]Maurice Gibbons, *The New Secondary Education* (Bloomington, Indiana: Phi Delta Kappa, Inc., 1976), p. 55.

PROJECT

3

LINKING COMMUNITY RESOURCES
WITH STUDENT PROJECTS

> ...The routes available to youth to become
> adults are insufficient. The artificiality of
> the present arrangement must be amended
> by the addition of authentic experiences.
> The adult world should be recoupled with
> youth...and youth should have learning
> opportunities in the practical and specific
> realm as well as those which are vicarious
> and theoretical.
> —*Task Force on Secondary Schools
> in a Changing Society, National
> Association of Secondary School
> Principals*[1]

Experience-based learning requires new ways of looking at traditional subject matter and new ways of planning what students will study and do. Projects are one important way of organizing a student's community-based learning activities into coherent subjects, themes or accomplishments that can be documented. Before projects can be planned with individual students, however, community resources must be analyzed for the kinds of learning activities they can provide.

Traditional ways of organizing knowledge into separate subject areas are seldom encountered in the community. For example, a city planner draws on several areas of knowledge at once when solving problems: design considerations, cost-effectiveness studies, tax rates, recreation needs, population growth, environmental issues, political realities. When you examine everyday situations at work sites in the community, you will find innumerable learning possibilities that can be written into student projects. The following list, for example, is a brief sampling of the scope of two different jobs—travel agent and plumber:

	TRAVEL AGENT	PLUMBER
Reading	Reads brochures, current tourist literature	Reads trade journals, follows product development, etc.
Mathematics	May need to compute tax rates, discounts, etc.	Computes measurements, reads schematics, understands scaled drawings
Communications	Writes out airline tickets, sends for reservations	Talks with customers, orders supplies
Science	Provides information on required immunizations, precautions for certain destinations	Knows reactions of chemicals on pipes, equipment
Social Science	Advises clients on cultural customs, needs of local citizenry	Keeps current on city/county codes
Humanities	Familiar with cultural centers, special events in travel areas	Quality of life; design problems
Business/Office	Arranges for rental cars; charts out itineraries, completes maps, guidebooks	Often runs one-person shop; keeps records, billings
Health/PE	Familiar with inoculations and other requirements for passports	Has awareness of sanitation regulations, gives household tips
Industrial Technology	Knows technological development of different areas of the world—can plan industrial tours	Uses specialty tools, understands mechanics of plumbing systems
Coping Skills	Uses patience and tact when providing assistance for travelers regarding destination, reservations	Answers customer complaints about billings, high repair costs, etc.; perseveres even when a plumbing problem is difficult to solve

LIFE SKILLS AND STUDENT LEARNING

Examining occupations in relation to traditional subject areas is one way to organize community-based learning experiences. Instead of trying to make community learning experiences fit the traditional school curriculum, however, many experience-based programs have adopted five organizing areas (termed life skills) that help young people integrate the knowledge and skills society expects of them.

These five areas are critical thinking, functional citizenship, personal/social development, creative development and scientific investigation. No matter what your subject area, you may recognize one or more of these life skills as processes you are trying to help students learn.

The following pages list the objectives of these five areas and give a *sample starter project* for each. It should be noted that the life skill objectives are purposely broad so that specific objectives can be stated for each project undertaken by students. The general objectives articulate a framework that is achieved through specified outcomes for individual projects.

Starter projects have suggested activities that can be performed at a variety of community sites. Specific objectives and activities are negotiated with each individual student to ensure personal appropriateness. Having all students begin with a starter project in each life skills area is a useful introduction to the concepts and processes inherent in the life skills. Students will be using those concepts and processes in subsequent projects.

Critical Thinking

Desired Outcome: Students will increase their ability to gather, analyze and interpret information and seek solutions to problems.

Objectives: Students should be able to do the following:

1. Identify a problem or issue.
2. Gather and sort information related to the problem and—
   a. Recognize that statistics, observations, language and feelings are different types of information that form the basis of our knowledge about situations.
   b. Be able to understand that these different types of information are a common language rather than mystical jargon.
3. Interpret information related to the problem, recognizing the impact of biases both in the data and in themselves.
4. Develop a variety of alternatives and reach a decision or tentative conclusion.
5. Evaluate the results of their actions and be prepared to take an alternative course of action to deal with the problem or issue.

Why critical thinking is important. Critical thinking is one of the basic life skills because it serves as a logical way of organizing the various learning processes students encounter. Learning objectives for critical thinking describe a set of problem-solving techniques to help students manage their learning both in school and throughout their lives.

Critical thinking requires the systematic analysis of a problem and the application of some data and criteria in order to identify a solution. We all follow this process either formally or informally as we make decisions. The more aware we are of the elements in the process, the better decisions we are capable of making. For example, a student may want to buy a car. An analysis of the situation requires thoughtful selection of data (information), thinking about alternatives and finally applying some value elements (criteria) in making the final decision. Anything less would not constitute critical thinking but would be acting on impulse.

To conclude the example of the car, the student would need various data such as the condition of the car, comparative prices, costs of insurance, finance charges and assured income before deciding whether to purchase it or not. After these data are gathered and preferably listed, then alternatives such as riding the bus, getting a less expensive vehicle or going without lunches to buy gasoline should be thoroughly considered. In the final step, the student should apply some value criteria to the whole process and select the appropriate course of action. "How badly do I need a car? Is it for pleasure or do I need it to get to work earlier? Would it be more energy-efficient to ride the bus? Will I be able to go without lunches to buy gas? Should I do this?" These questions are all in the category of value criteria and are just as important as objective data in the critical thinking process. When students become aware of the systematic process of critical thinking, they are ready to develop lifelong critical thinking habits.

Experience-based learning assures practice in critical thinking because it depends so much on student/adult negotiation to set learning goals and plan activities. As students learn to manage their own time and learning, school staff will have many opportunities to evaluate their skills in this area.

The following *starter project* in critical thinking helps students practice critical thinking by working through three identified problems. Subsequent individually negotiated projects will draw on these problem-solving skills even more. That is why we recommend the critical thinking starter project as the first step for students if you are implementing the project process. A secondary purpose of the critical thinking starter project is to teach students to help write their own projects.

Starter Project: Critical Thinking

SUBJECT/TITLE: How to Solve a Problem When You See One
COMMUNITY RESOURCES: Any site of your choice
SCHOOL RESOURCES: Texts on preparing reports, sample projects,
          other students, staff
PURPOSE: To use a typical problem-solving strategy in three different
          situations and apply it to the writing of a project you can
          complete at a community site. The critical thinking method
          has five distinct parts: (1) identify a problem or issue,
          (2) gather and sort information related to the problem,
          (3) interpret that information, (4) develop alternative solu-
          tions and define a course of action, (5) evaluate the results
          of your action.

SUGGESTED ACTIVITIES:

1. Think of a real problem that is important to you and that you
   might be able to solve using the critical thinking process. In a
   discussion with staff, talk through the solution of this problem
   using the five-step method outlined above.
2. At a community site of your choice, discuss a hypothetical or
   site-related problem with a resource person who might be
   able to help you solve it. Write a report that discusses the
   problem in terms of the five problem-solving steps, even though
   you may not actually carry these steps out at this time.
3. Now apply the critical thinking process to the "problem" of
   writing projects. Identify and locate all the information you can
   about what a project is, the format it follows and how one is
   negotiated between you and school staff. Prepare a written
   summary of how you approached this task and resources you
   used. Make sure this report includes a complete definition
   and description of the steps required to write projects (ask
   staff for guidelines).
4. Based on what you found out in Step 3, develop at least three
   ideas for projects you might like to do and sketch out the title,
   resources, purpose, activities and possibilities that might be
   developed for each.
5. Choose one you would like to carry out and write it up as a set
   of activities you can do, with specified products or results.
6. Be prepared to defend your outlined project during a conference with the staff. Explain how the critical thinking process
   affected your approach to this project. With the staff, review
   the elements of the project you have written and revise it as
   necessary.

PRODUCT POSSIBILITIES: Written reports, lists, taped discussions with
          resource person, project plans

Functional Citizenship

Desired Outcome: Students will increase their understanding and application of democratic processes in interpersonal actions and in the private sector as well as in local, state and federal government.

Objectives: Students should be able to do the following:

1. Demonstrate that they understand the principles of democracy by comparing the activities of individuals and private or public institutions to those principles.
2. Explain and give examples of strategies for social and political change.
3. Analyze how systems of governance come into being and identify the assumptions on which those systems are based.
4. Demonstrate an understanding of the structure and functions of the three branches of American government.
5. Understand and give examples of how decisions are made and carried out at various levels of government.
6. Develop familiarity with the American tax system so students can identify its main purposes, sources of income and uses of monies.
7. Show an understanding of the distribution of power in American government through the use of examples.
8. Analyze the ways in which laws are made and enforced in a democracy.
9. Analyze the operations of organizations of their choice.
10. Understand why participation and responsibility are necessary in a democratic society.
11. Identify ways that citizens can participate in their government and society.

Why functional citizenship is important. There is little question that increased awareness of government and the responsibilities of citizenship is highly beneficial both to the student and to society. Learning objectives for this area stress that to be truly functioning citizens, students must be able to combine an understanding of how their government works with the actual exercise of democratic principles in their day-to-day activities.

Citizenship is inherently functional; we pay taxes, vote and abide by laws. The concern of this life skill is to increase student awareness of the ways they can become more functional and effective in exercising their citizenship. By focusing on processes, students begin to see citizenship as active, not passive. They see that it is more than paying taxes, voting and abiding by laws. It is also more than knowledge about the structure of government. It means knowing how to participate most effectively in the decision-making processes and total life of a community. Functional citizens know their rights as well as their responsibilities. They also know about the resources and services available to them (parks, health clinics and libraries to name a few).

Projects in this subject area should bring the student into direct contact with a variety of social/political activities in the local community. For example, a student interested in social work might begin a project that examines the role of volunteer workers in social agencies; another student interested in sheet metal fabrication might choose to examine union structure as it relates to that technology.

The *starter project* in functional citizenship asks students to reflect on the nature of democracy and other governmental forms of decision making. Students examine their own roles in governmental decision making and discover ways to become personally involved in affecting social and political change. Students also look seriously at the governmental structure of different organizations, including specific community sites.

Starter Project: Functional Citizenship

SUBJECT/TITLE: My Role as a Citizen

COMMUNITY RESOURCES: Any adult citizens; any community site; government representative, either hired or elected; government agency including Internal Revenue Service; state tax officials; county tax assessor; attorney; unions; personnel officers; agencies concerned with occupational safety and health; public interest research groups; employer associations

SCHOOL RESOURCES: U.S. Constitution, government textbooks, newspapers and magazines, telephone directory

PURPOSE: To become aware of the role of government in American life and how citizens can and should participate in governmental processes

SUGGESTED ACTIVITIES:

1. **Reasons for government**
   a. Prepare a list of questions people often have about why government is or is not necessary.

    b. Using these questions, interview three adults in the community and record their answers.

    c. Write and discuss your own statement about why we have government. Be prepared to name categories of needs (society's and individual's) to which any government should respond and be able to apply the categories in analyzing specific modes of government.

    d. Discuss with your community site resource person how decisions are made at that site. Compare this information with what other students may have discovered at their sites.

    e. Research your local government and report on:
- The decision-making and responsibility structure
- Making, interpreting and enforcing laws
- How citizens can affect decisions

    f. Discuss how you can make decisions for yourself in the following situations: at home, with friends, at community sites, at school. With whom do you share decision making in each of these settings?

2. **Citizen responsibility**

    a. Select a social problem that concerns you. Investigate that problem as a concerned citizen and find out how you can help solve it using the following questions as a guide:
- What is the problem? Who is affected by it?
- What are the causes?
- Who is trying to deal with the problem?
- Is the government involved? How?
- What are you going to do about it?
- What must happen in order to solve the problem or improve the situation?

    b. Describe your plan of action in detail and secure staff approval before beginning your investigation.

3. **American tax system**

    a. At a privately owned business in the community, identify at least two kinds of taxes paid by the business and submit a report that covers the following topics:
- What is the purpose of each tax?
- How is each computed?
- How is each collected?
- Where does the money go?

    b. Identify at least four kinds of taxes (other than income taxes) you might expect to pay as a citizen. Answer the same questions suggested in (a) above and add two more:
- Do you understand and agree with each tax?
- What alternatives might you suggest?

4. **Work-related regulations and codes**
List three laws or codes that apply to your community site and discuss the following questions with your resource person and school staff:
   - Who enforces these regulations?
   - What is their purpose?
   - Does your resource person feel the codes are serving their purpose?
   - What are the good and bad points of the codes as you see them?
   - How do these codes affect you as a citizen?
   - How can ineffective codes be changed?

5. **Practicing citizenship**
   a Provide a working definition of citizenship.
   b. Define the term "lobby."
   c. List five ways citizens can participate in the decision-making process at the city, county, regional, state or national level.
   d. Explain why such participation is essential in a democracy.
   e. Select one activity from *each* of the following groups:

   Group A
   (1) Attend a meeting of your local city council.
   (2) Attend a meeting of your local school board.
   (3) Attend a meeting of another governing body approved by the staff.

   Group B
   Select an issue or candidate and at the above meeting either:
   (1) Speak on behalf of the issue or candidate.
   (2) Speak in opposition to the issue or candidate.
   (3) Write a statement on behalf of the issue or candidate.
   (4) Write a statement in opposition to the issue or candidate.

   Group C
   (1) Attend and/or participate in a lobbying activity.
   (2) Join and participate in a citizen action group.
   (3) Help conduct a political poll.
   (4) Volunteer some time to a local public interest or community service group.
   (5) Locate and meet a precinct leader and become involved in a precinct activity.
   (6) Write a letter to the editor and get it published.

POSSIBLE PRODUCTS: Reports, written statements, taped interviews, photographic displays, published letter, participation in community activities, organizational charts

Personal/Social Development

Desired Outcome: Students will increase their ability to understand and accept responsibility for self, personal behavior and effects of actions and attitudes on others.

Objectives: Students should be able to do the following:

1. Demonstrate that they understand themselves by—
   a. Identifying, assessing and using information from a variety of sources to bring about personal growth and development
   b. Demonstrating a positive self-image
2. Demonstrate self-direction and responsibility by—
   a. Coping effectively with daily tensions and pressures
   b. Initiating action to further personal growth and development
   c. Making their own decisions and choices
   d. Setting realistic learning goals with a minimum of stress
   e. Describing and using various strategies of decision making in determining courses of action and goals
   f. Evaluating decisions and their end results
   g. Understanding the consequences of behavior in relation to themselves and others
3. Deal positively with human sexuality by—
   a. Understanding male/female roles as they have developed in various societies
   b. Explaining the influences of femaleness and/or maleness on their own personal development
   c. Understanding the effects of human sexuality on an individual's selection of goals and courses of action
4. Use personal information to enter into and maintain effective interpersonal relationships by—
   a. Describing individual and group behaviors in nonjudgmental terms
   b. Demonstrating involvement in group processes by talking, listening and looking at other group members
   c. Listening and contributing in individual or group discussions without interrupting or dominating the interaction
   d. Agreeing and disagreeing with members of a group without demonstrating hostility

Why personal/social development is important. As a life skill, personal/social development deals with what is perhaps education's most generalized and least measurable purpose: providing students with resources and experiences to help them develop and refine their attitudes toward themselves and society. Objectives include growth in such personal management skills as mental health, self-direction, self-analysis, interpersonal relations and responsibility.

Personal/social development is concerned here with creating individual awareness of the potential for self-fulfillment—not only what others think we can become but what we ourselves want to become. There are several dimensions to self-insight: What we enjoy doing and with whom. How we like working with people. What we like most and least in our relationships with others. What we enjoy doing when we are alone. What others praise us for on the job—the unusual skills and talents that others recognize in us and we recognize in ourselves. What we feel keeps us from achieving our perceived ideal self. By thinking about these questions and more, we can gain new insight into ourselves and heighten our awareness of what we can continuously become during life.

Projects written in this area should encourage students to look at themselves, exercise self-direction and responsibility and enter into effective interpersonal relationships with a variety of people. Through community site activities, students encounter personal management skills they will have to exercise in adult life and work—for example, getting along with others, being on time, choosing appropriate times and situations for frankness, expressing abilities and talents. Student interaction with adults in various community settings gives them a chance to reassess what they know about themselves, redefine future goals accordingly and develop the flexibility necessary to cope with the fact that not only are they entering a rapidly changing world but their self-concepts and goals will be changing as they grow and mature.

The *starter project* in this area asks students to describe themselves in an objective yet positive way and to apply the critical thinking process to examine who and what they are. Students then interpret what they have observed about themselves, identify a behavior they wish to change and define a course of action to achieve that change. They also reflect on themselves as they relate to interpersonal activities and consider how they perceive female and male roles in their own lives and in society. Students conclude the project by summing up their experiences in self-descriptions.

Starter Project: Personal/Social Development

SUBJECT/TITLE: What (Can I Do) About Me?
COMMUNITY RESOURCES: Any community site, personnel officers, state bureau of labor, women's studies programs
SCHOOL RESOURCES: Library, self-help books, magazines, other students, counselor, Equal Rights Amendment, affirmative action regulations, Title IX guidelines, equal employment legislation
PURPOSE: To know yourself better as an individual and as a member of a group and to learn some skills that can help you change your behavior to a syle that is more satisfying

SUGGESTED ACTIVITIES:
1. Positive self-description
   a. List ten of your personal strengths and ten personal weaknes-
      ses (some could be outward or physical; others may be in-
      side).
   b. Based on your list of strengths, show the good, positive you in
      one of the following ways:
      • Make an advertisement for yourself.
      • Use drawings, photographs and other materials to create
        a visual representation of you as *you* see yourself and you
        as *others* see you.
      • Write an autobiography.
      • Write a long, laudatory eulogy for yourself that will leave
        the reader teary-eyed.
   c. In your own words, define the following terms:

(1) assertiveness	(11) participant
(2) behavior	(12) personal goals
(3) behavior modification	(13) responsibility
(4) coping	(14) risk
(5) dominate	(15) self-awareness
(6) facilitate	(16) self-concept
(7) feedback	(17) self-direction
(8) group process	(18) social roles
(9) ideals	(19) strategy
(10) interpersonal	(20) trust
relationships	(21) values

   d. Ask school or city library staff or literature or psychology
      teacher to recommend a book that deals with a person who is
      looking deeply at his/her life and attempting to make
      changes. Read the book; then write a letter to the main
      character showing that you understand the changes this
      person went through and the processes involved.
2. Changing behavior
   a. Identify some behavior you would like to change in yourself
      and describe it either in writing, cartoons or on tape.
   b. At a community site, collect information about this behavior in
      the following way: select a period of time to observe yourself,
      count the number of times the behavior occurs, prepare a clear
      and simple chart or graph that depicts your data.
   c. Interpret the graph or chart and explain how this behavior
      could be affecting other people. Ask your resource person and
      someone else who knows you to read what you have written
      and see if it is an accurate interpretation. Amend it as needed.
   d. Plan a strategy for changing this behavior by—
      • Setting a goal
      • Listing all the things that work against your changing this
        behavior

- Listing all the things that could help you change this behavior
- Ranking each list starting with the item that's most important or easiest to do
- Setting a deadline to check how far you've come
- Evaluating your progress by talking it over with someone you trust

3. Being an effective group member
   a. Observe a group situation at school, home, church or community site and make notes to yourself about how the group seems to work.
   b. As a member of any group, practice using a group process skill called "perception check." Describe to a person in that group what you think the person's feelings are in order to check whether you really do understand what is going on "inside." Describe feelings without evaluating the person.
      Examples: *"I get the impression you'd rather not talk about this. Is that so?"*
      "You look like you felt hurt by my comment. Did you?"
      "Am I right that you feel disappointed because nobody commented on your new car?"
   c. Ask someone to observe you participating in a group and give you feedback on your group process skills.
   d. In a group setting with other students, evaluate your own ability to use group process skills.

4. Family effects on male and female roles
   a. Write a description of what you consider to be the ideal family.
   b. Read about family structures in at least three other cultures and prepare a chart that compares selected characteristics with your ideal family. Suggested categories for comparison:
      - Number of generations present in household
      - Chief decision maker
      - Person primarily in charge of child care
      - Chief provider of material goods
   c. Prepare a report displaying statistics that emphasize family structure and sex roles in the United States. Suggested data:
      - Percentage of families with single head of household
      - Sex of these heads of households
      - Percentage of mothers with children under six who are employed outside the home
   d. Choose some bases for comparison and compile a comparative study of your ideal family with a typical family either in the United States or in another culture. Try to analyze whether sex roles are related more to cultural patterns or to biological differences.

5. Sex role stereotyping
   a. For each of the following job titles, write down which sex comes to your mind first:
      - Secretary
      - Bank executive
      - School principal
      - Teacher
      - Hair stylist
      - Model
      - Truck driver
   b. Are you personally aware of exceptions? Explain.
   c. Pick a job title which is not normally associated with persons of your sex. Investigate and document the difficulties you might expect to encounter in trying to get that job. Are you aware of any sex discrimination related to hiring for this job? What recourse would you have if discrimination occurred?

PRODUCT POSSIBILITIES: Written reports, autobiography, eulogy, cartoon, graphs, charts, observation notes, essay

Creative Development

Desired Outcome: Students will increase their ability to identify the effects of and participate in creative processes.

Objectives: Student should be able to do the following:
1. Recognize and use the creative process in thinking, talking and writing.
2. Discuss the form and meaning of "art."
3. Identify and participate in creative experiences to develop skills and styles that satisfy their expectations.
4. Blend new and existing materials, ideas or concepts into unique or useful forms or experiences.

Why creative development is important. Creativity is an essential element of self-expression and contributes significantly to the individual's total growth. Creative development is, in fact, a valuable life skill that can help students find more satisfaction in both work and nonwork pursuits.

Creativity is related more to attitudes and the ways we act than to a specific product or result. Since creativity is by its nature a uniquely personal quality, learning objectives for projects in this area should serve as guidelines to help students recognize their own creative capacities and encourage them to become more confident about expressing themselves in creative ways.

Keep these elements in mind when writing student projects in creative development:
1. Creativity is a *process*, not a *product*, although it can result in a product.
2. The concept of creativity should not be limited to the arts; rather it is a way of understanding and dealing with all human endeavors and should be reflected in everything we do.
3. Projects should spur inventiveness and positive originality in any field rather than merely emphasizing participation in a particular art or craft.
4. While projects may address the history of art or the products of someone else's creativity, they should always stress the student's own creativity in the present.

Not everyone agrees on what creativity is or how it is brought about. We do know, however, that it finds expression in a variety of ways, from the little things each person does to think through a new situation to the more visible creative accomplishments of artists, architects and inventors. Encouragement, acceptance and conditions such as the following are necessary for optimum development of creativity:
- Exposure to different and contrasting cultural stimuli
- Openness to cultural stimuli

- Stress on becoming and not just being
- Free access to cultural media
- Tolerance for diverging views

Interaction with creative people in the community is also valuable for encouraging students to recognize and express the creativity in themselves.

The *starter project* in creative development asks students first to develop their own definition of creativity and then to look for examples of it in a variety of settings, including the community sites they are using. Students can interact with school staff, other adults and their peers in working out their ideas. However, they should take their own stand on what creativity is and defend and explain it in conversation with school staff and, as necessary, with resource people and other adults in the community.

The assessment of creativity is difficult since few precise definitions are acceptable to all. Many teachers center their evaluation on the product, which may or may not appear to be creative, but the *process* the student went through must also be considered. The process is just as important as the product. A few descriptive lines may be as much of a creation for one student as a poem is for another student. Or the act of breaking away from a traditional page layout in a report may be an important achievement. Look at creativity in a broad context, not just in the arts, keeping in mind that creativity can emerge in *any* area including art, music, dance, writing, dramatics, mechanical skills and social leadership.

Evaluation of any experience-based learning activity requires a sensitive communication between you and the student. It works toward the common goal of a better understanding of what the student has done and it prepares for subsequent learning activities. The creative development starter project will help you get to know what creativity means to each student; it will also provide a basis for giving individual feedback. Subsequent projects in creative development give the students a chance to exercise creativity as a skill.

Starter Project: Creative Development

SUBJECT/TITLE: Recognizing Creativity in New Ways
COMMUNITY RESOURCES: Any workplace in the community, museums and galleries, concerts, home television, arts and crafts stores, research laboratories, local performers, people in unique or unusual careers, self-employed people
SCHOOL RESOURCES: Library, magazines, art department
PURPOSE: To acquaint students with the creative process—how to recognize it and how to develop it
SUGGESTED ACTIVITIES:
    1. Definition of creativity
        Define the term "creativity" in writing after first reading various definitions and identifying examples of creativity in your own community. Point out how your examples fit your definition. Build a collection (e.g., a collage, scrapbook, photographs with

captions) of examples that reinforce your message. Be prepared to alter your definition if necessary as you work through this project.

(Hint for writing definition: List ten things you think are creative. On another sheet list words that apply to all ten creative things. Try to use those words in your definition.)

2. Using your definition
   a. Choose a creative idea that has had an impact on your life. Evaluate it according to your definition of creativity.
   b. Identify a community need that has not been met. Create and describe in detail a job that would both meet the community need and financially support you.
   c. Read accounts of the creation of life from several different religions; also read two current scientific theories of the creation of the universe. What do they all have in common? How do they differ? Do they all fit your definition of creativity?
   d. Select and study two pieces of recognized art at a gallery or museum; or listen to recorded music; or attend a live performance of dance, theater or music. Evaluate your selection as a creative event or object.

3. Career and leisure applications of creative processes
   a. Choose a situation at your community site which could be improved. Propose three creative alternatives. Select the one you think will best improve the situation. Discuss your choice and your reasons with your resource person.
   b. Select one activity from *each* of the following groups, or propose an alternative to your teacher:

   Group A
   (1) Spend an hour at a local art museum or gallery.
   (2) Attend some performing arts event.
   (3) Interview a local artist, performer, composer, writer, etc.
   (4) Critique a work of art, exhibit, musical piece, book, newspaper, landscape design, playground, building, etc.

   Group B
   (1) Select a creative medium and design and produce something that meets your definition of creativity.
   (2) Using "before and after" photographs, do some interior decorating in a room of your choice or do some outdoor landscaping.
   (3) Design a detailed plan for the physical improvement of your school or one part of your school.

   Group C
   (1) Keep a record of all costs for your activity in Group B and how long it took you; then create a detailed marketing plan for the product that resulted from your activity.
   (2) Create an advertisement for your product or services. Include prices.
   (3) Other:

4. Analyze the creative process
   a. Think about how it feels to create something:
      • Are you satisfied with your product?
      • What mental and physical skills did you use?
      • Is there room for improving these skills? In what ways?
      • Describe yourself as a creative person.
   b. Review your definition from Activity 1. Rewrite it if this project has changed your ideas.

PRODUCT POSSIBILITIES: Collage, photographs, written reviews, advertisements, taped interviews, invention, experiment, collection, play, poem, essay, any art or craft creation

Scientific Investigation

Desired Outcome: Students will increase their ability to recognize and apply rational procedures and methods, particularly in the analysis of technology's impact on natural environments and cultural values.

Objectives: Students should be able to do the following:
1. Use systematic, logical methods for testing the reliability of data.
2. Use cause and effect reasoning to explain a point of view.
3. Recognize precision, accuracy and self-discipline as necessary aspects of scientific investigation and discover by application the extent to which they either have these traits or are willing to develop them.
4. Discuss positive and negative consequences of advancing technology.
5. Describe a balance between technological progress and the quality of life.

Why scientific investigation is important. The existing level of technology in this country brings every person into direct contact with the results of science. Environmentalists have shown quite clearly what happens when we emphasize the products of science without understanding fully or attending to the effects of those products. Understanding scientific procedures of investigation and the impact of applied science on the natural environment and on human beings is essential.

Before the 1940's schools stressed one scientific method that leaned heavily on an interpretation of the writings of Dewey (1933). The prevailing concept was that the scientific method consisted of six steps:[2]

1. Defining the problem
2. Collecting data
3. Formulating a hypothesis on the basis of the collected data
4. Testing the hypothesis
5. Drawing a conclusion
6. Applying the conclusion

This method was stressed both as a general problem-solving technique and as a specific procedure for scientific discovery.

In 1961, the American Association for the Advancement of Science sponsored a major study designed to review the status of science in schools, beginning with the elementary level. This swung the emphasis away from science *content* toward scientific *processes*, and the more rigid scientific method gave way to a variety of generally accepted methods of investigation.

Today most science educators describe methods relating generally to what scientists do—observing, measuring, classifying, comparing, predicting, inferring and so forth. These methods differ for each problem. Few scientists would claim to follow precisely any one scientific method; instead they approach a problem with an intuitive application of various methods.[3]

Despite the many methods involved in scientific investigation, the logic of the earlier six steps still prevails:

- A problem is defined.
- Observations are collected.
- Observations are organized into patterns or correlations.
- A hypothetical solution to the problem is formed.
- The hypothesis is tested to see if it holds true under various conditions.
- A conclusion is drawn.

These six steps are in fact the old scientific method. And regardless of what is said about its obsolescence, all of these things are usually accounted for in any systematic process of investigation.

It is useful to point out to students how closely these steps relate to the logic of the critical thinking steps outlined in the starter project for that life skills area. It is also important for students to realize that scientific methods of inquiry or any other methods of problem solving do not necessarily yield the truth. Using systematic approaches to discovery, whether for ourselves or others, can only be expected to result in an increased likelihood of finding a true relationship or a relationship more closely approximating the truth.

Thus students should come to appreciate the role of uncertainty as a part of scientific investigation and to understand that human knowledge continually evolves. This is particularly important with respect to our attitude toward technology and its relationship to the environment and to our standard of living.

Learning objectives for scientific investigation emphasize logical, rational approaches applicable to many everyday problems. All students need not immerse themselves at great length in the facts and methods of a particular scientific discipline (biology, chemistry, physics, for example) to gain an understanding of scientific inquiry and its implications. Instead project activities should help students discover personally how to apply scientific methods of inquiry and how to recognize where applied science affects their lives. Using these methods will help students interpret more accurately what they subsequently read and study in the particular areas of science.

The *starter project* in this area encourages students to apply their unique interests and abilities to the realistic practice of scientific investigation. When negotiating subsequent projects with students, staff should try to build on activities practiced in this starter project, giving attention to both local and global implications of particular science issues and problems. In this way, students whose interests might be totally nonscientific are helped to perceive some of the ways in which science and technology affect society.

Interested students can plan projects for intensive community-based study of particular science fields. These projects might involve using resource materials from local public and private libraries and institutions and working closely with resource people who are experts in a given science. After exploring a local gypsum plant, for example, a student interested in chemistry might develop a project that focuses on more thorough investigation of that industry's application of chemistry.

Similarly, a student's general interest in science can often be given specific focus at a community site. For example, a student interested in working with people might explore a variety of medical/social community sites, become very interested in future study in medicine or psychology and consequently see the need to take a biology class in preparation for that study.

Starter Project: Scientific Investigation

SUBJECT/TITLE: Scientific Methods of Investigation

COMMUNITY RESOURCES: Almost any site can be used for Activities 1-4; Activity 5 is best accomplished using resources like research-oriented organizations, a museum of science and industry or a local planning commission

SCHOOL RESOURCES: Science texts and reference books, newspapers, magazines, lab equipment

PURPOSE: To acquaint students with scientific methods of problem solving and familiarize them with the extent to which science is involved in our lives

SUGGESTED ACTIVITIES:

1. Definition of science
   a. In your own words, describe steps that can be followed to solve problems scientifically. Check this statement with school staff to be sure you have accurately described steps for scientific investigation.
   b. In your own words, define the following scientific terms:

(1) analysis	(12) earth science
(2) atom	(13) experiment
(3) bacterium/virus	(14) hypothesis
(4) biology	(15) inductive thinking
(5) cell	(16) inertia
(6) chemistry	(17) light year
(7) chromosome	(18) mammal
(8) conclusion	(19) photosynthesis
(9) conservation of energy	(20) physics
(10) control	(21) scientific classification
(11) deductive thinking	(22) variable

   c. Identify two places outside the school where scientific methods of investigation are applied.
   d. Does careful application of scientific approaches to problem solving under controlled conditions always yield absolute truth or certainty? Discuss this with a resource person at one of the community sites identified above.
2. Identification of cause and effect relationships
   a. Prepare a written definition of cause and effect, with an example.
   b. Identify cause/effect reasoning in two magazine or newspaper articles.
   c. At a site of your choice, identify four examples of cause and effect.
3. Identification of scientific behaviors
   a. The following are activities often attributed to those who use scientific behaviors in their work. Using the following list, look for activities at your community site that suggest these types of behavior and activities that seem to demonstrate the opposite types of behavior:

(1) systematic behavior	(5) ability to identify
(2) critical thinking	cause and effect
(3) ability to use logical methods	(6) precision
(4) ability to rely on collected data	(7) accuracy

(8) self-discipline	independent decisions
(9) effective relationships	(12) ability to set and
with others	meet goals
(10) initiative	(13) ability to cope effectively
(11) ability to make	with stress

b. Rate yourself on these same factors.

c. Which factors would you need to develop in order to pursue a career in science?

4. Using scientific methods of investigation

a. Give ten examples of situations at one community site where scientific methods could be applied.

b. Select one problem from that site and apply each step of the scientific method you outlined in Activity 1a to reach some conclusion or solution to the problem.

c. Evaluate how well you used this method of investigation:

- Was I able to solve the problem?
- Did I correctly apply the scientific method?
- Did I adequately consider the possible alternative solutions?
- What biases did I have at the beginning of my research and how did I handle them?
- In what ways did I use mathematics to solve my problem?
- What skills have I developed that were particularly helpful in this process?
- What skills would I need to develop to become more efficient?
- Did I enjoy this experience? Why?

5. Finding science at work in the community

a. Select and visit a community site which advances science and/or technology or is an agency dealing with environmental or ecological issues. On that site, investigate an issue or an application of scientific methods. Use questions like these in gathering information:

- Where is the site located?
- Why is it in existence?
- What issues does it deal with or what products does it produce?
- How are scientific methods used?
- What is the social or cultural impact of this organization?

b. Determine with school staff how you will present your findings and then make that presentation at the conclusion of your investigation.

PRODUCT POSSIBILITIES: Oral discussion, written reports, taped interviews, experiments

BASIC SKILLS AND THEIR EVERYDAY APPLICATION

In addition to providing many learning opportunities related to subject areas or life skills, community sites can be analyzed for the many ways in which the basic skills—reading, mathematics and communication—are applied in everyday situations. Experience-based learning activities can then be designed to give students a chance to compare their basic skills abilities with the specific requirements of daily living and of careers that interest them. Students may be reading technical manuals, computing taxes and monthly expenses, explaining procedures to a customer, writing an office memo and so forth.

To help determine what kinds of activities, resources and settings are appropriate, try distinguishing between fundamental and applied basic skills as these are used at community sites. Fundamental skills are those proficiencies in a given discipline that are *prerequisite* to the actual performance of tasks, solution of problems or learning of concepts. Applied skills are those *used to perform* tasks, learn concepts and solve problems. Applied skills are used by students while completing tasks at community sites and achieving objectives in each life skills area.

For example, the applied skills of invoicing and pricing would have as their corollaries the fundamental skills of fractions, percentages, decimals; the applied skills of dealing with customers and writing ads would have as related fundamental skills the ability to organize thoughts, summarize main ideas, listen carefully, and understand and apply grammar/spelling skills. During site analysis it is helpful first to identify the applied skills and then to break out the fundamental skills.

COMMUNITY SITE ANALYSIS

The process of community site analysis is a key resource for developing individual, community-focused student learning plans. This process will help staff identify three kinds of learning opportunities at each site:

1. Onsite activities that can help students improve in basic skills
2. The relation of the job or site to the life skills or specific areas of the curriculum
3. Job skills needed at the site

Site analysis for the in-depth kinds of learning activities needed for individualized student projects should be done in an interview between a school staff person and site resource person. This method of collecting the information helps the resource person understand the kinds of things students will be doing onsite and helps the staff person know more about the site. It is usually an interesting experience for the resource person, too; resource people are often amazed at how many different skills and processes are applied daily at their sites.

Many experience-based learning programs use a specific form for community site analysis to facilitate the interviews and provide consistent kinds of information for all sites. The form is designed to gather two different levels of information—general data about the job and site and an in-depth task analysis of the resource person's job. All of this information is used to plan student learning activities at the site.[4]

General information includes:

1. Specific working conditions and requirements a student may encounter at the job (physical, clothing, equipment and safety requirements)

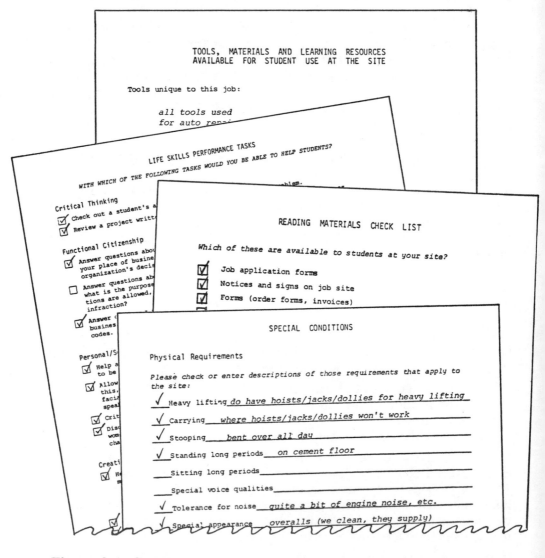

Figure 3-1. Sample community site analysis sheets used to gather general site information.

2. Site-related literature (manuals, catalogs, pamphlets and so forth) the student may use to learn about the job and practice basic skills
3. Potential life skill situations that may be encountered on that job and that could be incorporated into project activities for the site
4. Tools, equipment, materials and other learning resources available for student use at the site

The task analysis portion of the form includes:

1. Major tasks performed for a given job
2. Mathematics, reading and communications skills applied in that work setting, as well as applied job skills and life skills

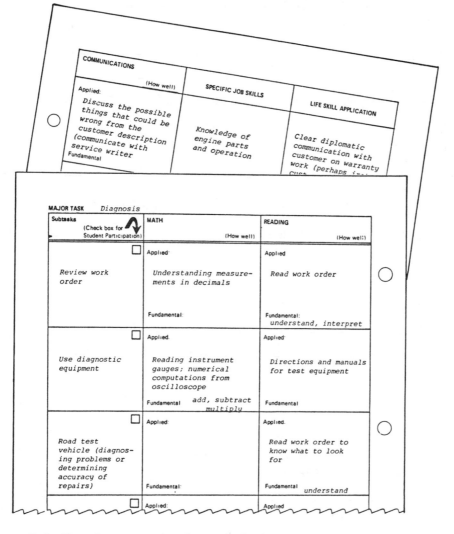

Figure 3-2. Sample community site analysis sheets used for in-depth analysis of job tasks and skills.

SPECIAL CONDITIONS

Physical Requirements

Please check or enter descriptions of those requirements that apply to the site:

✓ Heavy lifting *do have hoists/jacks/dollies for heavy lifting*

✓ Carrying   *where hoists/jacks/dollies won't work*

✓ Stooping   *bent over all day*

✓ Standing long periods *on cement floor*

___ Sitting long periods

___ Special voice qualities

✓ Tolerance for noise *quite a bit of engine noise, etc.*

✓ Special appearance   *overalls (we clean, they supply)*

✓ Tolerance for odors   *cleaning solvents, oil, gas, etc.*

✓ Driving ability   *moving cars*

Please list any other special physical requirements _general good_

    health and in shape to do physical work

Clothing, Equipment Requirements

✓ Driver's license ___ Hard hat ✓ Coveralls ___ Rain, foul weather gear

___ Uniform

___ OTHER

Safety Conditions

Please describe special safety restraints or conditions as designated by the resource person or contracts and agreements:

Safety in a garage - careful when moving cars and machines, no smoking, keep long hair out of way

Figure 3-3.

To complete the task analysis section the interviewer must help the resource person break down major work tasks into subtasks and the skills needed to perform each subtask. These skills form the basis for student learning opportunities in basic skills and life skills. Once this portion is filled out, learning objectives can easily be specified and then project activities written. (The process of writing learning objectives will be detailed in Chapter 4.) These learning objectives are then checked with the resource person for accuracy and sequencing.

The Community Site Analysis Process: A Simulation

Imagine that you are interviewing a resource person named Al at Brown Chevrolet to gain the information you'll need to help students plan learning experiences at that site. The following simulated interview illustrates techniques for gathering information using a community site analysis form. Any other community site could just as easily have been used for this example, but Brown Chevrolet was selected because everyone is basically familiar with such a business and the services it offers, thus providing a common ground from which to illustrate the analysis process.

Special Conditions (Fig. 3-3):

You: Let's talk first about what we call "special conditions"—things that might affect a student's physical comfort or safety. First, do any of the following physical requirements apply to a mechanic's job: heavy lifting?

 Al: Yes, quite a bit, although for the really heavy stuff like lifting transmissions, blocks and so forth, we have hoists or jacks.

You: How about carrying?

 Al: Sometimes—mostly in situations where hoists or jacks won't work.

You: Stooping?

(You continue down the list of physical requirements listed on the "Special Conditions" page and jot down Al's responses to each.)

You: What would you say about safety to a young person coming here?

 Al: We stress two main points all the time: be careful when you're moving equipment and cars around so you don't hurt anyone or yourself; and positively no smoking in the area where repairs are being made. We're strict about this—it's dangerous and we have to enforce it to the letter. Smoking where you're not supposed to automatically means you find another job.

Oh, another thing. I don't want to sound uptight, but we discourage long hair around here, too. If they have it longer than their collar they have to pull it back with a rubber band so it doesn't fall forward when they're working.

You: That's perfectly legitimate as far as we're concerned. Part of what we think is important for students to learn is that what an employer says to his employees goes.

```
                READING  MATERIALS  CHECK  LIST

    Which of these are available to students at your site?

    ☑    Job application forms
    ☑    Notices and signs on job site
    ☑    Forms (order forms, invoices)
    ☑    Catalogs
    ☑    Brochures or printed advertising
    ☑    Manuals and written instructions
    ☑    Schedules or lists
    ☐    Account statements
    ☑    Letters, memos, notes (a sampling)
    ☑    Reports, pamphlets or articles in publications
    ☐    Telephone lists or lists of extensions
    ☑    Address lists
    ☑    Labels or writing on packages
    ☐    Union or labor force contracts
    ☐    Personnel tests regularly administered
    ☑    Any other specific work-related materials
    ☐    List others

         _____

         _____

         _____


    Using the list above as a reference, select three pieces of written
    material you feel must be read in order to do the job satisfactorily.

    ____ Mfg's repair instructions _____

    ____ Instruct. for diagnostic equipment _____

    ____ Order forms/instructions/parts manuals _____
```

Figure 3-4.

Reading Materials (Fig. 3-4):

You: OK, it looks as if we've covered everything on the first page. Next I need to know what reading materials would be available to the student here in the shop—things an employee would actually have to read. This list can be pretty important because it will not only cue us and the student as to what information's available about the site, but it can also be useful if a student is looking for extra basic skills to practice.
Let me run through this list: job application forms?

Al: Yes, I could get some from the office manager.

You: Notices and signs on job site?

Al: Yes.

You: Anything like order forms, invoices and so forth?

Al: Sure, we've got plenty of those. In fact, students can be involved in completing all the written records we do.

(You continue down the "Reading Materials Checklist" and conclude by asking Al to pick out what he thinks are the three most important things a student should read while there.)

Al: Well, there really are a lot of things the workers have to read to do their jobs. But I guess the repair specifications we get from manufacturers on certain makes and styles of vehicles are really important. So are the instruction manuals for our diagnostic equipment. Maybe the third would be order forms and instructions for obtaining parts and supplies—and parts manuals themselves. Actually, it's surprising how much you do have to read around here!

LIFE SKILLS PERFORMANCE TASKS

WITH WHICH OF THE FOLLOWING TASKS WOULD YOU BE ABLE TO HELP STUDENTS?

Critical Thinking

☑ Check out a student's ability to recognize and solve a problem.

☑ Review a project written by a student that involves your place of business.

Functional Citizenship

☑ Answer questions about the ways in which various aspects of democracy impact your place of business; for instance, what role do employees play in your organization's decision-making process?

☐ Answer questions about business taxes that affect your business; for instance, what is the purpose of the tax, how is it collected and computed, what exemptions are allowed, who regulates the tax and what are the penalties for infraction?

☑ Answer questions about work-related regulations and codes that affect your business and employees; give your opinions about the relative merits of those codes.

Personal/Social Development

☑ Help a student identify and analyze a behavior he or she possesses that needs to be strengthened or eliminated.

☑ Allow a student to analyze a conversation in which you are involved. (To do this, a student will try to interpret nonverbal clues such as tone of voice, facial expression, body movements, etc., in an effort to understand how the speaker feels.)

☑ Critique a student's observations.

☑ Discuss equal employment codes and how these have affected the types of jobs women and men hold within your place of business. If job patterns have changed, explain how.

Creative Development

☑ Help a student understand creativity not just as expressed in painting, music or crafts, but as a process related to all aspects of life:

    a. Help the student identify creative business methods or operations.

    b. Allow the student to photograph creative products or methods at your business.

☑ Help the student identify a situation at your site that could be improved.

☑ Critique the student's proposed suggestions for improving that situation.

Scientific Investigation

☑ Help the student apply scientific methods, including the following steps: (1) observe a problem or process; (2) look for patterns and correlations; (3) formulate a theory or hypothesis; (4) use the hypothesis to make a prediction; (5) test the theory or hypothesis as it might impact your place of business; (6) draw a conclusion.

☑ Critique the student's recommendations.

☑ Help students identify cause and effect relationships and situations at your site.

Figure 3-5.

Life Skills Areas (Fig. 3-5):

You: Now, how do you feel about helping students work on project activities related to some of the following topics and tasks: "Check out a student's ability to recognize and solve a problem."

Al: Sure. We're solving problems every day as we make repairs.

You: Would you be willing to review a project a student might write about your shop? Some projects are actually designed and written by the students, but they have to be screened carefully by you or someone else at the site to make sure they are on target.

Al: That sounds fine. Can't think of anything terribly controversial that could come up!

(You continue down the page and list possible project tasks by paraphrasing each so that Al understands what the tasks might involve, and you check the box by each task Al agrees to.)

Job Task Analysis (Figs. 3-6 through 3-10):

You: Now we need to record what a mechanic's job consists of so we can figure out what a student could do to learn about it, while at the same time acquiring some important basic and life skills. We will be using this information to put together what we call learning objectives to use for designing projects.

Tell me about being a mechanic: what is the job all about, what do mechanics have to do, what work are they responsible for? Don't be concerned about the order in which you tell me things. As you talk, I'll jot down what we call "major tasks"—the big responsibilities in the job and "subtasks"—the smaller parts of each big responsibility. Then, when you've described it generally to me, I'll read back to you what I've got so we can agree before going any further. Maybe reviewing a typical day's or week's activities is a good way to begin, or you might find some of these cue words helpful *(see Fig. 3-6, next page).*

CUE WORDS

The following list of cue words can be used as prompters to help resource people specify the kinds of activities that are suitable for student learning at their sites.

READING	COMMUNICATIONS	MATH	
Identify	Compose	Add	Measure
Interpret	Copy	Balance	Multiply
Skim	Describe	Calculate	Percent
Understand	Direct	Calibrate	Ratios
	Discuss	Centigrade	Subtract
	Edit	Count	Use Money
	Enunciate	Decimals	
	Flexible Vocabulary	Degree of Angle	
	Inform	Degrees of Heat	
	Instruct	Divide	
	Interview	Estimate	
	Listen	Fahrenheit	
	Paraphrase	Formulas	
	Persuade	Fractions	
	Record		
	Summarize		
	Transcribe		

SPECIFIC JOB SKILLS			LIFE SKILLS APPLICATION
Administer	Develop	Mark	Analyze
Adjust	Diagnose	Memorize	Chart
Advise	Discriminate	Mix	Comprehend
Alphabetize	Draw	Nail	Create
Analyze	Drill	Post	Empathize
Appraise	Drive	Reason	Generalize
Arrange	Examine	Repair	Negotiate
Assemble	Excavate	Replace	Observe
Bore	Experiment	Score	Perceive
Build	Fabricate	Serve	Realize
Classify	File	Service	Relate
Clean	Finish	Setup	Resolve
Compare	Install	Solder	Solve
Compile	Investigate	Sort	Synthesize
Control	Layout	Spray	Translate
Coordinate	Locate	Test	Use Statistics
Design	Lubricate	Type	
Detect	Manipulate	Weld	

Figure 3-6.

Major Tasks (Fig. 3-7):

Al: OK, let me first go through in a very general way what a mechanic does. Maybe it would help to talk about one particular car coming into the shop. That should at least touch on most of the things we do here.

First of all, when someone brings a car in for repair you have to figure out what needs to be done. Most of the time they'll tell you something sounds wrong or "it's doing something funny," but they don't know what the problem is. It's up to the service representative to listen to their description of the problem and then write the description and possible causes on a work order. The work order is what mechanics use to figure out what has to be done. They usually check the car out to get more specific. For example, the work order may read "hum in transmission" or "rattle in dashboard," but the

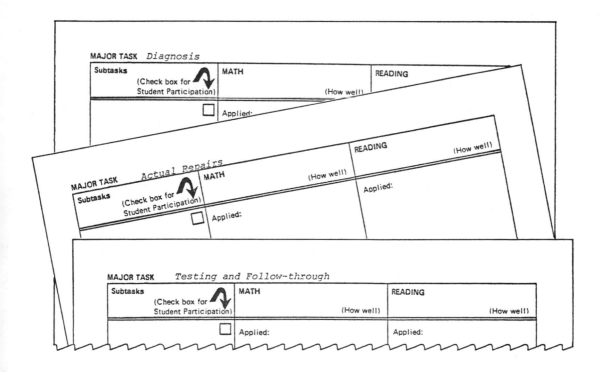

Figure 3-7.

MAJOR TASK   *Diagnosis*

Subtasks (Check box for Student Participation)	MATH (How well)	READING (How well)
☑ *Review work order*	Applied: Fundamental:	Applied: Fundamental:
☑ *Use diagnostic equipment*	Applied: Fundamental:	Applied: Fundamental:
☑ *Road test vehicle (diagnosing problems or determining accuracy of repairs)*	Applied: Fundamental:	Applied: Fundamental:
☐	Applied: Fundamental.	Applied: Fundamental:
☐	Applied: 	Applied:

Figure 3-8.

mechanic has to start investigating what it actually is—maybe by taking the car for a test drive or using some of our diagnostic equipment.

You: That seems like it would be the first major task the mechanic does —trying to figure out what's wrong with the car.

Al: Right. Until you do that you can't do anything. We call this first step "diagnosis."

(You write "diagnosis" in the "Major Task" space at the top left of the first task analysis page; see Fig. 3-7.)

You: OK, so then what does the mechanic do?

Al: Fixes it! Once you figure out what's wrong, you do whatever work is necessary.

You: So major task number two becomes—what shall we call it? Actual repairs?

Al: Right. And then the only thing left for that particular job is testing what you've done and wrapping things up—you know, cleaning up your work area and writing the final order.

You: Good. We'll call that "testing and follow through."

Subtasks (Fig. 3-8):

You: OK, let's go back now and try to dig into a little more detail about each of these three major tasks. We want to find out a little more about what makes up each one—in other words, what their subtasks are. Let's begin with diagnosis.

Al: I'd say it's pretty simple, really. The mechanic reads the work order and, if necessary, clarifies what's written on it with the service writer. Then the mechanic investigates, looking the car over, testing it on the equipment, taking it out on the road if necessary.

You: Good. How about my breaking those things out into their own subtasks just as you described them: review work order, use diagnostic equipment, road test. Can students actually do the subtasks themselves?

Al: Yes, with our supervision.

(You proceed in a similar way with the two other major tasks and extract for each the subtasks that make them up. Each one that can be performed by students is checked.)

From Subtasks to Basic Skills (Figs. 3-9 and 3-10):

(The next step is to break down each subtask even further into skills a student could learn while performing each.)

You: What we have to do now is examine each of these subtasks for math, reading, communication, job skills and life skills the student could learn to do. For "review work order," tell me a little more about what a student would need to know in order to be able to do that adequately.

Al: First, be able to read somebody else's writing and interpret what the service writer meant. That would involve being familiar with terms related to auto repair and understanding measurement tools, such as calipers and so on. Then you have to be able to communicate with the service writer and even sometimes with customers, especially for warranty work. Naturally, once in awhile you get someone who's mad about something, so the mechanic has to be a reasonable person who can handle that type of thing.

You: Let me check this. Necessary math skills would be understanding measurements—at what level?

Al: Decimals, for instance.

You: OK. Would necessary reading skills usually just be reading a handwritten work order and understanding or interpreting someone else's directions?

(Al nods yes)

You: And communications skills would involve talking with both the service representative and possibly a customer to narrow down the problem? Now, what about specific job skills for diagnosis?

Al: Well, you've got to be familiar with engine parts and operation.

You: OK. And what about life skills—things you have to do generally that are related to specific school subjects or human relations?

Al: I guess you have to be able to talk with the customer—know how to handle someone who's really upset with their car or thinks you're not getting at the problem.

You: All right, let's go on to the next subtask, "Using diagnostic equipment."

(Continue through all the subtasks in a similar manner and fill in information on the form as you proceed. Figures 3-11 and 3-12 at the end of this chapter represent a completed analysis of one major task. Separate forms would be filled out for each major task identified for a job.)

MAJOR TASK *Diagnosis*		
Subtasks (Check box for Student Participation)	**MATH** (How well)	**READING** (How well)
☑ *Review work* *order*	Applied: *Understanding measure-* *ments in decimals* Fundamental:	Applied: *Read work order* Fundamental: *understand, interpret*
☑ *Use* *diagnostic* *equipment*	Applied: *Reading instrument* *gauges; numerical* *computations from* *oscilloscope*	Applied: *Directions and* *manuals for test* *equipment*

Figure 3-9.

COMMUNICATIONS (How well)	SPECIFIC JOB SKILLS	LIFE SKILL APPLICATION
Applied: *Discuss the possible* *things that could be* *wrong from the* *customer description;* *communicate with* *service writer* Fundamental:	*Knowledge of engine* *parts and operation*	*Clear diplomatic* *communication* *with customer on* *warranty work* *(perhaps irate* *customer)*
Applied: *Writing out results* *on work order--* *recommendation for* *customer repairs*	*Learn to use the* *oscilloscope, other* *test equipment* *(increment of change)*	

Figure 3-10.

MAJOR TASK _Diagnosis_

Subtasks (Check box for Student Participation)	MATH (How well)	READING (How well)
☑ _Review work order_	Applied: _Understanding measurements in decimals_ Fundamental:	Applied: _Read work order_ Fundamental: _understand, interpret_
☑ _Use diagnostic equipment_	Applied: _Reading instrument gauges; numerical computations from oscilloscope_ Fundamental: _add, subtract multiply_	Applied: _Directions and manuals for test equipment_ Fundamental:
☑ _Road test vehicle (diagnosing problems or determining accuracy of repairs)_	Applied: Fundamental:	Applied: _Read work order to know what to look for_ Fundamental: _understand_
☐	Applied: Fundamental.	Applied: Fundamental:
☐	Applied:	Applied:

Figure 3-11. The first page of a completed analysis for one major task in a mechanic's job. Identifies subtasks and skills needed to do those tasks.

COMMUNICATIONS (How well)	SPECIFIC JOB SKILLS	LIFE SKILL APPLICATION
Applied: *Discuss the possible things that could be wrong from the customer description; communicate with service writer* Fundamental:	*Knowledge of engine parts and operation*	*Clear diplomatic communication with customer on warranty work (perhaps irate customer)*
Applied: *Writing out results on work order-- recommendation for customer repairs*	*Learn to use the oscilloscope, other test equipment (increment of change)*	
Applied: *Writing a service order; discussing with other mechanics or customer* Fundamental:	*Feeling car's vibrations; hearing a miss, wind leak, etc.*	*Diagnosis by feel and sound*
Applied: Fundamental:		
Applied:		

Figure 3-12. Second page of the completed analysis for one major task in a mechanic's job. Further defines skills needed to do the subtasks identified on the first page.

Using Site Information to Plan Projects

Once the site analysis has been completed, staff will have information they need to plan learning projects with individual students. Chapter 4 explains how a site analysis is translated into learning objectives and how student projects are negotiated to fit both the student and the site.

FOOTNOTES

[1]National Association of Secondary School Principals' Task Force on Secondary Schools in a Changing Society, *This We Believe: Secondary Schools in a Changing Society* (Reston, Virginia: NASSP, 1975), p. 16.

[2]John Dewey, *How We Think* (New York: Heath, 1933).

[3]Thomas S. Hall, et al., "Science Teaching in Elementary and Junior High Schools," *Science* 133 (1961): 2019-24.

[4]The Site Information form described in Chapter 2 for community explorations parallels only the first half of the more detailed site analysis form illustrated in Figs. 3-1 through 3-12.

4

WRITING STUDENT PROJECTS

> The value of activity increases when it
> is personal, when one's own concern
> generates it, when one is committed,
> and when one's abilities and viewpoint
> are expressed. The process and the
> outcome should matter to the student.
> Value also increases when the activity
> characterizes the real world, rather
> than the school world, in problem
> solving necessary in life rather than
> in practice exercises. And the value
> for learning increases when the
> activity challenges, when it tests the
> students' ability to make ideas work,
> to overcome obstacles, to learn from
> mistakes and to achieve the goals they
> set.
>
> —*Maurice Gibbons, The New*
> *Secondary Education*[1]

Student projects for experience-based learning combine the best instructional techniques of the one-room schoolhouse with the finest innovations on today's educational scene. The process accomplishes several important things:

- Restores two-way communication between teacher and student
- Integrates different subject areas

99

- Requires student practice in the basic skills
- Requires students to be accountable and think through problems logically
- Measures performance rather than book knowledge
- Helps students use community learning resources in a planned, in-depth way

Four aspects of project writing are discussed in this chapter: how to translate each site analysis into learning objectives, how to relate projects to students' assessed basic skill needs, how to plan projects with students based on learning objectives and needs, and how to use some basic project-writing steps.

FROM SITE ANALYSIS TO LEARNING OBJECTIVES

From an analysis of the learning potential at each community site (see Chapter 3), objectives can be written to specify the many different activities a student can perform either at the site or in relation to the job or site. To be most useful to you in project planning, these objectives should be written to capture elements of both outcome goals and behavioral objectives. For example, from the sample site analysis at Brown Chevrolet (pages 85-97 , Chapter 3), here are just a few of the learning objectives that could be specified:

- The student will be able to write work orders that accurately describe the needs of the customer.
- The student will be able to add, subtract, multiply and divide with 100 percent accuracy as required for use of diagnostic equipment.
- The student will be able to communicate results of the road test to other mechanics and the customer.

Objectives written at this level allow you to state clearly what students should be able to do while still retaining flexibility in tailoring activities to the varying interests, needs and abilities of your students.

The Completed List of Learning Objectives

Your completed list of learning objectives for a given site will be quite extensive and should capture the learning possibilities in each of the major tasks and subtasks identified during site analysis. Work systematically through the information recorded for each task discussed during site analysis, listing as many learning objectives as possible from the subtasks and skills that have been identified. Figure 4-1 illustrates a completed list of the learning objectives written from the site analysis simulated in Chapter 3.

Objectives by Extension

Other objectives can be derived from the site analysis *by extension*, as illustrated on page 103. These objectives will involve the student in activities derived from but not directly linked to participation in actual job tasks. These extended objectives will vary, depending on curriculum needs and the degree to which students are allowed to be actually involved in work tasks. The site is likely to be just one of several resources for this type of objective.

Extended objectives make each community site a truly flexible learning resource. They can lead to a more reflective and analytical approach to the job and site and are easily specified. For almost any site, students can do the following kinds of activities:

1. Historical, legal or environmental research
2. Collection and conversion of information into statistical reports, organizational charts, diagrams, graphs and flow charts
3. Computation of costs, profits or taxes
4. Written reports in various forms
5. Oral or audiovisual presentations
6. Application of problem-solving processes such as critical thinking or scientific investigation

---

LEARNING OBJECTIVES

The following objectives have been written from the community site analysis for *Brown Chevrolet* and reflect activities a student can do at that site.

MAJOR TASK: DIAGNOSIS
Subtask: "Review Work Order"

1. The student will become familiar with work orders used on the site and indicate an ability to—
   a. Read the work orders used to communicate the repairs that are needed to the service manager and the mechanics.
   b. Write work orders; the student will either obtain blank work orders or make facsimilies and demonstrate an ability to write work orders that accurately describe the needs of the customer.
2. The student will observe the ways in which the service manager discusses problems that the customer is having with his or her car; the student will observe the communication skills that are needed and also will be able to, when possible and allowed, take these descriptions and write them into work orders.

Figure 4-1. Completed list of learning objectives for Brown Chevrolet (community site analyzed in Chapter 3).

Subtask: "Use Diagnostic Equipment"

3. The student will be able to—
   a. Read instruments and gauges.
   b. Perform numerical computations from the oscilloscope.
   c. Add, subtract, multiply and divide with 100 percent accuracy as required for use of diagnostic equipment.
   d. Read directions and manuals on how to operate the testing equipment.
   e. Use electronic equipment to diagnose engine problems.
   f. Write out results of diagnosis on work orders.

Subtask: "Road Test a Vehicle" (for diagnosing problems)

4. The student will be able to—
   a. Read the work order to know what to look for.
   b. Understand the required work on a particular car by reading other work orders.
   c. Road test the car and determine by vibrations what repairs might be indicated.
   d. Hear a "miss."
   e. Listen and observe for wind leaks and so forth.
   f. Write any repairs that are needed on the work order and discuss with other mechanics or the customer.

MAJOR TASK: ACTUAL REPAIRS

Subtask: "Disassemble a Car for a Final Diagnosis"

5. The student will be able to—
   a. Read manuals to determine types of repair needed.
   b. Read work orders to interpret repairs as needed.
   c. Discuss with other line mechanics and the service manager the diagnosis for the disassembled car.
   d. Be able to read micrometers, calipers and other precision gauges.
   e. Measure with 100 percent accuracy for size of replacement parts.

Subtask: "Actual Repairing"

6. The student will be able to—
   a. Compute the pounds per square inch using a torque wrench.
   b. Read three work orders.
   c. Fill out purchase order for parts.
   d. Use hand tools as necessary for particular repairs.
   e. Spell the names of the ten most frequently used tools with 100 percent accuracy.

Subtask: "Reassembly and Filling Out Time Accounting Cards"

7. The student will be able to—
   a. Compute and record the time required to complete a job to the nearest tenth of an hour.
   b. Read directions on forms.

Figure 4-1. *(continued)*

c. Become familiar with the system for keeping track of time on trouble-shooting jobs and be able to fill in the forms to report this accurately.

d. Be able to read a time clock.

MAJOR TASK: TESTING AND FOLLOW-THROUGH

Subtask: "Electronic Retest"

8. The student will be able to—
   a. Calibrate an oscilloscope.
   b. Compute information from numerical gauges.
   c. Read the gauges and instruments and demonstrate an understanding of how they operate and the type of information obtained from them.

Subtask: "Road Test"

9. The student will be able to—
   a. Recheck a work order by road testing a car and writing the results of the test.
   b. Communicate the results of the road test to other mechanics and/or the customer.

Subtask: "Credit for a Completed Job and Cleaning Up After Work"

10. The student will be able to—
    a. Explain the importance of cleaning tools.
    b. Write up final orders for turning in to cashier with the key.
    c. Identify any other tasks that are necessary in wrapping up the final job.

OBJECTIVES DERIVED BY EXTENSION*

11. The student will prepare a chart of the organizational structure of the service department that includes the positions of the service manager and upper management.

12. The student will interview people at the site to get an overall picture of the range of jobs performed.
    (This could include mechanics, service advisers, office staff and the general manager. The intent of this objective is to familiarize the student with other positions that might be available in an operation the size of this one. Activities could include writing descriptions of key positions in the service department and in other departments, including statements of major responsibilities for each person interviewed, typical tasks performed, basic education, training or experience requirements for each of the positions and any other data that would be necessary or important to the person being interviewed.)

13. The student will study the environmental issues associated with the automobile industry.

Figure 4-1. *(continued)*

*These objectives are derived from activities at the site but are not directly linked to information gained during site analysis.

(This could include what happens with used parts, oil and so forth, and the responsibility that the automobile industry assumes in ecological problems.)

14. The student will show an understanding of the relationship of well-tuned engines to air pollution.
    (This could be part of a more in-depth study of ecological problems.)
15. The student will conduct research on the taxation of automobiles. *(Another research topic could be the laws that regulate the auto repair business, such as any legal responsibilities to guarantee repairs, price-fixing restraints and so forth.)*
16. The student will conduct research on the considerations that go into car design including functional and safety considerations, visual appeal and cost factors.

Figure 4-1. *(continued)*

Relating Objectives to Actual Tasks

As you can see from Fig. 4-1, writing learning objectives from the site analysis results in a long list of objectives that have both direct and indirect relationship to actual job tasks. Remember that these are only *potential* site objectives; how involved students will be permitted to become in specific job tasks will influence precisely how you plan the actual learning objectives.

When the list of potential site objectives is developed to your satisfaction, you should identify how involved the student could become in actual work tasks at the site relating to each objective. This will help you when you are developing project activities from the learning objectives and are deciding who should certify the student's satisfactory performance of the activities, as well as what criteria should be used for that evaluation.

The following coding system might be used:

1. *Not Observe (NO)*: The student cannot even observe the job activity (too confidential, legal restrictions, sanitary regulations, safety factors).
2. *Observe Only (OO)*: The student can only observe the job activity (no hands-on allowed).
3. *Attempt/Practice (AP)*: The student can attempt and practice the job activity (but cannot expect to learn to perform at the level of an employee).
4. *Practice and Learn (PL)*: The student can reasonably expect to learn to perform as well as an employee after practicing (keeping in mind the length of time the student will be at the site).

You might write the appropriate code letters beside each learning objective in preparation for project planning with students. Some learning objectives may involve more than one level of participation, and a student might pursue these by degrees.

Remember that even activities falling into the *Not Observe* and *Observe Only* categories can be used as a basis for student learning objectives and project activities. For example, a student interested in knowing about brain surgery could interview a surgeon or surgical nurse to find out what goes on in the off-limits surgery and recovery rooms. Similarly, a student in a psychiatrist's office could do a research report based on written literature or films about confidential aspects of that job.

Getting the Resource Person's Okay

After you have converted the analysis of a community site into learning objectives and identified the degree of onsite student involvement for each objective, you should have the objectives and student involvement levels approved by the resource person who will work with students at the site. This gives the resource person an opportunity to see in advance the kinds of learning activities you will be negotiating with students. The resource person can check your interpretation of the site analysis before you actually begin project planning with an individual student. Involving the resource person in these preliminary steps of project planning is essential before the student arrives onsite.

ASSESSING THE BASIC SKILLS NEEDS OF STUDENTS

In order to translate the site learning objectives into valid learning experiences for each individual student, you will need to assess the students' abilities and needs in the areas of math, reading, writing and oral communications. Regardless of the students' ability levels in these areas, you can plan learning activities that utilize the reality base of the onsite activities. For example, a student with solid math skills might be able to meet Objective 7(a) in Fig. 4-1 on the first attempt. For another student, attempting this objective could reveal a learning need, causing you to plan background math practice in the identified areas of need. This student might need to practice timekeeping, simple addition or following directions, but the student would clearly see the reason for working on these skills.

Basic skills assessment information can be developed for each student from several sources:

1. Past educational experiences, including transcript data and observations of past performance
2. Ability tests commonly available in schools
3. Individually administered diagnostic tests such as informal reading inventories
4. Initial student journal entries, reviewed by school staff for indication of each student's skills
5. Basic self-assessment exercises performed by students at community

sites during explorations or ongoing project work (the student practices several job-related basic skills tasks to see whether present abilities and interests match the skill levels and involvement required to perform the job)

6. Student comments about their skills in response to questionnaires and interviews

You can use all of these as sources for a general overview of the student's language and computation skills. For example, a student might be strong in certain math skills, average in writing/communication skills and weak in reading skills. You can go beyond this overview, however, and use individualized assessment activities with students as diagnostic tools to pinpoint exact skills and difficulties. This precise diagnostic information can then be the starting point for planning learning activities specific to the student's abilities, interests and goals.

Once a student is actively involved in ongoing learning activities, the evaluation of these activities can provide basic skills information that is as useful as the initial assessment information in planning subsequent activities. For example, if a student scores well on standardized tests but cannot communicate complex ideas in writing, you can plan sequential reading, discussing, writing and analysis activities to help the student develop needed writing skills.

Basic Skills Exercises at the Site

Specific activities can be worked into projects to help students improve their basic skills. These activities are planned in keeping with each student's needs and reflect realistic work activities at a site. The following example lists suggested activities to help a student improve communication skills:

1. The student reviews the list of site-related reading materials developed as part of the site analysis (see page 86).
2. From this list, the student selects three different kinds of reading materials that have been checked, such as:
   - Instuction manual or information pamphlet
   - Routine memo or letter
   - List of names and addresses
3. For each of the above items the student will demonstrate competence appropriate to the item. For example:
   - Instruction manual or information pamphlet
     The student will read and explain or demonstrate the action required by a designated passage.
   - Routine memo or letter
     The student will read a memo or letter and satisfactorily explain orally or in writing (a) the main points, (b) the writer's purpose and (c) specific facts and details. This could also be demonstrated by composing a reply to the letter or memo.

- List of names and addresses
  The student will demonstrate ability to locate five names on an alphabetical listing and accurately copy the names, addresses and telephone numbers (if given).

Lists of site-related objectives can be planned for all the basic skills.

GUIDELINES FOR PROJECT PLANNING

Now that you have translated site learning potential into learning objectives (see Fig. 4-2) and assessed student basic skills needs, you are ready to sit down with a student to plan an experience-based learning project. Ideally, project planning is highly individualized. It is a negotiation process in which both you and the student play an equal part:

1. Matching each student's expressed and assessed interests and learning needs with the site learning objectives that seem most appropriate for the student
2. Writing out specific project activities that will meet the learning objectives in terms of the individual student's interests and needs

This process of project planning can be an exciting experience for both of you. No special training is required for successful project planning, but the following are some suggested techniques to help the process work smoothly.

Help Students Accept the Challenge of Individualized Learning

Experience-based learning is a departure from more traditional, passive forms of education; it requires much more student involvement in planning their own learning. You may have to help students become accustomed to this more individualized way of learning before you can have effective project planning sessions.

You might begin with small group discussions about the ways students can make learning activities fit their personal needs and goals. Challenge them to start defining their own short-term needs and reasonable long-term goals. Help them describe what they want to do and learn in terms that seem real (not just saying what they think you want them to say). Help them begin to identify things they need to learn to make their lives better now and in the future.

Figure 4-3 is a sample Goal Questionnaire used in some experience-based learning programs to help students start thinking in the personal terms that are so necessary to effective planning of individualized learning activities. This questionnaire can be administered individually and then used as the starting point of a small group discussion about the ways students can get involved in planning their education. During this small group session, introduce a sample project such as the Creative Development starter project (see page 74). Discuss this project with the students, explaining clearly both the overall intent of the project and the primary learning objective for each separate activity. Then illustrate how various other activities, personalized according to individual students' goals and abilities, could meet the same learning objectives. This kind of group discussion helps prepare students to negotiate individualized learning projects that still meet identified curriculum objectives.

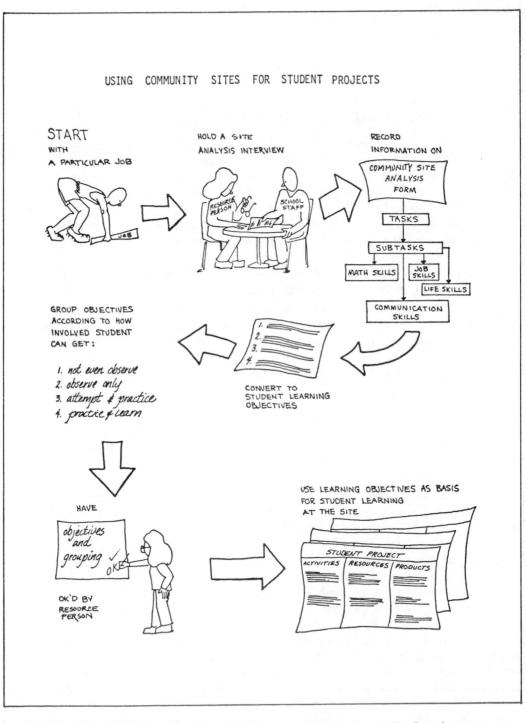

Figure 4-2. Steps to follow in relating the learning potential of each community site to project planning.

GOAL QUESTIONNAIRE

Skills/knowledge you (will) want or need	Learning activities you could do to get them	Ways school could help you reach your goals
Every day:		
1.	1.	1.
2.	2.	2.
3.	3.	3.
A few months from now:		
1.	1.	1.
2.	2.	2.
3.	3.	3.
In five years:		
1.	1.	1.
2.	2.	2.
3.	3.	3.
In 30 years:		
1.	1.	1.
2.	2.	2.
3.	3.	3.

Figure 4-3. A chart to help students start thinking about their education as a service to themselves.

Put the Student at Ease

Experience-based learning thrives in an open, candid and honest atmosphere. You should lay the groundwork for good communication with students by seeking their active participation in planning activities that fulfill school requirements and make sense to them. A self-assessment questionnaire that asks the student to analyze skills and needs, past schooling and learning experiences, and preferred learning styles and methods provides you and the student with a good starting point for individualizing project activities (see the sample Learning Style Self-Assessment form, page 129).

Review the Ground Rules

If a student has any questions about community-based projects, clear them up when you and the student first meet. It might help to show the student the sample project on pages 132-139 and those in Appendix A to illustrate the variety of learning activities that are possible.

Some things about projects—like the kind of products to be developed— are negotiable; other factors are more difficult to alter once the conditions have been written up. For example, if history is the subject area and the project theme, then historical research and concepts should be incorporated into the project. Likewise, basic skills are always emphasized, particularly those in which the student most needs improvement. You and the student should decide together which factors about the project are fair game for change and which are givens.

Be Open to Questions and Ask Some of Your Own

Project negotiation may be unlike anything the student has ever done before. Keep checking to make sure the student understands exactly what is happening and what will be expected. Ask questions such as:
- Does the whole project make sense to you?
- Can you explain why it is important?
- How does this learning experience fit into your life now? In the future?
- What's the next logical learning experience?
- What part of the project looks hardest?
- How can you get help when you need it?
- What's the most important part of this project?
- If you think you are falling behind on the project, what will you do?

Prod the student to ask questions if something is unclear. This practice in questioning is good preparation for the same techniques the student must use on community sites. It should also prepare the student for later evaluation of the project. It is the student's responsibility to negotiate a project that is worth doing well.

Push into Uncharted Territory

Challenge the student to explore areas of ever greater difficulty rather than repeating familiar paths. In writing project activities, try to build in successive challenges for the student. The advantage of projects built from community site experiences is that knowledge and skills can be demonstrated in new ways. Students probably have been led by the hand or told what they need to know about themselves and the world during most of their school lives. Experience-based learning, on the other hand, offers the chance for young people to discover things for themselves with the school's support.

Help Students Look Inward

Provide opportunities for the student to reveal feelings, self-concepts and opinions that may be stumbling blocks to personal growth. Honesty and trust shared during project planning may well carry over into relationships with other adults in the community. Use conference time as another way for both of you to gather data on the student's strengths and weaknesses and deal with these in planning project activities. Remember that ideas and suggestions are usually confidential—something shared only between the two of you.

Encourage Students, Yet Keep in Touch With Reality

Try to end each project planning conference on an encouraging note. While there may still be some rough spots in the project, the student should leave with the feeling that what you have planned together is attainable and important. Even though you are asking the student to try some things that are new and difficult, you are also offering understanding and help when it is needed.

Help the student understand the role of the resource person, too, and the fact that all may not be sweetness and light at community sites. Students should realize that their projects and community experiences may not be one long success story, but both they and the resource people will be learning together—from their mistakes as well as their successes.

THE PROJECT FORMAT

Properly designed, the project form serves as an organizing device and a recordkeeping tool. Your own course requirements will naturally determine the project format that works best for you. The project form presented here has the following parts:

1. A **cover sheet** (see Fig. 4-5, page 116) with space for—
   - Subject or life skills area addressed by the project
   - Project title
   - Individuals and sites in the community serving as resources for completing the project
   - Student rationale for doing the project and what the student expects to learn from it (written after negotiation and before the student begins work on the project)
   - Teacher justification, stating what the project is designed to help the student learn (including basic skills emphasis) and why it is an important part of the student's learning plan (final evaluations and recommendations will be made in relation to this baseline statement)
   - Space for the student, teacher and key resource person's signatures indicating they agree to the purposes, activities and products outlined in the project
   - Timeline for the project work (date the project will be started by the student, planned completion date, actual completion date)
   Completed cover sheets can be duplicated and used as summary records of student project work.
2. A separate **sheet for each project activity** (see Fig. 4-6, page 118) specifying—
   - Number of the activity (students will usually proceed through activities in numerical order, each activity leading logically to the next)
   - Target date for completion of the activity
   - Actual tasks the student will do to complete the activity
   - People and other resources (both in the community and in school) that may be useful to the student in completing the tasks outlined for the activity
   - Products for each task in the activity (what the student and school staff person have agreed on as the results or ways the student will demonstrate completion of each task)
   - How each product will be evaluated (criteria describing the level of performance the student should achieve on each task)
   - Student and staff comments on how well the student accomplished the activity
3. A final **evaluation sheet** for the entire project (see Fig. 4-7, page 126) with space for—
   - Overall teacher evaluation of the student's completed work on the project and the extent to which the initial purposes of the project were achieved
   - Student self-evaluation
   - Recommendations from the teacher for future projects and learning activities that would be helpful to the student, based on newly learned skills or needs revealed in this project

NINE STEPS TO SUCCESSFUL PROJECTS

The following pages outline nine basic steps that distinguish student learning projects in the community from other kinds of contracts often used today for individualized instruction. The steps are illustrated by completed forms showing how project information is recorded for student, staff and resource person use. These illustrations are drawn from existing experience-based learning programs and are included to help you visualize the project-writing process.

The nine steps for writing and completing experience-based learning projects are as follows:

1. Know your student.
2. Determine project theme.
3. Determine the potential of community resources to help the student meet curriculum goals.
4. Specify project activities.
5. Suggest resources for activities.
6. Describe products to be developed.
7. Decide how the products will be evaluated and by whom.
8. Set target dates and be sure the resource person agrees on project activities that will be completed onsite.
9. Evaluate the completed project with the student.

JEFFERSON HIGH SCHOOL
Center City, Illinois

Official Student Record and Transcript

Name _____ Date of Birth _____ Male ☐ Female ☐
Name of Parent or Guardian _____

Grade _____

Subject
_____
_____
_____
_____

GOAL QUESTIONNAIRE

Skills/knowledge you (will) want or need	Learning activities you could do to get them	Ways school could help you reach your goals
Every day:		1.
		2.

STUDENT PROFILE

Name _____

CAREER INTERESTS

LEARNING STYLE SELF-ASSESSMENT

Either fill in or put a check mark by the answer or answers below that best describe you and your needs (check as many responses as you wish). When you are done, talk your responses over with your teacher.

In what physical situations do you learn best?

__ quiet place   __ alone
__ noisy place   __ lecture
__ small discussions   __ individual conferences
__ large group discussions   __ other _____

BASIC SKILLS NEEDS

What are your favorite subjects?   Why?

_____   _____
_____   _____
_____   _____
_____   _____

What turns you on to learning? If you could choose ways to learn, which would you choose and what kinds of materials would you like to use?

LEARNING STYLE

WAYS   MATERIALS

__ projects   tape recorders
__ written assignments   videotape
__ reading and answering questions   __ typewriter
__ group discussions   __ pen and paper
__ interviews   __ mass media activities
__ observations   (collages, cartoons, etc.)
__ research   library resources (books,
__ attending classes   magazines, etc.)
__ "hands on" activities   __ other _____
__ other _____

OTHER

When given an assignment, can you work alone or do you like someone to check in with you now and then?

__ need to have directions explained more than once or twice
__ mostly self-directed but also like to check in with someone now
   and then
__ need to be told more than once to start a task and to complete it
__ self-directed and responsible enough to complete assignment
   independently

Figure 4-4. Various resources for becoming familiar with a student's needs, abilities and interests.

☐ Know your student

Three types of information are needed about each student before writing an experience-based learning project: career interests, basic skills levels and personal learning styles. Project writing consists essentially of student and teacher pulling these pieces of information together into a coherent set of activities through careful, face-to-face negotiation. As noted earlier, it may be helpful to precede the one-to-one project-writing conference with small group discussions of the students' interests and abilities so the students have a chance to use their peers as a sounding board.

Where the Student Wants to Go from Here

Often gathered from career interest inventories, expressed interests and a goal questionnaire that you can easily design (see Fig. 4-3), individual student goals—some long-range and others short-range—should never be considered permanent. Career development, after all, is a continuous process of exploring, matching, planning and sifting out alternatives.

A second kind of analysis you will want to make is a transcript check or review of where the student is now in meeting school requirements. How much time does the student have for this particular project? If another project is underway or has just been completed, should there be a tie-in?

What the Student Already Can Do

Assessment information is often gathered from standard instruments such as the Comprehensive Test of Basic Skills, Palo Alto Math Test and Wide Range Achievement Test; previous school records; recent performance on other learning experiences; and feedback from parents, employers and others in a position to know. You can interpret this information for diagnostic purposes to help you plan activities that will lead the student to improve skills, experience success and be continually challenged.

How the Student Learns Best

Data can be gathered from the Learning Style Self-Assessment Inventory (see page 129), personal interviews during individual conferences, negotiation and actual observations of how the student works. Thinking about their learning styles will encourage students to analyze and reflect on past and current experiences in order to plan future ones.

Student Profile

Student information can be summarized on a Student Profile form for reference during project writing (see page 131). This profile should be viewed as a worksheet to be updated as you learn more about the student's needs, abilities and interests.

STUDENT NAME   *Sonja Carmichael*   SUBJECT *Art & Bus. Math*

PROJECT TITLE   *Company Logos as Graphic Art*

COMMUNITY
RESOURCE
PEOPLE/SITES   *Hugh Attrell, Graphicom Inc.*

            Local advertising agencies

            Gallefsen's Gallery

            Public Library

STUDENT RATIONALE
FOR THIS PROJECT:

It seems to me there is no better way to use my skills and interests than in the area of designing company letterheads and signs. I've seen some neat ones that say a lot very simply.

TEACHER JUSTIFICATION:

Sonja's natural ability in design coupled with her usual self-initiative deserves the time she will spend looking into this kind of commercial art. Her need to sharpen math skills will be enhanced by looking at the economic side of graphic art from the artist's point of view.

I agree to the purposes, activities and products outlined in this project.

Sonja Carmichael   1/15/77
Student   Date

Sharon Bergstrom   1-15-77
Teacher   Date

H. Attrell   2/1/77
Key Resource Person   Date

Starting Date *2-10-77*

Planned
Completion
Date   *2-22-77*

Actual
Completion
Date   *2-22-77*

Page 1 of ___

Figure 4-5. Sample project cover sheet.

② Determine project theme

When you have compiled learning information about the student, you are ready to sit down together and sketch out what the overall thrust for the project will be and how it can be justified as a valid learning experience. From this point on, you will be applying the guidelines for successful project planning discussed earlier (see pages 107-112).

Determine Subject Area and Title

If you like the life skills approach described in Chapter 3, use one of those designations. If a course title such as American history, consumer economics or practical writing will work better, use it. The project should also have a title that describes the focus of the activities.

Clarify Project Purpose from Two Perspectives

Fundamental to experience-based learning is the need for student agreement that the learning is worth doing. On the project cover sheet, the student should state clearly why this project is a reasonable investment of time and what will be learned as a result. You, too, must ratify the plan by noting how the project will meet previously identified needs and what the expected accomplishments will be. The two rationale statements are crucial starting points for writing activities and will serve as a constant reference point for overall evaluation.

③ Determine the potential of community resources to help the student meet curriculum goals

You will make life easier for yourself and design better projects if you consider carefully two important factors:

1. Characteristics of the community site and the learning objectives that have been identified for that site
2. Subject-related learning objectives

Each project planning session gives you the opportunity to link student abilities, interests and needs with the rich learning potential identified through the site analysis process described in Chapter 3. Remember also that the life skills objectives listed in Chapter 3 and what the student may have accomplished in a starter project for the subject or life skills area should be reflected in the planning of subsequent projects in that area. The life skill or subject area objectives are useful organizers and they also help you tie project activities into long-term educational goals for students and parents. Projects offer one of the best ways to show how knowledge from a variety of disciplines is integrated in the real world. Weave in as many subject-related objectives as you feel can be effectively met and logically fit, but avoid trying to cover so many bases that the project becomes a hodge-podge.

Student Name _____Joseph Olsen_____   Page _6_ of _8_

(A) ACTIVITY _5_ :   TARGET DATE: _2/16_

    a. *Now that Joseph has investigated the nature of child abuse and agencies involved in preventing child abuse, he will research child abuse laws now in effect.*

    b. *Joseph will then prepare a statistical summary of the number and rate of reported child abuse cases in the county.*

(B) COMMUNITY SITE RESOURCES
  State representatives, county health department, Legal Aid Society, state legal code at city library
IN-SCHOOL RESOURCES
  School nurse, library, newspaper file

(C) PRODUCTS

    a. *Summary of state laws on child abuse*

    b. *Graph or chart showing 5-year trend of reported child abuse cases in the county*

(D) HOW EACH PRODUCT WILL BE EVALUATED

Clarity and simplicity of language

Mo BJ Brown
s/attorney or legislator

Accuracy of data, format, clarity

Mrs J. Rollins
s/math teacher

STUDENT COMMENTS

I never realized how many cases go undetected and how you really can't tell the whole story in numbers.

STAFF COMMENTS

You really did find out a lot of things. Want to prepare a presentation for the next parent school meeting?

Figure 4-6. Sample project activity page with coding to project-writing steps 4 through 7.

4 Specify project activities—A in Fig. 4-6

Now that you have determined curriculum objectives, community site characteristics and potential site-related learning objectives, you need to decide what activities the student will do and how they will be organized— where the student will begin (Activity 1) and end (last activity). The project must emerge as a logical plan of action, with activities that move the student from discovery of what is to the creation of something new and different. Use your professional creativity and skill as a curriculum builder. Try one of these approaches as you refine techniques that work for you:

1. **Deductive:** Student takes a general concept (e.g., morality) and applies it to specific daily situations (e.g., how a public health clinic handles confidentiality with minors).
2. **Inductive:** Student identifies a specific problem (e.g., parent's complaint about a high heating bill) and relates it to broader issues (e.g., energy consumption patterns as monitored by public and private utilities and agencies).
3. **Logical task sequence:** Student completes one task after another to see how an orderly progression results in an intended outcome (e.g., a head chef follows a definite routine, no matter what cuisine is planned).
4. **Chronological sequence:** Student completes logical task sequence as above, but observes time differences (e.g., project activities are built around a bank teller's typical day).
5. **Critical thinking approach:** Student identifies a problem or issue, gathers information, interprets the information, chooses among alternative courses of action and evaluates results (e.g., determines how to inform employees about options in a new health insurance plan).
6. **Scientific approach:** Student observes a situation or process, investigates, hypothesizes, predicts, tests the theory or hypothesis (e.g., effects of a customized bus schedule brochure on ridership from an apartment complex).

The activities themselves are the specific tasks the student will perform in the course of the project. You can often get ideas for activities from conversation with the student concerning a particular interest, skill or hobby. Whenever possible, you should encourage students to take the lead in designing activities that will stretch their abilities and be personally meaningful and challenging. The activities are numbered in sequence and one activity is written per page (as in Fig. 4-6), with a target date for completion of the activity agreed on by you and the student.

Use the following criteria as checkpoints after you and the student have listed project activities:

1. **Do the activities fit the organizational pattern you used?**
   The sequencing of activities will be determined by the approach you and the student have defined (deductive, inductive, logical task sequence, chronological, critical thinking approach, scientific approach and so forth).

2. **Do the activities meet the objectives the student and you worked out?**
For example, if you and the student have combined awareness of how government affects individual rights with improvement of speech skills, which of the following activities would accomplish that objective?

One way: Write and present a three-minute oral argument on how city government as a political entity must conform to state land use laws.
A better way: At a meeting of the city council, present a three-minute summary of how individual citizens in your community are protected by city, regional and state land use planning codes. Staff and students in attendance at the meeting will critique the presentation.

3. **Do the activities emphasize basic skills practice?**
All projects should help students make improvements in their basic skills. If a student needs to work on reading, for example, try to weave the application of a variety of reading skills into all activities: reading for overall sense, hidden meanings, reference, recall, errors in logic, relaxation; reading straight narrative; reading pictures, charts, maps and graphs.

4. **Do the activities offer variety?**
The kinds of activities a student can perform are limited only by your imagination. Use action verbs such as *try out, analyze, observe* and *generalize* to suggest activities and products that can be done.

5. **Do the activities trace back to community site tasks?**
Whenever possible, tie project activities directly into the tasks that site resource people carry out. For example, if a typical site task is to record customer complaints and prepare a daily report, a student task can be to write down three customer complaints and paraphrase each for the resource person's daily report.

6. **Is at least one activity suitable for a group effort?**
Experience-based learning relies heavily on independent learning but also recognizes that students need group interaction both at a site and back at school. How can this group interaction be accomplished?

One way: Have the student lead a class or group discussion of an issue encountered during a project, such as consumer rights and responsibilities.
A better way: Select an issue that has actually occurred at a site, such as a customer who refuses to pay a bill. Have a group of students work together to prepare a case for presentation in Small Claims Court.

Admittedly, it's tricky to meet all these criteria, but it can be done with practice. It is probably most difficult to provide realistic and suitable math activities and to fit site-related activities into the selected organizational pattern. Keep in mind that the criteria will speak to the ideal; applying each criterion can become unnecessarily time-consuming. When that happens, don't hesitate to include important activities, even if they don't exactly fit the organizational pattern you are using. The main consideration is the learning experience your students will be having. Remember that criteria for project activities are guidelines, not rigid prescriptions.

5   Suggest resources for activities—B in Fig. 4-6

Resources for project activities can include materials, people and places in the community and in the school. Remember that experience-based learning puts top priority on face-to-face interaction between students and adults in the community, but it is usually important also to do extensive background research in printed and other materials.

Community-Based Learning Resources

Students in experience-based learning usually access community resources in two ways:

1. Through an extended community site placement
   Example: A student interested in silversmithing and leatherworking as art forms and as potential avenues for self-employment might spend time at a cooperative crafts studio.
2. By checking specialized places for ideas and supplementary assistance
   Example: The same student visits an art gallery to observe trends in silver and leatherwork, a museum for historical insights, a public library for related reading and two retail outlets that take crafts on consignment.

School-Based Learning Resources

Three general types of resources are available in most school situations:

1. School staff willing to share their classrooms, labs, shops, professional materials and expertise with students not regularly enrolled in their courses
   Example: For the same student as above, resources include art teacher, shop teacher, chemistry teacher, teachers with special hobbies or interests in leather or silverwork
2. School facilities such as library, resource centers, textbook supply room, study halls
   Example: Periodicals, textbooks from art appreciation class, history department resource center
3. Other students with special hobbies or interests
   Example: Sophomore student who won art festival award for silver jewelry

Resources you and the student discuss are suggestions only; students should not consider them in a limiting sense. It is important to encourage students to seek out other appropriate sources of information in the school and community. Help the students expand their concept of learning resources and try especially to make them more aware of current and local resources.

6   Describe products to be developed—C in Fig. 4-6

For each activity or each task within an activity, you and the student will agree on specific results or products that will demonstrate the student's use of resources to achieve stated levels of performance (see Step 7). Project products can take many different forms. They can be verbal, visual, written, spoken, displayed, performed—the possibilities are unlimited. **Each product should give the student an opportunity to practice one or more basic skills: reading, writing, math, speech.** Each should also provide you with a suitable basis for evaluating whether learning objectives have been met.

When you suggest a variety of products you may encounter some resistance from students who are accustomed to written work, especially students who have excelled in those situations in the past. In experience-based learning the emphasis is often different: the product will likely receive more visibility than the traditional classroom assignment, and it will often be evaluated by an expert in the field.

Help students see that there are any number of ways to demonstrate the mastery of information, but avoid being gimmicky just for the sake of variety. For example, a student could create a self-sustaining terrarium and describe its principles in a project related to ecology. On the other hand, a macrame wall hanging of a student's family tree would be a questionable way for the student to demonstrate an understanding of genetics.

Keep product ideas like these in mind:
- Oral presentations
- Still photographs, films, videotape
- Natural products like a garden
- Displays, such as air pollution samples
- Tape recordings (both audio and video)
- Handicrafts (quilts, leatherwork, carpentry)
- Graphs of data, flip charts, wall posters, murals
- Original dance, music presentations, plays
- Service to others (at senior citizens center, day care program)
- Handling responsibility (running a switchboard, teaching a class)
- Publication of articles (in a newspaper or magazine)
- Business letters (written for self or on behalf of another person)

7   Decide how the products will be evaluated and by whom—D in Fig. 4-6

Now comes the task of individualizing the yardsticks to be used to measure each product. Sometimes you or another staff person will do the measuring; sometimes the student's performance will be measured by a community resource person with expertise in the subject area. Either way, the criteria must be clearly understood by you, the student and the certifier. Writing the criteria down is important as a clear record of this understanding.

Usually the criteria are stated as performance levels that relate to the student's personal abilities, interests and goals (identified in Step 1). These criteria should never limit a student's potential; ideally activities should achieve a balance between challenging a student and presenting opportunities for success.

Site Related Criteria

Products that naturally emerge from daily events at a community site are best judged by the adult expert who is serving as key resource person. You as the teacher of record will be monitoring the type of learning in which the student is participating as well as the quality of the completed work. Whenever appropriate, however, let the resource person decide if the product is acceptable by standards used to measure employee performance or some other reality check.

Basic Skills Criteria

You as the professional educator must evaluate the basic skills performance of students. If, for example, initial student assessment has indicated a weakness in math, fair spelling ability and strong skills in organizing written material, you and the student might agree on a product that calls for written notes for an oral presentation to other students on the mathematical processes involved at a particular site. In evaluating this product, you would probably set higher performance standards for the student's communication skills and look for reasonable progress in math understanding and application.

Subject Matter Criteria

Here again your judgment counts. Discuss where the student is in meeting expected outcomes. How well the student performed on the starter project in a particular subject area might also be considered—always trying to build on previous accomplishments.

Importance of Criteria

The important point to remember in setting criteria is that experience-based learning flourishes best if you can achieve a radical departure from the standard grading system. It is also important to note that apple polishing games are meaningless in the context of reality-based projects and performance criteria. Take whatever time is necessary to discuss evaluation methods with your students and put everything you can in writing. This will go a long way toward aligning the student's and the program's expectations and avoiding later feelings of frustration or surprise.

⑧ Set target dates and be sure the resource person agrees on project activities that will be completed onsite

Keeping on Schedule

Part of maturing is learning to be responsible and meet deadlines. This is particularly true when students are working independently on personalized projects. During the negotiation process students and staff should agree on starting and estimated completion dates for the entire project as well as for individual activities within the project (see spaces for this information on Figs. 4-5 and 4-6). If target dates slip, further negotiation must take place to set new dates.

Deadlines will sometimes slip because project activities often take longer than either you or the student might reasonably expect. However, the personal freedom coming from frequent movement to and from the community may lead a student to neglect obligations in favor of the sheer experience of it all. You must be able to judge individual variations in learning styles and rates. One person may be stalling while another is exercising honest caution or reconsidering alternatives.

Keep accurate records of student target dates. Plan regular conferences with students to check on their progress. Time management and accountability are important concepts students will be learning as they work on projects. Staff must help students meet deadlines and give advice to those having difficulty. Special workshops on task planning may be necessary for some students. See Chap. 6, pages 173-175, for more specific ways you can help students set schedules for themselves and follow through.

Sealing the Agreement

This step applies largely to projects requiring considerable time at resource sites. Protocol dictates that you and the resource person agree on the feasibility of all community-based project activities before they are undertaken.

When negotiating projects that involve outside resources, proposed activities must be checked to be sure they do not conflict with school or company policies, safety regulations, union rules and so forth. Ask the resource person whether the tasks require training or experience the student may not have. Do the activities expect too much learning too fast? Should the learning of other skills be handled first? Might the student interfere with ongoing work at the site? Finally, the resource person should look at the criteria for evaluation of site-related activities. Are they reasonable? Does the resource person feel comfortable making judgments in terms of those criteria?

Space is provided on the project cover sheet for signatures of the student, teacher and resource person (see Fig. 4-5) signifying they agree with the stated activities.

FINAL PROJECT EVALUATION

Student Name ___Susan Secanti___

Project Title ___Materials Lab Tests___

OVERALL TEACHER EVALUATION

Susan, you finally did it! This project is a demonstration of your ability to be punctual, responsible and systematic! Your lab notebook is a beautiful example of challenging scientific inquiry handled in a professional manner. All year I've been after you about your haphazard work; this notebook shows your real potential. Use it. As I indicated in earlier evaluations, you have a very effective writing style that can become quite sophisticated with practice.

STUDENT SELF-EVALUATION

I really enjoyed seeing this one through! I discovered I can really get into the scientific way of thinking. It's like detective work--following the clues step-by-step, weighing the evidence, reaching a conclusion, then testing yourself to be sure the conclusion is right. This project really showed me how to think.

RECOMMENDATIONS

Use your final essay as a model of quality writing. Your outline seemed especially helpful. Remember that technique as you do more writing.

SIGNATURES:

Susan Secanti   3-17-77
Student   Date

Elna Lewson   3-17-77
Teacher   Date

Student Name ___Susa___

ACTIVITY _5_:

a. Weighing and
    gypsum sampl
    lab work an

b. Read the va
    keep recor
    the numbe

COMMUNITY SITE
    Lab equipme
    other sites
IN-SCHOOL RE
    Science te

PRODUCTS

a. Cert
    per
    100

b. G
    s
    mat

STUDENT COMMENTS
I had trouble with some of the statistics on this activity and finding the best way to write them up. But Bill Purcell helped me understand what I was doing.

STAFF COMMENTS
Good descriptions of the tests. From your technical records I can see that each test was very carefully documented.

Evaluations ➡ from individual activity sheets

Figure 4-7. Sample project evaluation procedures.

6 Evaluate the completed project with the student

Monitoring student progress on each activity and looking back on the whole project after it is over is an important learning experience for both the student and you as the instructional leader. During the life of the project, you and the student will meet regularly to see how things are going and review each completed activity. You may renegotiate due dates, products or certain criteria, depending on the student's progress and changing conditions. When the project is completed, you should review the comments that have been made on the individual activity sheets as a beginning point for your final project evaluation.

Activity Evaluation

While either you or a resource person may evaluate individual activities, overall certification and evaluation of the student's educational growth rests on your shoulders. As the one who knows the student, the project goals that were originally established and the performance criteria that were negotiated and written down, you will have to determine if each activity has been achieved as everyone hoped.

If criteria for judging products were carefully prescribed at the outset, your job will be easier. For example, the following could be easily evaluated:

- Susan will perform all 15 points of the air pollution instrument check to the satisfaction of her resource person.
- Jerry will log the day's incoming mail as accurately as possible, making no more than three mistakes.
- Mark will submit a letter in standard business form with no misspelled words urging a change in legislation and send it to his Congressional representative.

Overall Project Evaluation

After the project is completed and you and the student have discussed how well the idea worked and how much was learned, it is time to summarize student accomplishments for future records. Remember there is seldom a time when a project is all good or all bad. Strive for balanced evaluation comments that will give the student a realistic sense of what has or has not been accomplished. If you are working in a nongraded situation, it is reasonable to require that all activities be completed at a high level of achievement according to the student's abilities.

Student Self-Evaluation

The student rationale on the project cover sheet (Fig. 4-5) serves as one basis for the student's own assessment of what has been accomplished and learned. Checking back to that original statement of why the project was important and what the student hoped to learn from it, the student can now decide how well those goals were met. You might also help the student in this self-evaluation by asking questions such as these:

- How did this experience change your plans?
- What was the most frustrating thing about your experience?
- What new sources of information are available to you now as a result of this project?
- Can you think of two ways you've changed as a result of doing this project?

Recommendations

The real educational purpose of evaluation is the chance to help the student integrate immediate learning with previous and future experiences—to see the consequence of choices and to weigh those in terms of future plans. It is never too early to begin writing the next project. The wrap-up recommendations provide the chance to step back and put one set of experiences into perspective while looking ahead to the next.

PUTTING THE STEPS TOGETHER

To see how the nine project-writing steps look when completed for one student, consider the following example of Jane Hilliard. Jane is an average student who has found new interest in learning thanks to a project using a variety of school and community resources. The examples take you from Jane's Learning Style Self-Assessment (Fig. 4-8) to a Student Profile (Fig. 4-9) and through one complete project (Fig. 4-10).

FOOTNOTE

[1]Maurice Gibbons, *The New Secondary Education* (Bloomington, Indiana: Phi Delta Kappa, Inc., 1976), p. 56.

1 Know your student

LEARNING STYLE SELF-ASSESSMENT

Either fill in or put a check mark by the answer or answers below that best describe you and your needs (check as many responses as you wish). When you are done, talk your responses over with your teacher.

In what physical situations do you learn best?

_x_ quiet place	___ alone
___ noisy place	___ lecture
_x_ small discussions	_x_ individual conferences
___ large group discussions	___ other _____

What are your favorite subjects?   Why?

Social Studies	*Here and now problems*
Business Education	*Good job market*
English	*My grades*
Math	*All except algebra*

What turns you on to learning? If you could choose ways to learn, which would you choose and what kinds of materials would you like to use?

WAYS   MATERIALS

_x_ projects	_x_ tape recorders
___ written assignments	___ videotape
_x_ reading and answering questions	___ typewriter
___ group discussions	_x_ pen and paper
_x_ interviews	___ mass media activities
_x_ observations	(collages, cartoons, etc.)
_x_ research	_x_ library resources (books,
_x_ attending classes	magazines, etc.)
___ "hands on" activities	___ other _____
___ other _____	

When given an assignment, can you work alone or do you like someone to check in with you now and then?

___ need to have directions explained more than once or twice
_x_ mostly self-directed but also like to check in with someone now and then
___ need to be told more than once to start a task and to complete it
___ self-directed and responsible enough to complete assignment independently

Figure 4-8. Example of a student's completed Learning Style Self-Assessment.

SIDE TWO

Learning Style Self-Assessment (continued)

Can you complete an assignment within a reasonable amount of time?

__x__ takes me longer than it should to complete assignments
_____ feel frustrated when I can't complete a task and just give up
_____ can easily finish a task in time
__x__ often need to be reminded about deadlines

What are the hardest things for you to do in school?

__x__ take tests	_____ follow the rules
_____ read	__x__ attend class
_____ math	_____ meet deadlines
__x__ do homework	_____ other _____
__x__ sit and listen to a teacher	

What do you think you need the most work in right now?

_____ listening to and following directions	_____ writing
	_____ spelling
__x__ understanding what is expected of me	__x__ mathematics
	_____ reading
_____ getting along with people	_____ nothing
_____ expressing myself	_____ other _____
_____ participating in discussions	
__x__ dealing positively with conflict	

How can staff help you most?

I want some practical things that will help me get ahead in this world instead of all this theory.

Other comments about yourself and your learning style.

If we could do something by ourselves sometimes, I think we would all be better off.

_Jane Hilliard_____   _9-1-75_
Student   Date

_Faye Silver_____   _9-1-75_
Teacher   Date

Figure 4-8. *(continued)*

1 **Know your student**

STUDENT PROFILE

Name ____Jane Hilliard_____   Date __9/75_____

CAREER INTERESTS

*Jane is not really sure how to pin down several career
possibilities--especially with some interesting aptitudes
showing up already: people-management and highly technical
skills. College aspirations also need to be fitted in, not
because of parent prodding but a sincere interest on Jane's
part.*

BASIC SKILLS NEEDS

*CTBS scores back up my observation of above-average capability.
Even with good reading and math scores, however, enrichment
is still needed there. Vocabulary development is also a future
need. Jane likes to get involved in solving nitty-gritty
problems, and basic skills practice can be worked into most
activities. She should be encouraged and motivated toward a
high development of her skills.*

LEARNING STYLE

*Some tendency to procrastinate and keep putting off work until
the last minute. Is not willing to admit difficulty in this
area, but knows it's been a problem in the past. Responds
well to positive reinforcement and will follow through on
activities of personal interest.*

OTHER

Needs work on ability to schedule time in units.

Figure 4-9. Sample completed Student Profile form.

3 Determine potential of community resources
(you and student work from site analysis
and listed objectives)

STUDENT NAME   _Jane Hilliard_   SUBJECT _Psychology_

PROJECT TITLE _Restaurant Chain Management_ ◄

COMMUNITY
RESOURCE
► PEOPLE/SITES   _Prime Rib House, Jo Ann Blakely_

Mayer Laboratory, Ron Sanchez

2 Determine
project theme

STUDENT RATIONALE
FOR THIS PROJECT:

_The project I did at Mayer Laboratory showed me how a business
has to organize itself in a competitive market. Last summer I
worked at Prime Rib House and would like to do this project
there since I saw the operation from the dish hustling side
before. I think I would like a career in food service management._

TEACHER JUSTIFICATION:

_Jane is still looking at people-oriented skills and has many of
the qualities needed for a career in business management. A job
like that requires the ability to think through personnel problems and help each one reach full potential. Jane will work on
strengthening skills in writing, emphasizing clarity and brevity._

8 Set
target dates
and seal
agreement

I agree to the purposes, activities
and products outlined in this project.

Jeane Hilliard   3-12-76
Student   Date

Faye Silver   3-12-76
Teacher   Date

Jo Ann Blakely   3-15-76
Key Resource Person   Date

Starting Date _3-19-76_

Planned
Completion
Date   _5-1-76_

Actual
Completion
Date   _5-1-76_

Page 1 of _7_

Figure 4-10. Sample completed student project: cover sheet (project activity and evaluation sheets are on the following pages).

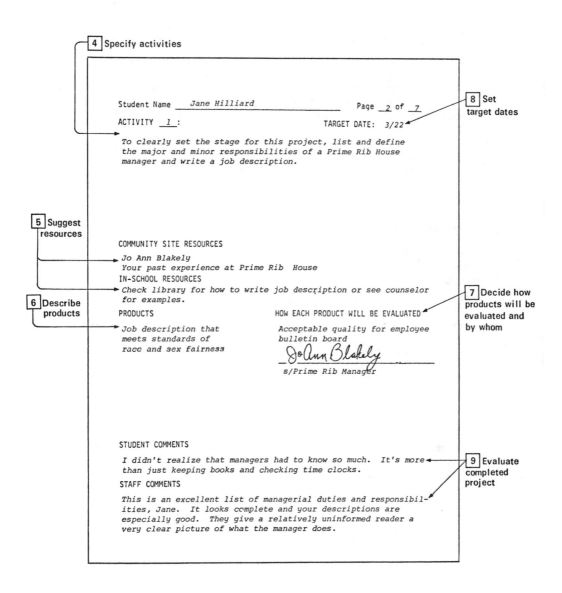

4 Specify activities

Student Name ___Jane Hilliard___   Page _2_ of _7_

ACTIVITY _1_ :   TARGET DATE: _3/22_

8 Set target dates

To clearly set the stage for this project, list and define the major and minor responsibilities of a Prime Rib House manager and write a job description.

5 Suggest resources

COMMUNITY SITE RESOURCES

Jo Ann Blakely
Your past experience at Prime Rib   House

IN-SCHOOL RESOURCES

Check library for how to write job description or see counselor for examples.

6 Describe products

PRODUCTS   HOW EACH PRODUCT WILL BE EVALUATED

7 Decide how products will be evaluated and by whom

Job description that meets standards of race and sex fairness   *Acceptable quality for employee bulletin board*

Jo Ann Blakely
s/Prime Rib Manager

STUDENT COMMENTS

I didn't realize that managers had to know so much.   It's more than just keeping books and checking time clocks.

9 Evaluate completed project

STAFF COMMENTS

This is an excellent list of managerial duties and responsibilities, Jane.   It looks complete and your descriptions are especially good.   They give a relatively uninformed reader a very clear picture of what the manager does.

Figure 4-10. *(continued)*

Student Name ___Jane Hilliard_____   Page _3_ of _7_

ACTIVITY __2_: TARGET DATE: 4/1

   a. *Since you worked at Prime Rib House, there has been a change in managers. Compare the professional styles of these two managers using specific examples to back up all statements.*

   b. *Now, how do these differences affect the business operation? Based on your observations and gathered information, list the significant elements of style for each and the most likely effects of those elements on restaurant operations.*

COMMUNITY SITE RESOURCES

  Jo Ann Blakely
  Your recollection of former manager

IN-SCHOOL RESOURCES

  Books on women in management or other nontraditional roles

PRODUCTS	HOW EACH PRODUCT WILL BE EVALUATED
a. *Written comparison of two professional management styles (personal characteristics should enter only as they affect the workplace)*	a. *Only those characteristics related to the workplace are to be reported, based on actual observations and not hearsay*
b. *List significant elements of style and most likely effects of each*	b. *Provide a factual example for each element of management style*

STUDENT COMMENTS

  When I left my job at Prime Rib, some of the folks didn't think Jo Ann could cut it as a manager. Now have they changed their minds!

STAFF COMMENTS

  Very well-organized and perceptive observations, Jane. You did an admirable job getting all the information down in a clear style without rambling. I was also pleased at the way you tried to separate out your personal beliefs.

Figure 4-10. *(continued)*

Student Name ___*Jane Hilliard*___   Page _4_ of _7_

ACTIVITY _3_ :   TARGET DATE: *4/15*

Now that you have observed two managers and analyzed their effect on work patterns, see if you can write work objectives for each position at Prime Rib.

COMMUNITY SITE RESOURCES

Jo Ann Blakely
See if you can sit in on a community college management course

IN-SCHOOL RESOURCES   *for a few days, too*

Management by Objectives by Peter Drucker

PRODUCTS	**HOW EACH PRODUCT WILL BE EVALUATED**
Work objectives for each staff position at Prime Rib	*Certification of creativity, effectiveness and plausibility*

JoAnn Blakely
s/Prime Rib Manager

STUDENT COMMENTS

This was hard to do since most people don't stop to think about all the elements of a job--even managers!

STAFF COMMENTS

If all your objectives were carried out, you would have an extremely efficient restaurant. Ms. Blakely's comment that your objectives should be stated more positively is a good one.

Figure 4-10. *(continued)*

Student Name ___Jane Hilliard_____   Page _5_ of _7_

ACTIVITY _4_ :   TARGET DATE: _4/21_

Using the objectives written in No. 3, design a training orientation session for "your" employees.

COMMUNITY SITE RESOURCES

Jo Ann Blakely, previous resource people, employee orientation materials from other firms

IN-SCHOOL RESOURCES

School counselor

PRODUCTS

Orientation design/plan describing all activities, using charts and a time-line with accompanying narrative

HOW EACH PRODUCT WILL BE EVALUATED

Consider questions like these:

1. *What would you as a manager want to tell employees about your expectations?*
2. *How would you motivate your employees to do the best job possible?*
3. *What effect do you think your style would have on employees?*

STUDENT COMMENTS

Jo Ann thought I did a good job, but I still wonder if anybody would want to sit through all that talk.

STAFF COMMENTS

Try to stress more information-giving activities, remembering that in your role as manager you are in a position of influence. Employees will need a clear concept of company policy to integrate with your management style and objectives.

Figure 4-10. *(continued)*

Student Name ___Jane Hilliard___   Page _6_ of _7_

ACTIVITY __5_ :   TARGET DATE: 4/25

Any large business requires teamwork to accomplish its purposes. What can you as a manager do to help your employees function as a team? Design at least three strategies to meet the goal of cooperative teamwork.

COMMUNITY SITE RESOURCES

Jo Ann Blakely, Ron Sanchez

IN-SCHOOL RESOURCES

School counselor

PRODUCTS

Describe in writing and orally three strategies that fit your management style

HOW EACH PRODUCT WILL BE EVALUATED

For each strategy, make sure there is a clear objective with specific steps to carry it out.

STUDENT COMMENTS

Getting people to work together must be the one thing that gives managers gray hair!

STAFF COMMENTS

Your strategies for promoting effective teamwork are a good start at figuring ways to work as a productive manager. You've included both professional and social techniques and that's a good bet for general morale purposes.

Figure 4-10. *(continued)*

Student Name _____*Jane Hilliard*_____   Page _7_ of _7_

ACTIVITY _6_ :   TARGET DATE: *4/30*

*Managers must naturally be prepared to handle personnel situations
as they occur. Prepare a response to three hypothetical problems
after talking over your approaches with Ms. Blakely and/or
Ron Sanchez.*

COMMUNITY SITE RESOURCES

Jo Ann Blakely, Ron Sanchez

IN-SCHOOL RESOURCES

Any personnel management materials you can find

PRODUCTS	HOW EACH PRODUCT WILL BE EVALUATED
Prepare tape recording of your responses to 3 situations:	*Clearly stated problem and your intended action.*

1. *One employee meets all ob-
    jectives but still has
    slightly negative attitude.
    Is somewhat aloof and un-
    friendly and seems not to
    care too much. What will you do and how?*

2. *Two key employees don't get along, even though they are competent
    and compatible with everyone else. You are concerned about effect
    on customers as well as performance. How will you handle this one?*

3. *You believe staff morale is quite low. How will you substantiate
    this feeling and approach staff?*

STUDENT COMMENTS

*You have to admit that my voice even sounds tough...
but in a gentle sort of way.*

STAFF COMMENTS

*Your responses were good, but a little general. Saying "shape up"
could mean almost anything! Make your expectations very clear
(some managers put expectations in writing as a way to hold
employees accountable).*

Figure 4-10. *(continued)*

9 Evaluate completed project

FINAL PROJECT EVALUATION

Student Name ___ *Jane Hilliard* _____

Project Title ___ *Restaurant Chain Management* _____

OVERALL TEACHER EVALUATION

*Your responses on this project indicated you have the qualities
necessary to be a sensitive and firm manager of people. The
combination of these two qualities is important for an efficient
workplace. I like the way you applied a lot of what you
learned at Mayer Laboratory to this project. Your ability
to transfer these skills and knowledge will be very useful
and productive for you. Good work, Jane.*

STUDENT SELF-EVALUATION

*Wow! Management is much more involved than I thought, but
the problem-solving is really fun. I had to use my imagination to come up with ways to solve some of the people
problems, and I think I learned a lot from this. I'm
beginning to see how simply getting along with people every
day is a lot like management.*

RECOMMENDATIONS

*Let's consider trying these **creative** "people managing" skills
out in an entirely different **community** setting. The
Neighborhood Associations Office at City Hall might be an
interesting site for another project. See me if you're
interested.*

SIGNATURES:

Jane Hilliard _____   5-3-76
Student   Date

Faye Silver _____   5·3·76
Teacher   Date

Figure 4-10. *(continued)*

5

LOCATING RESOURCE PEOPLE AND INVOLVING THEM IN THE PROCESS

> Something should happen early to give each kid
> a community experience to remember. Each, for
> example, should be placed in an interview situa-
> tion with a charismatic contact—hopefully the
> sort of person he never would have taken the
> time to talk with otherwise—so that he comes
> away shaking his head in amazement that
> "people like that" exist and will respond to him
> as an individual. It should be the sort of contact
> who will make him feel that he is special, and
> that the project is special, and that because he
> took the time to visit, that contact's day was
> made a little better.
>
> —*Moments: The Foxfire*
> *Experience*[1]

The community and its day-to-day activities can provide a wealth of educational opportunities and resources for student learning. Adults and their workplaces offer expertise and hands-on experiences that cannot feasibly be provided within the classroom. To tap this knowledge and experience and turn it into effective learning activities for students requires (1) advance planning, (2) a well-defined set of procedures for recruiting and orienting community resource people and (3) clear statements of what is expected from everyone— resource people, students and school staff alike. Naturally if teachers are to have time to contact community resources and prepare them for student place- ments, they must arrange to free themselves from some classroom responsi- bilities. This will require a commitment to experience-based learning on the

141

part of the school administration and possibly a cooperative agreement with another teacher to share classroom duties and community recruiting.

Site recruitment is simply the process of making specific community sites available for student learning. There is no mystique to it, but there are some procedures that can make it relatively easy. Once they have said "yes," community participants then need to be briefed on their roles. They also need a certain amount of ongoing psychological support to help them work effectively with students. The following pages will help you think about these processes of recruitment and orientation.

KNOWING WHO AND WHAT TO LOOK FOR

Anyone in the community is a potential resource person for student learning, whether their work is manual, technical, volunteer or professional. There are as many potential learning sites for students in the community as there are places of business.

Flip through the Yellow Pages of your telephone book and you will discover the breadth of possible learning experiences in your community. Or think of subjects like these and who in the community might use them:

ART:

Sites	Examples of people at work
Crafts gallery	Artist, salesperson
Museum	Curator, restoration expert
Print shop	Typesetter, designer, photographer
Florist	Flower arranger
Furniture store	Interior designer
Television station	Director, cameraperson, set designer, graphic artist
Bakery	Cake decorator
Department store	Window designer

CHEMISTRY:

Paper manufacturing company	People involved in sizing, rolling and coating paper
Pharmacy	Pharmacist, drug supplier
Dental clinic	Dentist, hygienist, lab technician
Hospital	Anesthesiologist, nurse, dietician
Local industry/manufacturer	Researcher, lab technician, salesperson, marketing expert
Sewage treatment plant	Researcher, tester, technician
Dry cleaning establishment	Dye expert, chemical wholesaler
Photographic supply store	Salesperson, photo lab technician
Print shop	Press operator, photographer

DRIVER EDUCATION:

Sites	Examples of people at work
State police	License examiner, patrol officer
Garage	Mechanic, tow truck operator
Airport	Air traffic controller, flight instructor
Driving school	Instructor
Transit system	Driver, route scheduler, maintenance crew
Auto repair	Salesperson, mechanic, auto body specialist
Race track	Driver, mechanic
Taxi company	Driver, dispatcher
Construction site	Heavy equipment operator

EARTH SCIENCE:

Landscape architect	Soil analyst, plant specialist, civil engineer
Municipal zoning, planning, maintenance services	Engineer, surveyor
Extension service	Soil analyst, plant specialist
Nursery	Gardener, plant and soil specialist
Army Corps of Engineers	Engineer, technician, surveyor
Water conservation district office	Engineer, soil analyst, geologist
County sanitation department	Sewage engineer
Weather station	Meteorologist
Assay office	Soil and mineral analyst, geologist
Parks department	Landscape architect, gardener, tree surgeon

ECONOMICS:

Bank	Teller, manager, economist
Insurance office	Investment specialist
Credit union	Loan officer, clerk
Import/export company	Manager, buyer
Consumer agency	Analyst, researcher
Retail and wholesale business	Accountant, buyer, salesperson, fiscal officer
College	Loan officer, economics professor
Advertising agency	Market analyst

FOREIGN LANGUAGES:

Sites	Examples of people at work
Bank	Foreign exchange—code clerk
Wine distributor	Importer
Travel agency	Travel agent, tour guide
International airlines/ airport	Flight attendant, customs agent, port official
Church	Missionary
Military base	Interpreter, overseas officer
Steamship line	Interpreter
Import shop	Buyer, correspondence secretary
Migrant labor community	Teacher, social worker
Automobile dealer	Foreign car importer
Publishing house	Editor of multicultural materials

HEALTH:

Hospital, clinic	Doctor, nurse, aide, therapist, dietician, lab technician
Day care center	Director, teacher
Rehabilitation center	Therapist, counselor, doctor
Survival training school	Teacher
Health spa	Fitness expert, weight-loss counselor
YMCA–YWCA	Lifeguard, instructor, fitness specialist
Local industry	Safety engineer
Mountain rescue unit	First aid instructor, rescue crew
Fire department	First aid instructor, rescue crew
Police department	Emergency squad, counselor

WRITING:

Radio or TV station	Scriptwriter, editor, news analyst, reporter
Advertising agency	Copywriter
Publishing house	Publisher, editor, author, proofreader
Engineering firm	Service manual writer, technical editor
Print shop	Designer, proofreader
State government	Speech writer, public relations
Law office	Lawyer, legal aide, secretary
Church	Minister

The definition of an off-campus resource can even be broader than a place of business or community institution. Students can start with their own home or neighborhood and gather valuable information from a parent, sister or brother, aunt or cousin—or the engineer down the street. During their out-of-school hours, students are often involved in situations that offer ready-made resources for experience-based learning activities: part-time jobs, church, interest groups like the Civil Air Patrol, hobby clubs like CB radio or stamp collecting and community recreation programs.

Now that you are getting used to the idea of nonclassroom resources, open your eyes to what your own school might offer for nonclassroom learning, too. It is, after all, a rather large community in its own right housing a variety of services:

School People	*Information They Might Have*
Faculty	Content specialities, hobbies
School nurse	Health expertise
Bus drivers	Traffic and pedestrian safety, transportation planning
Social worker	Home and interpersonal problems
Security staff	Behavioral patterns
Attendance officer	Attitudes toward school
Maintenance personnel	Carpentry, plumbing, electronics roofing, masonry, glaziery
Custodians	Environmental health, organizational abilities
Secretaries	Office skills, public relations
Administrators	School management issues, school law, public relations
Other students	Avocational skills, hobbies

School Places	*What They Offer*
Library	Materials, coding and storage systems
Media center	Audiovisual equipment and materials
Cafeteria	Nutrition, meal planning and preparation, equipment, weighing/measuring
Boiler room	Scientific principles, safety regulations and practices
Science lab	Equipment and expertise, chemicals, standards, processes
Vocational lab	Equipment and expertise, application of basic skills, raw materials
Athletic facility	Equipment and expertise, systems for health maintenance, printed materials on physical fitness, fitness tests
District maintenance shops	Equipment and expertise
Counseling office	Specialists, printed materials
School newspaper office	Expertise, equipment, materials, photography
Music department	Expertise, equipment, materials, mathematic and musical skills
Campus grounds	Environmental issues, land use, landscaping, neighborhood planning
Hallways	People, traffic patterns, environmental planning

How Resource People Can Help

The resource people you ask to work with students can play a variety of roles in experience-based learning activities:

- **Model.** Students will look up to resource people to see what it's like to be an adult, employee, employer, citizen, community member, producer and consumer.
- **Supervisor.** Students will be working under the watchful eyes of working adults who are skilled in specialized tasks.
- **Instructor.** This role often comes into play when students want or need to learn some particular thing only the resource person knows. The content being taught might include job skills, academic skills, personal/social skills and so forth.
- **Counselor.** Closely allied with the instructor role is the guidance role. Resource people often help students think through career, personal and academic questions—sometimes merely by listening sympathetically.
- **Evaluator/certifier.** In this important capacity, the resource person actually certifies when given tasks have been completed by the student at acceptable levels of performance.

Who Makes a Good Resource Person?

Successful resource people need on-the-job time to devote to instructional activities without feeling they are neglecting their work. They must also have a positive attitude toward young people and the desire to interact with students in learning situations.

One community-based program described the ideal resource person as follows:

People we look for are outgoing and open-minded about things; they don't have a lot of locked-in negative concepts. Their attitude is positive. They tend to be helpful and willing to cooperate. They don't get scared off when you ask, "Will you help us evaluate the student?"

They are self-disciplined: they know what they're doing and why they're doing it; they know what has to be done on what time schedule and they can stick to it. But they are still flexible in their attitudes toward students and have a high degree of patience.

All of this adds up to what could be called emotional stability in a person. This stability is capped off by positive expectations about young people and confidence in students' abilities to make their own life decisions.

Of course, perfect resource people are rare; each will have a different style with students and some student and resource styles may not match. Such differences, however, are part of what students should encounter—part of learning how to get along in the world. Of course, serious mismatches should be avoided and student placements changed if they don't work out to the satisfaction of both student and resource person.

BUILDING A NETWORK OF SITES

Your community site network should represent a range of occupations and community services with enough variety to permit students to select experiences in a number of different interest areas. Naturally you will be looking for people willing and able to work with students at sites that are reasonably accessible.

You should check out what other school-community sharing of resources is going on in your area. Your school district probably has a work experience program and may also be one of the growing number that are giving students credit for off-campus participation in community service projects. Programs like Junior Achievement and Scouting also ask community volunteers to help, usually contacting them through the schools. As more and more school districts offer community-based experiences to students, systematic efforts to catalog and schedule those interactions have been devised. Consult with your building principal and high school work experience coordinator to determine what kind of cooperative planning is already underway or can be started in your district to coordinate community use.

Estimating Site Availability

A quick estimate of a community's potential for supporting student onsite experiences can be obtained by gathering the names and addresses of local businesses and organizations from readily accessible sources like these:

1. The Yellow Pages of the telephone directory, where businesses are grouped together by type
2. A Chamber of Commerce business directory and assistance from a Chamber of Commerce official familiar with the community, who may be able to tell you not only the nature of particular businesses but also various site and personnel characteristics such as size of the work force
3. In larger metropolitan areas, formalized directory services that list firms and personnel alphabetically in various ways—by firm name, kind of business, name of key executives and so forth

Look around the community and you'll probably come up with a long list of possible learning sites for students. Score yourself on the following quiz to see what the possibilities are.

Check the kinds of sites available in your community:

___Bank	___Museum	___Schools
___Hospital or clinic	___Fire department	___Insurance office
___Attorney's office	___Flower shop	___Seamstress
___Service station	___Welfare office	___Car dealership
___Manufacturing firm	___Department store	___Day care center
___YMCA-YWCA	___Typewriter repair	___Hardware store
___Courthouse	service	___Church
___Library	___Supermarket	___Senior citizens
___Art gallery or	___Jewelry store	center
crafts shop	___Optometrist	___Post office

SCORING

Sites Available	*Potential for Experience-Based Learning*
1-5 sites available..............It's a starting point.
5-10 ....It's looking better.
10-15 ....You're average.
15-20 ....No problem at all.
20-30 ....You'll never keep them down on the farm.

If you are considering placing a fairly large number of students in experience-based learning situations, you may want to contact a representative number of sites and citizens informally to determine if the community generally supports the notion of community-based learning and is willing to try it. Some districts have found it useful to arrange individual or group meetings with key people to explain experience-based learning concepts; listen to their reactions, comments and questions; and ascertain if they would be willing to support such activities. In this manner, you can:

1. Seek suggestions for the kinds of learning activities individuals can see happening in the community.
2. Let individuals know how they can be actively involved in planning for experience-based learning.
3. Seek the names of additional people such as company supervisors whose clearance will be needed for actual student placements.

Determining Sites You'll Need

If you have surveyed potential community support for your intended learning activities, you will have some idea of the kinds and number of sites that may be available. The next task is to decide generally what occupations should be represented in the network to meet student interests and needs.

Ideally, the interests of students should be assessed at about the same time potential community support is being informally surveyed. As soon as you know which students will be involved in community-based experiences, provide some means to have them indicate their career interests so you can get an idea of the kinds of sites that should be recruited. Assessment of students' career interests can be as simple as asking them each to name three occupations or career fields they would like to explore. There are also many different career assessment instruments available to educational programs.

Most experience-based learning programs find they initially need more "people-oriented" sites (police department, schools, day care programs, a hospital, legal aid office, drug treatment center). Gradually students begin to move toward specialties (lawyer, self-employed shop owner, architect, special education teacher, insurance adjuster). Some of these more specialized resources can be recruited later as you need them.

It is important to distinguish between a community site and the individual resource people whose specialties can be tapped at the site. Each community site or place of business has the potential for offering students a number of different occupations, skills or interests. For example, at an insurance company students could investigate or learn through several different kinds of work: claims adjusting (including perhaps telephone adjusting and drive-in claims adjusting), actuary, receptionist, general office, bookkeeping, sales. Students may be interested either in these discrete occupational areas and identifiable jobs or in an entire business operation. Keep that in mind when projecting the need for both kinds and numbers of community resources. A network of 50 businesses, offices and agencies, for example, might result in 150 or more potential learning stations within the sites.

Avoiding Too Many or Too Few

The number of sites needed depends on the number of students who will be involved in your experience-based activities and the ways that sites will be used. If you overrecruit, you risk disillusioning resource people who are not used right away. It is also difficult to complete a large number of site analyses all at the same time. If, on the other hand, you underrecruit or recruit the wrong sites, you may not be able to meet student needs and find yourself burdened with recruiting more sites at the same time you begin to work with students. This is difficult both because of the time you need to give to planning learning activities with students and because resource people quickly recruited to fill gaps are often poorly prepared for their role.

No formula has yet been devised for a perfect match between available sites and student choices, but using student interests as a starting point and trying to offer a broad representation of community resources can help you come close. Best initial recruitment efforts will undoubtedly have to be supplemented by ongoing recruitment to update your network on a continuing basis, according to student need.

Why Resource People Like to Help

Experience-based learning usually sells itself. People in the community will have varied reasons—some they can articulate, some they cannot—for agreeing to work with students in community-based educational activities. The business sector has taken an increased interest in experience-based learning because this kind of activity has potential for—

- Contributing to a better prepared future work force
- Bridging the gap between young people and adults
- Providing hands-on learning and expertise that can be neither effectively simulated nor economically provided within the schools— providing a better educational program without appreciable cost
- Increasing community understanding and appreciation of the education process

In addition, community participants helping students learn about their jobs often gain a new appreciation of their own work—a sense of pride in what their occupation contributes to the workplace.

Resource people agree that what they most enjoy about their role is the opportunity to give of themselves on a person-to-person basis. Employers do not expect to come out ahead in any way other than personal satisfaction and the knowledge that they and their employees have made a worthwhile contribution to the lives of some young people.

You will probably hear reasons like these when resource people say, "Yes, I'll help":

- Belief that community-based learning can provide exciting opportunities to high school students
- Dissatisfaction with their own traditional high school education or that of their children, usually expressed as, "I wish this opportunity had been available when I was in school"
- Desire to help young people develop positive attitudes toward work and positive relationships with adults
- Desire to participate in the life and growth of the community

How to Recruit Community Resources

Recruiting community sites to take part in experience-based learning requires some legwork. There's just no way around it. Recruitment can be done by letter, but it is best done in person or at least with a personal interview as a followup to positive responses to a letter.

If you can recruit sites in person, visits to sites should be by appointment and scheduled during regular working hours. Whenever possible, the visit should be preceded by a letter of introduction from someone in the community—a parent or school or advisory board member, for example, and ideally one who knows the person being recruited. Such a letter gives credibility to the recruiter and to the request and can encourage the site to participate.

It is important to identify in advance the appropriate contact person at each site—the person in charge or who has the authority to commit the company or business to the learning activities. Find out who is in charge by consulting a business directory, calling the personnel department at the site or getting a referral from someone who is familiar with the site.

If recruitment is carried out by letter, the letter should be specific in explaining student placements in easily understood terms, covering the kinds of students who will be served, objectives of the placements and kinds of involvement that will be asked of community sites and individuals. Such a letter should have an attached form (see Fig. 5-1) or postcard with return postage and address so the site contact can indicate interest. Positive responses to a mailed inquiry should be followed up with personal contact between school staff and resource people to make specific arrangements for student placements.

SAMPLE RECRUITMENT FORM
(enclosed with introductory letter and
stamped, addressed return envelope)

Please check one or more of the following options if you would like to help the schools provide experience-based learning for students. Return this sheet in the enclosed envelope. Program staff will then plan specific activities with you.

_____   Students can explore jobs at our business for three to
          four days.*

_____   Students can come to our business for several weeks to
          complete learning projects.*

_____   We have personnel who can visit the school to talk to students.

_____   The following individual(s) are interested in serving on an
          advisory board for experience-based learning:

          _____

          _____

          _____

Name: _____

Business: _____

Address: _____

Phone: _____

*Hours arranged at mutual convenience.

Figure 5-1. Sample form used to recruit community sites for experience-based learning.

The Value of Personal Interviews

If you have the resources, a personal meeting is the most efficient way of recruiting sites because it not only helps the site person understand how participation can be worked out but also helps school staff gather information on student learning possibilities at the site. One way to accomplish personal recruiting with limited staff is to use a team of recruiters—a combination, for example, of teachers, business people from the school board, advisory group members and/or parents. Students who have already been in experience-based learning might also assist in recruiting. The number of recruiters needed is, of course, conditioned by the size of your community and number of sites you need to contact.

A recruitment interview will generally cover these topics:
- Description of the learning activities and students
- Description of the resource person's role and roles of the school staff
- General overview of the site's functions and organization
- Analysis of the learning potential of the site (see Chapter 3)

Recruiters should be well-versed in the intent of student placements. Explanatory materials can be left with the contact person for review when convenient. Care should be taken, however, not to leave too much reading material; a simple description of the proposed learning activities is sufficient. Encourage questions throughout the interview; help the contact person see what the site can offer students in terms of interesting and challenging learning experiences. Show samples of previous student work at community sites if you have already had student placements (sample exploration records and student projects, for example).

What the site can offer is, of course, dependent on what the contact person is willing to offer, but the interviewer can help the contact person visualize how students could be involved in specific activities at the site. If in-depth learning through student projects seems formidable at first, the two- to three-day exploration sequence might be suggested as one way a site could be initially involved.

Agreeing on Site Involvement

Decision makers at community sites will be especially interested in the following details, which can affect agreement to participate:

1. **Insurance coverage** protecting sites from liability related to student onsite learning (see Chapter 6 for more on legal, insurance and other administrative questions)
2. **Legal provisions** for students to participate in site activities as learners rather than earners
3. **School staff support** that will be available to the resource people

When questions have been answered and both parties agree on the desirability of the site for student learning, all that remains is to determine the degree of involvement acceptable to the employer and formalize the agreement in writing. This involves negotiating two remaining particulars:

1. **Number of students** who can be accommodated (not necessarily at one time)
2. **Degree of student involvement** acceptable to the site

The interviewer will know generally at this point what resources in time, people and materials are available at the site and how willing the contact person is to allocate them for student use. On the basis of this preliminary understanding, the interviewer can help the contact person specify the extent of student involvement that will be acceptable to the site. To determine this, the interviewer should take the initiative by asking such questions as, "Can you take five students, one at a time, for explorations?" "Are you willing to work with students for several weeks on projects?" If the contact person is shy about hosting several students or committing the site for long-term visits, the interviewer can suggest short-term student placements for specific project activities so the resource people have a chance to see how the process works.

Each site's agreement to participate should be recorded in writing. A Statement of Intent (see Fig. 5-2) which the interviewer asks the contact person to sign is one way to record the agreement.

Matching Interview to Situation

The way recruiters proceed during the interview will depend on the time available, the type of learning site being recruited, the role of the contact person at that learning site and the personality and habits of the contact person. For example, if the interview is with a top management person in a large corporation who will not become a resource person, emphasis should be placed on the goals of experience-based learning and provisions the district is taking regarding such things as insurance coverage and student transportation, with less time on student learning activities. If, on the other hand, the interview is with someone who will also be the resource person for students, more information can be given about learning activities to help prepare that person for actual placements.

The interviewer should watch for clues that indicate how the contact person is feeling about the idea of experience-based learning. If the employer is "sold," don't keep selling; complete the Statement of Intent and conclude the interview. Conversely, if the employer is convinced that experience-based learning will not work at that site, attempt briefly to identify the reasons but avoid pressure tactics. Thank the contact person, leave descriptive material and exit graciously. Above all, leave a good impression. Individuals may "come around" long after the first recruitment interview, when they have time to reconsider and realize that student schedules can be adjusted to accommodate site situations.

```
                         STATEMENT OF INTENT


   TO:      (Administrator, school, address, phone number)



   FROM:    Company/Agency _____

            Address _____ Zip _____

            Phone _____
```

Our firm will provide learning experiences for a maximum of ___ student(s),
ages ____. We will have the opportunity to meet the students prior to
beginning their learning period. We reserve the right to cancel our
participation at any time. The time the student will be with our firm
will be by mutual agreement between both parties but will not exceed
five days per week or seven hours in any one day without a written
waiver from the student's counselor.

We understand that students will be here only for a learning experience
and under no circumstances shall they be allowed to become commercially
productive for us. We further understand that the student is not to be
paid for the time spent at our workplace.

It is agreed that students will comply with our rules as specified, will
report promptly for work assignments or will call their assigned
resource person if unforeseen circumstances interfere.

The following learning stations will be available for _____
(if more space is needed, insert a page):   *(type of student use)*

```
   1.  Job/Department: _____  Location: _____
                                                   (floor, room, etc.)
       Resource Person: _____  Phone: _____


   2.  Job/Department: _____  Location: _____
                                                   (floor, room, etc.)
       Resource Person: _____  Phone: _____


   3.  Job/Department: _____  Location: _____
                                                   (floor, room, etc.)
       Resource Person: _____  Phone: _____



                              _____
                              Signed

                              _____
                              Title

                              _____
                              Date
```

Figure 5-2. Sample written statement of community site agreement to participate in experience-based learning.

Recruiting Union Sites

If students are to gain a general understanding of the trends and issues operating in the world of work they need to understand the philosophy and contributions of organized labor. It is, therefore, important to make both union and nonunion sites available for student learning if possible.

Union representatives may have difficulty understanding how hands-on experiences for students can be accomplished within the laws and regulations governing the involvement of minors at work sites and without posing a potential threat to the job security of adult workers. They may fear that introduction of students on job sites means competition with regular employees for jobs or possible exploitation of the students for free labor.

The following general approach is suggested for recruiting union sites:
1. Ask the site contact person about union contracts at the site and obtain the name(s) of union representatives there.
2. Discuss any projected changes in the company's work force with the contact person. Students entering the site while employees are on layoff may be suspect.
3. When possible, volunteer to initiate the union contact yourself. This gives you or another school representative the opportunity to explain the intent of student placements directly to union officials and answer their questions firsthand.

When talking with union representatives, explain the exploration process in detail. Explorations are a good entry for a site hesitant about getting involved. Describe also how project activities fit into the curriculum. Emphasize that onsite learning is carefully planned and monitored so it will be educationally productive for the student and not financially productive for the employer. Give some examples of student onsite learning activities.

Before leaving, make sure the union representative understands the conditions under which the site is participating. When necessary, develop a memo of understanding or agreement with the union to supplement the Statement of Intent, delineating the students' planned activities at the site and their relationships with site resource people.

When a student placement actually begins, be sure the student meets the shop steward if there is one (closed shop). Be sure the shop steward has a clear understanding of the educational purposes of the proposed activities and the site's agreement to participate. Answer any questions the steward may have. Follow up with the union representative(s) at regular intervals to answer additional questions which may develop from having a student at the job site.

At sites where several trade or craft unions are present—for example in the building or construction industries—students might spend a short time with each of several different crafts (plumber, electrician, carpenter, welder and so forth) to sample the business as a whole. Union offices themselves might be developed as sites for student learning. Some central union offices are receptive to providing onsite learning experiences for students, having them attend union meetings, steward training classes, grievance meetings, arbitration cases and collective bargaining sessions. Suggest that the business agent invite the student as a guest to a regular union meeting.

Special Considerations for Some Sites

Agencies or individuals dealing with confidential or client-privileged information such as doctors, lawyers, psychiatrists, counselors, ministers, banks and credit unions may express concern that client confidentiality cannot be maintained if students are placed at their site. In these instances, recruiters and site contact people can negotiate areas of work that are available and not available to student observation or involvement. Students can learn without participating in every aspect of a given occupation, and the realities of working around situations requiring confidential information can in themselves be educational for students.

Individuals with hourly incomes or those compensated on a straight commission basis may feel they cannot spare time for one-to-one, intensive interaction with a student. For these and any other kinds of limitations, individual agreements can usually be worked out for student site experiences that fit the desires of the contact person and the availability of time, personnel and resources. You might suggest they take only minimal time from their schedule to work with students by using their down time—lunch, coffee breaks, early mornings—or by identifying substitute or additional resource people in their firm to share the responsibility. Perhaps students could accompany such individuals for specified periods while they pursue their regular activities. Students might also have learning activities that do not require constant interaction with site personnel.

Criteria for Site Selection

An onsite interview is an important way to determine if a site will be a healthy place for students to learn. On-the-spot professional judgment should be operating in the selection of community sites, and the following are basic criteria for this judgment:

1. **Willingness to participate.** An employer's willingness to participate should include acceptance of the fact that some students will be more challenging to reach than others. The employer should also show a willingness to let students become genuinely involved in learning about site operations and people's roles on the job.
2. **The site's potential for student learning.** You should ask the contact person specifically which site personnel will be available to the students, what those personnel do in their jobs and what actual tasks the student could do with those personnel. Based on these questions, you can generally tell if the site will be a productive learning resource for students.

KEEPING TRACK OF SITES

To place students in the community, you will need an up-to-the-minute site inventory and records of site usage. The site recordkeeping system should have the following four qualities:

1. **Simplicity**—making it easy for staff to record only what is necessary and find it when they need it
2. **Accessibility**—making information on community sites readily available to students for site selection
3. **Comprehensiveness**—providing records of all pertinent information about each site and about the program's interaction with each site
4. **Portability**—allowing program staff to use needed records both in their office and in the field

SIDE ONE

Company Name: *Walk-In Legal Aid*	Phone: *555-3880*
Address: *1921 N.E. Meridian*	

Contact: *Ann Vandam*

Type of Business: *Provide legal assistance to indigent persons*

Learning Stations	Resource Person	Activities
Alternatives	*Rose Martin*	*Intake interview Phone research*
Investigation	*Grant Hickman*	*Investigate alleged crime, canvas for witnesses, write reports*

SIDE TWO

Comments: *Requires that you be able to monitor your own time, be a good reader and be able to write reports*

Must ride bus (lines 41 and 44 from south corner of school grounds)

Scheduling Requirements: *Flexible scheduling; however, you may have to spend some full days onsite*

Figure 5-3. Sample file card for easy student and staff access to the current site inventory.

Card File: Current Site Inventory

An alphabetical card file can serve as a current site inventory and permit easy reference to brief site information. For each site recruited, a card is added to the file listing the site name, address, contact person, resource person(s) and general site requirements or restrictions related to student learning (see sample in Fig. 5-3). This file should be housed where it is accessible to both students and staff and can be supervised.

File Folders: Cumulative Site-Related Materials

You may also want to establish a cumulative site file with folders for each site that include narrative descriptions by the program representative who recruited them, site-related literature and everything about those sites gathered in the course of developing them for student learning. This might include site analysis information, completed student exploration records and lists of learning objectives—anything that will help students select sites and students and staff plan learning activities. You might also mark participating sites on a community map posted near the site file to help students see the various sites available to them and help them plan transportation.

Staff Notebook: A Portable Summary of Site Activities

Whoever is responsible for liaison with participating sites and resource people should have a looseleaf notebook summarizing key site information and student learning activities. When a site is recruited, the site name, address, telephone number and contact person can be entered on forms designed to fit in the binder (see Fig. 5-4), and the forms can then be filed alphabetically in the notebook.

Each student placement at a site should be noted, as well as visits to the site by school staff. The forms thus become a brief cumulative record that a staff person can take along on site visits. These forms should clearly indicate the frequency of site use (or lack of use if an available site has not been selected at all by students—a possibility if recruitment is not based directly on student interests).

For purposes of future reference and to avoid repetitive contacts, a record should also be kept of (a) sites identified earlier as potential learning sites but not yet interviewed and (b) sites interviewed but not selected for recruitment.

Adding Sites to the Network

There are several reasons why you may have to recruit new sites after student placements have begun:

SIDE ONE

Brown Chevrolet   555-1234
Business   Phone

14572 N. Wayside Blvd.
Address

Charles Goddard   same, ext. 206
Contact Person   Phone

Statement of Intent Signed ___9/15___

LEARNING STATION	DATE OF ANALYSIS	RESOURCE PERSON	PHONE
whole business	10/15	Charles Goddard	same ext.206
sales dept.	"	" "	"
shop	11/21	Myrna Long	ext. 35
office	"	Al Armstrong	ext. 16

CONDITIONS AND COMMENTS:

Time Arrangements ___to be negotiated; full days preferred___

Clothing Requirements ___shop-overalls supplied___

Safety/Equipment _____

LEVELS OF STUDENT INVOLVEMENT:		DATES OF STUDENT SITE USE:
☑ Exploration	☑ Individual	10/20 - 10/24 2/10 - 2/14 12/15 - 12/16
	☑ Group/No. __3__ (maximum)	3/5
☑ Learning		11/28 - 12/23
☐ Other		

Figure 5-4. Sample site record form.

SIDE TWO

SITE VISIT RECORD:

DATE	STUDENT	PURPOSE OF VISIT
10/5		Interview w/Charles Goddard to analyze learning potential
10/20	Kelly Robbins	Checked on Kelly's first day of exploration
11/21		Interview w/Myrna Long and Al Armstrong
11/28	Kelly Robbins	Phoned to confirm learning activity w/Myrna Long
12/7	Kelly Robbins	Checked w/Kelly and Myrna in shop
12/15	Carol Lee	First day of exploration
12/23	Kelly Robbins	Performance review w/Kelly and Myrna Long

Figure 5-4. *(continued)*

1. Students' career interests will change and new interests will develop.
2. Certain occupational areas may not be sufficiently represented to meet student requests.
3. Some sites may withdraw or be terminated.
4. Specific student learning plans may require new resources.
5. You may decide to offer more kinds of experience-based activities.
6. Management at an active site may change, requiring that you "recruit" the new contact person or find a substitute site.

New sites are identified through the same sources of information used in initial recruitment—the expressed interest of not-yet-recruited sites, personal references, business directories and so forth. Specific sites can often be recommended by parents, members of an advisory board or school board and site personnel already participating. Many times, the students themselves can recommend sites that fit their interests.

Placement Procedures and Attendance Records

Figure 5-5 summarizes one system that experience-based programs have used to verify student placements and attendance. A sample Student and Resource Person Contract form (Fig. 5-6) is part of that recordkeeping system.

ORIENTING RESOURCE PEOPLE

The first task in preparing resource people is to let them know what is expected of students and what they must do to assure that students are learning. Resource people should also be familiar enough with those expectations to explain them to their fellow employees and anyone visiting their site.

Staff must make certain that all resource people—

1. Understand the reasons for the students' visits to their sites
2. Know how they can help the students complete specific learning activities at the site
3. Receive pertinent information about the students with whom they will be working before placements begin
4. Feel generally prepared for the new experience and the arrival of students at their sites

As an aid in this orientation process, the Northwest Regional Educational Laboratory has developed *The Community Resource Person's Guide for Experience-Based Learning*, a handbook that helps resource people understand explorations and student projects. It also suggests how resource people can analyze their own job or site's learning potential and provides helpful hints on interacting effectively with students from junior high to community college age (see Appendix C).

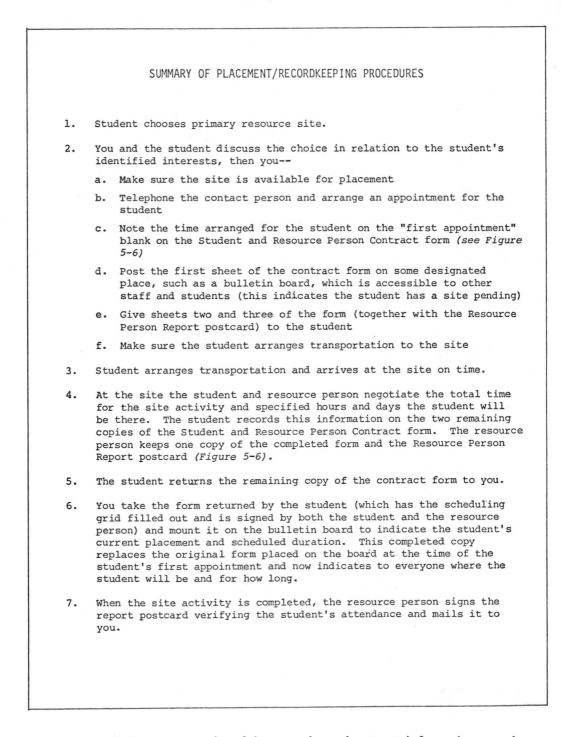

SUMMARY OF PLACEMENT/RECORDKEEPING PROCEDURES

1.   Student chooses primary resource site.

2.   You and the student discuss the choice in relation to the student's identified interests, then you--

    a.   Make sure the site is available for placement

    b.   Telephone the contact person and arrange an appointment for the student

    c.   Note the time arranged for the student on the "first appointment" blank on the Student and Resource Person Contract form *(see Figure 5-6)*

    d.   Post the first sheet of the contract form on some designated place, such as a bulletin board, which is accessible to other staff and students (this indicates the student has a site pending)

    e.   Give sheets two and three of the form (together with the Resource Person Report postcard) to the student

    f.   Make sure the student arranges transportation to the site

3.   Student arranges transportation and arrives at the site on time.

4.   At the site the student and resource person negotiate the total time for the site activity and specified hours and days the student will be there. The student records this information on the two remaining copies of the Student and Resource Person Contract form. The resource person keeps one copy of the completed form and the Resource Person Report postcard *(Figure 5-6)*.

5.   The student returns the remaining copy of the contract form to you.

6.   You take the form returned by the student (which has the scheduling grid filled out and is signed by both the student and the resource person) and mount it on the bulletin board to indicate the student's current placement and scheduled duration. This completed copy replaces the original form placed on the board at the time of the student's first appointment and now indicates to everyone where the student will be and for how long.

7.   When the site activity is completed, the resource person signs the report postcard verifying the student's attendance and mails it to you.

Figure 5-5. An example of how student placement information can be systematically recorded.

Three-part form used to note the student's first appointment and schedule of times the student will be at the site.

STUDENT AND RESOURCE PERSON CONTRACT

Name_____

Site_____ Dept._____

Resource Person

First

STUDENT AND RESOURCE PERSON CONTRACT

Name_____

Site_____ Dept._____

Resource Person

Firs

STUDENT AND RESOURCE PERSON CONTRACT

Name_____

Site_____ Dept._____

Resource Person_____

First Appointment_____

Date - Time

Week Of	M	T	W	Th	F

Resource Person Signature   Student Signature

If there are any negotiated changes to this contract, please notify school staff.

Postcard used to verify student attendance.

RESOURCE PERSON REPORT

Did the student meet the hours and appointments involved in this contract (was the attendance satisfactory)?

Student Name _____ Yes _____ No _____

If not, what day(s) did the student miss?

_____

Comments: _____

_____

_____

Resource Person

Figure 5-6. Sample forms to verify student placement and attendance.

The Value of Group Orientation Sessions

Orientation information can be shared during recruiting interviews or even when scheduling student placements, but the recommended way of orienting resource people is in at least one group session prior to actual involvement with students so resource people have an opportunity to exchange questions, opinions and suggestions with school staff and each other. One session at the beginning of the year, however, may neither anticipate nor respond to the resources' needs for information and support. Chances are, too, that you will be adding resource people to your network as the year goes along.

Some programs offer a sequence of four orientation sessions during a school year to focus on the following purposes:

- Session 1: Orienting new participants to their role as resource people before they receive students at their sites
- Session 2: A problem-solving clinic where experienced resource people help answer the questions of community people new to experience-based learning
- Session 3: Building skills that resource people feel they need to better serve both the students and the activities—skills in helping students and evaluating performance
- Session 4: A year-end feedback session to give resource people an opportunity to evaluate processes and procedures

Planning Orientation Sessions

If you decide to plan a sequence of group sessions for resource people, remember to keep materials, procedures and approaches in these sessions straightforward and concise. It is always difficult to ask busy people to attend more meetings, so you owe it to them to make the meetings as useful and brief as possible.

Weigh the pros and cons of various presentation techniques so that each group session is interesting and appropriate to its purpose. Group discussions invite contributions from all participants: new ideas pop up, everyone gets involved and no one person has to carry the rest of the group as leader. Panel discussions are good, too, and can include seasoned resource people as well as students and staff. Use of visual aids such as videotapes and overhead projectors as well as student materials and samples helps to clarify what students will do at sites and how the resource people can help. Role playing can also be useful, allowing resource people to put themselves in the students' shoes and act out site situations.

One Resource Person's Observations

The following interview with a resource person who has participated in experience-based learning may help you plan effective agendas for orientation sessions. These observations may also be useful during site recruitment.

1. **What characteristics does a resource person need?**

Each time we have a new student we learn something. Resource people must be willing to spend some time learning about the individual students with whom they'll be working. At each site you need resource people who enjoy their jobs. You need enthusiastic people, not just those who are putting in time. People can't satisfactorily show someone else what they do unless they really like doing it themselves.

A resource person should be natural and not try to "put on" for students. If you try to show your job as more important than it is, a student will perceive this and mark you as a phony.

2. **What are some things a resource person can do to help a student maintain interest?**

You must walk a fine line between limiting a student's experience unnecessarily and having the student become economically productive at the site. The student should be given real tasks to do, but should never replace an employee. Think of things to keep a student involved, not just watching. For example, ask the student, "Could you mix this for me," or "Please watch this gauge and record changes," and so forth. Students need to do activities related to the actual job being explored or learned, not menial tasks around the place.

At our site we show films on the industry to vary the presentation of information. We let students sit in on meetings so they can see how business actually functions, and we use a variety of resource people at the site so students get a good idea of the variety of jobs available.

3. **How can a resource person help a student who has problems with reading, writing and math?**

Look for ways to challenge students in keeping with their own learning levels. Some of the training materials we use for certain jobs are very challenging, for example. But some are also so difficult they would turn off students if they were introduced to them immediately. We try to start out slowly and avoid using too much technical jargon.

4. **How do you discuss problems of personal hygiene or grooming without hurting or alienating the student?**

We haven't had many problems with this. If it's something minor such as a student wearing a T-shirt with "I live to boogie" across the front, I feel it's better to let the student learn what kind of dress is appropriate by observing employees. If, on the other hand, it were something entirely off base for a regular employee, I would tell students very frankly that a change was necessary if they wished to stay here. In the case of long hair, students would be required to fix it some way to ensure safety around machinery. Above all, be straight with students and tell them if something is a problem.

5. What are the primary benefits a resource person receives?

If matched well with students, resource people will find themselves talking with individuals who really are interested in what they're doing; that will be satisfying in itself. Some of us are isolated in our work; the student gives us someone to talk to about what we're doing. The hardest part of any job is communication—trying to tell other people about your ideas. A student gives us a chance to brainstorm ideas with a new person.

Observations such as these go a long way toward helping community people *and* school people understand what students can gain from experience-based learning. One clear message is that resource people and students begin to appreciate each other as individuals, without regard to age difference except as it gives the resource people a perspective that the students want to hear.

Be sure to thank resource people for their efforts with students. Many ways can be found to express public appreciation for their contributions including an annual recognition banquet, newspaper articles and photographs of students and resource people working together, certificates of appreciation and letters of commendation from the district superintendent or chairperson of the school board to the resource person's supervisor. Remember that these resource people and sites are volunteering their time and energy to help the schools provide learning experiences that cannot be duplicated or even effectively simulated within the classroom. For this cooperation, they deserve all the recognition you can give them.

FOOTNOTE

[1]Eliot Wigginton, *Moments: The Foxfire Experience* (Washington, D.C.: Institutional Development and Economic Affairs Services, Inc., 1975), p. 19.

6

MANAGING THE PROCESS

...push back the desks and sit down on
the floor with the kids and really
listen to them...see what they can all
come up with *together* that *might* work
in the context of their own particular
school and community—and then try to
find ways to make it work....
            —*Moments: The Foxfire*
            Experience[1]

Generally, people using experience-based learning have not encountered as many obstacles to community-based activities as they expected, and there are usually reasonable solutions to administrative problems that may arise. Road-blocks will be fewer if the decision to adopt experience-based learning is jointly made by teachers, administrators, school board and possibly a citizen's committee. Find out everything you can about your community's goals and priorities for education, district policies concerning curriculum, financial implications and staff support for the basic concepts.

Administrators and teachers desiring to implement experience-based learning must attend to some of the following issues and provide appropriate information to others in the district and community who will be affected by the learning activities:

1. Know exactly what you want to accomplish through experience-based learning.
2. Establish regular contacts with teachers, counselors and administrators so others in the school system know what will be going on.
3. Know what school services are available to the teachers and students who will be involved in experience-based learning (testing, counseling, reading labs and so forth).

167

4. Plan ways experience-based learning can help other teachers and students in the school and vice versa.
5. Review all course and credit requirements that students must meet and make sure students in experience-based learning continue to satisfy those requirements.
6. Determine evaluating, grading and reporting policies for experience-based activities.
7. Decide early how experience-based learning credit will appear on students' transcripts.
8. Develop liaison with other school programs using community sites as resources.
9. Make specific plans for coordinating student transportation to community sites with school schedules and policies.
10. Clarify whether hall passes and other school rules apply to students who will be leaving campus during the school day for experience-based activities.

In your planning provide answers or recommendations for critical questions such as who will have administrative responsibility for experience-based learning, what staff development will be provided for those who want to implement it with students, how the experience-based activities will be coordinated with the rest of the curriculum, what resources are available for carrying out planned activities and what courses or programs will be infused with experience-based learning. Other questions are raised in the pages that follow, with answers based on the administrative experiences of those who are actually placing students in the community.

WHY EMPHASIZE STUDENT ACCOUNTABILITY?

A major goal in experience-based learning is to increase students' abilities to make and act on choices and to accept responsibility for the consequences of those choices. A good accountability system helps implement that goal. You should view the accountability system—and the negotiation that is a necessary part of it—as an important guidance tool, a mechanism for turning every behavior into a learning experience:

● Standards of behavior must be clearly defined for students and reflect general community expectations as well as regular school requirements.
● Consequences should flow naturally from the standard in question.
● Personal conferences between the student and appropriate adults should be built into each action.

Students need to know in a general way what is expected of them and what can happen as a result of certain behaviors, including the types of penalties that might be imposed. However they also need to be able to count on staff showing a concern for them and a willingness to listen to what they say. Figure 6-1 illustrates the way one experience-based program has spelled out expected behaviors and consequences for its students.

```
                    STUDENT ACCOUNTABILITY SYSTEM


   WHAT IS EXPECTED          WHO GETS INVOLVED          WHAT HAPPENS

Appropriate conduct while    Parent            When there is evidence
representing school                            that a student is doing
(recognizing legal as well   Resource          less than satisfactorily
as personal responsibilities) Person           on any of the expectations,
                                               a conference will take
High level of cooperation    Staff             place with the student
with resource people/staff/                    to clarify concerns.
students                     Administrator     It is during this
                                               meeting that appropriate
Educational productivity                       natural consequences
                                               must be put in writing.*
Planning and goal setting
                                               If improvement has not
Completing work on time                        occurred after an
                                               established period of
Signing in/out appropriately                   time, a conference will
                                               be held with parents/
Keeping appointments                           staff/student to reach
                                               new agreements.
Following transportation
agreements                                     Failure to fulfill
                                               penalties and improve
Showing care for facility                      in meeting responsibilities
and equipment                                  calls for an immediate
                                               conference involving
                                               parents/staff/student
                                               and appropriate school
                                               administrator.

                                                 Types of Penalties

                                               Make-up work
                                               Loss of free-time
                                                 privileges
                                               Daily reports to staff
                                               Written agreements or
                                                 "contracts"
                                               Repayment of inconvenience
                                                 time
                                               Loss of credit
                                               Loss of site access
                                               Probationary period
                                               Suspension from program
                                               Dismissal from program

*By "natural consequences" we mean that courses of action should be
 negotiated that logically address or relate to the student's behavior
 and are not imposed arbitrarily.
```

Figure 6-1. Example of how expectations can be spelled out in advance for students in experience-based learning.

The student accountability system outlined in Fig. 6-1 is initiated whenever a student is not meeting negotiated learning agreements or some behavior is considered counterproductive. The accountability system provides for three sequential levels of student/adult interaction:

- **Level 1:** The first conference is usually between a student and the individuals most immediately affected by the behavior to resolve the problem between the people directly involved.
- **Level 2:** If the difficulty is not resolved, then it may be time to bring a parent or guardian into the negotiations. Again, the goal is to work out a solution that is appropriate to the problem with adults who can help, as well as establish communication with those adults responsible for the student.
- **Level 3:** If the difficulty persists in spite of actions at the first and second levels, an administrator may become involved.

Staff immediately involved with the student are often the ones to decide when to go on to the second and third levels. There may be several negotiations and conferences at each level, and attempts are always made to exhaust the resources of one level before going on to the next. For example, if a student is late turning in project products, the student's staff adviser may try several reminders before deciding to call on parents for help. Likewise, several conversations with both parents and students may be reasonable before deciding to go to administrative levels.

At each conference level, school staff, student and the student's parent (unless the problem is minor) try to agree on what the student will do to improve behavior and what consequences will result if the agreement is not met. Together, all come up with a plan to eliminate the problem—including support for the student in the home environment. Agreements, deadlines and consequences should always be written down and signed by all concerned. In this way, further conferences and consequences do not come as surprises to the student but instead follow naturally on the student's previous decisions.

Application of the student accountability system is based on a conviction that responsibility for student learning and behavior can be transferred only gradually from adult to student, depending on the individual readiness of the student. The best way to deal with a problem is simply to invite the student to sit down and talk about it on the spot. The student is encouraged to talk out causes and effects of the behavior in question. Together, student and staff member try to interpret the action honestly and negotiate a solution. Depending on the seriousness of the problem, the staff member may formalize the interaction by noting the behavior and the conference on a form (see Fig. 6-2), which helps everyone involved in the interaction understand why it was necessary and what the participants have agreed can be done about it.

A written agreement or contract, signed by the student, may also be used to specify changes to be made within a certain time frame (see Fig. 6-3). If a problem continues, additional consequences are discussed and terms renegotiated. Further disciplinary action is involved only if reasonable solutions cannot be found and the student's actions continue to conflict with school standards.

ACCOUNTABILITY WRITE-UP

Copies to: ___ Administrator
             ___ Student
             ___ Parent
                 Other Staff:
                 ___ _____
                 ___ _____

Student Name _____

Date _____

EXPECTED BEHAVIOR

___ Appropriate conduct while representing
    school (legal as well as personal
    responsibilities)

___ High level of cooperation with resource
    people/staff/students

___ Educational productivity

___ Planning and goal setting

___ Planning and completing explorations

___ Planning and completing projects

___ Establishing competency target dates

___ Signing in/out appropriately

___ Keeping appointments

___ Following transportation agreements

___ Showing care for equipment and facility

___ Submitting journals

___ Other _____

    _____

COMMENTS: _____

_____

LEVELS OF ACCOUNTABILITY

Conference

___ Administrator

___ Resource person

___ Parent

___ Staff

Consequences

___ Make-up work

___ Written agreements or "contracts"

___ Repayment of inconvenience time

___ Loss of free-time privilege

___ Loss of project credit

___ Loss of exploration credit

___ Loss of site access

___ Probationary period

___ Suspension

___ Dismissal

___ Other _____

    _____

_____   _____
Staff signature   Date

_____   _____
Student signature   Date

Figure 6-2. Sample record of staff/student agreements regarding behaviors and consequences.

Following an accountability conference, decisions negotiated with the student are put in the form of a written contract to which the student agrees and then signs. Following is the text of such a contract, designed for a student who repeatedly was absent from sites and was more than a month behind on her journal entries. The student gave numerous reasons for lack of performance. Staff, realizing her propensity for rationalization, wrote the contract specifically to rule out further excuses other than those carefully examined by staff and the student's parents.

ACCOUNTABILITY CONTRACT

Ruth will select another site for exploration purposes by 3:00 p.m. May 1, that site to be entirely new, not one she has already visited.

She is to meet exactly the times, hours, schedule and all other arrangements on that site. 'If she has any physical reason for not meeting these arrangements, she is to inform her staff adviser first, her resource person second and her mother third. All must verify whatever reason she gives.

Each exploration record must be turned in on the exact date specified and be of acceptable quality to receive full credit.

Ruth is not to attend any other site than the one to which she is assigned and is not to accompany any other students to their sites, no matter whose permission she gains first.

She will keep an appointment with her staff adviser on Monday, May 9, to discuss the remaining three projects and plan dates for completion.

Ruth will be caught up with her journal entries by May 9.

Ruth understands that if any of the above listed provisions are broken she will be asked to leave the program. Responsibility for graduating with her class is entirely hers. It is our estimate that if she continues to perform at her present level, graduation will not be possible. If she meets all negotiated dates and utilizes sites to the satisfaction of staff, the possibility of timely graduation is still there.

_____   _____
Student signature   *Date*

_____   _____
Staff signature   *Date*

_____   _____
Parent signature   *Date*

Figure 6-3. Sample agreement between student, staff and parent on how the student can meet expectations.

Student Management of Time

Students need reasonable periods of time within which to accomplish course objectives. This time frame may be defined by traditional grading periods or staff may devise some other framework. Some experience-based programs divide school calendars into "action zones" as a way of making clear to students the importance of managing their time wisely. Tasks are recommended that should be completed for each zone or portion of the year. Students are not strictly required to meet all expectations listed in an action zone but use the zones as a basis for negotiating target dates that will help them complete all activities.

Action zones provide a clear guide to the performance/behavior expectations set forth in the student accountability system. Their intention is two-fold:

1. To help students manage their time more effectively and be responsible for themselves
2. To organize monitoring activities so school staff know where each student is in relation to requirements

Staff estimate the number of learning activities that should reasonably be completed within each zone. Then each student and a staff adviser together plan the day-to-day actions necessary for the student to accomplish as much or more than the number of learning activities suggested for the zone. All target dates are put in writing so students and staff can keep track of how performance is shaping up.

During the first zone, staff work with students to help them recognize the need for and take initiative in planning individual activities and weekly schedules. Gradually, the need for staff assistance in time management decreases as students gain skill in accepting these responsibilities.

At the end of each zone, students meet with staff to discuss the tasks they have finished and what they still have to do. They then negotiate new target dates for unfinished activities and set a time to discuss completion. If a student fails to meet these new target dates, another staff/student conference is initiated, with the possible application of accountability consequences.

For students who cannot manage time, zone dates are *mandatory* until the students develop self-management skills. For students who show a reasonable ability to direct themselves, the zones are *recommended* target dates to help them get going and perceive their tasks in terms of available time. Individual differences in learning styles and rates will require variations from this basic timeline. Within reasonable limits, students must be free to interrupt prescribed patterns as their experiences lead them to make new decisions about their goals. Variations should be negotiated with staff whenever needed.

<table>
<tr><td colspan="5" align="center">Jack Jones</td></tr>
</table>

		Jack Jones

(form)

```
                                              Jack Jones
                                         _____
                                           Student Name
End of Zone____6_____        Absences this zone    __2__
Date__March 17, 1978___         Absences this semester _3_
```

	Required This Semester	Required This Zone	Completed This Zone	Completed To Date
Journal Entries	12	4	3	6
Competencies	7	2	2	4
Explorations	6	2	3	4
Projects	5	1	1	2

Comments and Recommendations:

Jack gets so busy he sometimes doesn't stop to think about his choices. This shows in his problem with writing journal entries. For the next month he should make two appointments a week with his staff correspondent to talk about his journal entries.

Staff signature

Comments and Response:

I've talked to Jack about keeping up with his journal entries. He likes all the other activities so well, he's really going to try on the journal, too.

Parent or Student signature

Figure 6-4. Sample form for recording how each individual student has met program commitments within a specified period of time.

Keeping Track of Student Time Management

At the close of each zone, the teacher or adviser working with a student on experience-based learning activities can complete a form (see Fig. 6-4) to answer the following general questions:

1. What has the student accomplished in this zone in relation to what was specified?
2. What was not accomplished?
3. What barriers seem to be in the way?
4. What can be done to help the student?
5. What should be communicated to the student? Who will do it?
6. What should be communicated to parents? Who will do it?

Question 3 through 6 can be addressed in the form of recommendations for what should happen next. These recommendations can be discussed with each student individually. If the form provides a place for student or parent response, it can serve as a grading period report, thus alleviating the need to duplicate that process. Extra space for other staff comments and signatures can be provided on the form if several staff are working together with students in experience-based activities.

Time accountability is one of the most important and visible responsibilities young adults must master. Staff should be fair with students, but also firm, honest and consistent in following through on consequences. Reasonable changes in plans are expected as students become increasingly involved with managing their own learning. At the same time, students should experience the consequences of their decisions and learn to weigh the results as they plan tasks and follow interests.

Students involved in more than one project at a time may need advice on setting priorities. What a student has been able to accomplish in one zone of time should be related to anticipated future workload, and the student should be encouraged to make realistic assessments of how much work to undertake in the next zone—perhaps more, perhaps less.

Involving Parents

Helping students make and keep schedules for their learning tasks is a good opportunity for parents to become more involved in their children's education. If a student is having difficulty keeping up with learning plans, staff may choose to invite the student's parent or guardian in to discuss courses of action. All participants in such a conference might complete a task sheet similar to the one in Fig. 6-5, displaying each learning task with its target dates. When a task is complex, it can be broken into mini-tasks with interim target dates for each. Parents can post a copy of the task sheet at home and regularly talk with their son or daughter about how much progress has been made and ways that the work can be accomplished.

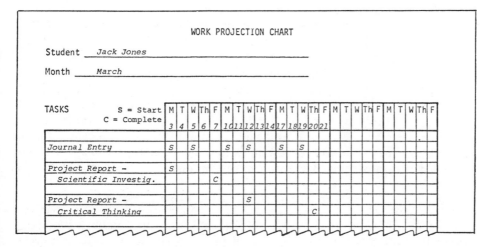

Figure 6-5. Sample task sheet to help students monitor their own completion of program activities within specified times.

SHOULD YOU HAVE AN ADVISORY COMMITTEE?

The operational success of community-based learning—whether a full-time educational effort or one part of a school curriculum—depends on the availability of community resources (working people, work settings, equipment and materials). One way to access these resources is by establishing an advisory committee that represents the community and those who will be involved with your experience-based activities (business, labor, parents, students and the school district).

High visibility in the community need not be a requirement for all committee members. The fact that people wear more than one hat in their civic life—that a parent can also represent a group such as the Urban League, for example—can help you achieve broad representation without having too many members in the group.

Representatives of students and parents might be nominated for their positions by their respective groups. School board members and administrators can recommend key people. Labor offices can recommend individuals and so can your local Chamber of Commerce office. In addition, individuals who have retired from business and labor and remained active in community life may have both time and invaluable experience to offer.

Before contacting potential members of an advisory committee you need to be clear about (a) how much time you will ask them to give, (b) the areas in which you want them to act as advisers and (c) the degree of influence they will have.

WHAT KIND OF LEARNING CENTER DO STUDENTS NEED?

The management of a full-time experience-based learning program requires some kind of learning center from which staff and students can operate. Because there is so much movement of students to and from the community, some programs prefer to house their staff entirely apart from the traditional school program. Others have found a school-based learning center to be preferable.

Even with experience-based activities infused into a more traditional curriculum, you may want to establish a learning center as a clearinghouse for community activities (part of your classroom, a separate place in the building or entirely off campus). Students should learn in a real world setting as much as possible. The learning center is simply a central location for the information they need to find resources in the community. The space should provide a pleasant, relaxed atmosphere that is conducive to independent study.

HOW MUCH WILL ALL THIS COST?

Costs for experience-based learning activities do not have to be significantly different from regular school program costs. What you decide to do depends largely on how well you can use what you already have in new and better ways. For general planning purposes, however, try listing categories like the following:

Personnel

Programs that use community sites for student learning experiences will need to find a way to cover two essential functions: coordinating community site activities and monitoring student school-based activities. Earlier chapters have suggested some ways these two functions can be shared by teachers who team up to provide experience-based learning.

If you are relying on yourself and others who are already attached to a school district in one way or another, then the major provision you will need is probably an extended contract to allow time to plan and prepare for experience-based learning. Some districts with experience-based learning provide for staff days during the summer or other in-between times to recruit sites and prepare resource people for student involvement. For schools weaving experience-based learning into ongoing efforts, staff inservice training and released time for planning should be considered. Many staff using community resources also utilize instructional aides to help students and handle paperwork.

Equipment

Basic equipment required will depend on your priorities. It is hard to run individualized, community-based activities without easy access to telephones, typewriters and duplicating equipment. Highly desirable extras are tape recorders and cameras. Our recommendation is to start with the essentials and add extra items as you determine the need and find the financial resources. Community resource people will often identify equipment and other learning resources that students may use at work sites.

Materials

Teachers and other specialists in your school district can probably help you identify existing instructional materials that are geared to individualized study. Look for assessment instruments and a variety of basic skills materials. If you are setting up a learning center separate from your school campus, your need to accumulate materials will be greater and, of course, will increase your costs. In addition to general learning resources, all students need their own copies of specific materials related to various experience-based learning processes (journals, competency guides, exploration records). Whether you develop your own versions of these or purchase them, costs for these consumable items will be comparable to those needed in other school activities (see Appendix C).

WHAT ABOUT LEGAL, HEALTH AND SAFETY CONSIDERATIONS?

Insurance

Schools planning to develop community-based activities must investigate local conditions and existing insurance provisions to determine if the following kinds of coverage can and should be provided:
1. General liability to cover participating learning sites, resource people and students and to protect the site from all risks, liabilities, claims or demands for personal injury or property damage
2. Personal injury protection for students at learning sites
3. Transportation coverage for students and staff enroute to and from learning activities in the community

School districts already involving the community in education have generally found that their existing district liability policies protect students at learning sites in the community. Contact your district insurance agent to determine provisions. For protection of resource people and community sites, it may be necessary to provide additional insurance against possible negligent behavior on the part of students participating in off-campus learning.

Personal injury protection for students can be provided either by the student's own medical and accident coverage, verified by parents, or by the district's coverage for students participating in school activities. Some districts ask parents to buy into the school accident insurance plan covering students in school-related activities, and some states have a statewide plan protecting students in school-related work situations. Existing district transportation insurance is often used to cover students and staff enroute to and from experience-based activities.

Explain insurance provisions to site contact people during recruitment and ask them to sign a Statement of Intent (see Fig. 5-2, page 154) as soon as they have agreed to take part. If you have the kind of coverage where it is applicable, a copy of the Statement of Intent can then be forwarded to the insurance company handling your liability policy and the company can enact an indemnity covenant on the employer's behalf. This procedure establishes a "hold harmless" relationship with the community site and makes your school district and its governing agency liable for student actions and behavior at the site.*

Health and Safety

In the career environment, students must follow the same health and safety rules that govern employees at the site they are visiting. To ensure student safety on job sites, school staff should arrange for student use of any required special safety or health gear. Such gear might include goggles,

---

*All aspects of indemnification should be reviewed by your district's legal counsel and insurance company.

welding outfits, hard hats or safety shoes. Community sites may agree to provide these items for students, or local business or labor groups might help in making such items available.

Child labor laws allow involvement in potentially hazardous occupations if the following conditions are properly met:[2]

1. The terms of the involvement are spelled out in a written agreement, signed by the employer* and school coordinator or principal.
2. The involvement is incidental to the student-learner's training.
3. The involvement is intermittent, for short periods of time and under the direct and close supervision of a qualified, experienced person.
4. Safety instructions are given by the school and correlated by the employer* with on-the-job training.
5. A schedule has been prepared of organized and progressive work processes to be performed on the job.

WHAT ABOUT TRANSPORTATION?

Transportation plans will vary greatly depending on the number of sites you have recruited, size of your community, quality of public transit, funds available and amounts of time students are expected to spend in the community. Transportation considerations include:

1. Determining school or district insurance coverage, if any, for students when using various means of transportation:
   - Public transportation system (insured public carrier)
   - Personal or family car
   - Student car pool
   - Volunteer adult driver (e.g., resource person)
   - School-operated vehicle
   - Bicycle
2. Getting parents' permission
3. Deciding how to finance student transportation
4. Deciding how far geographically you can go to recruit community resources and still manage an effective transportation schedule

In any case, a transportation agreement form should be signed by parents before students are permitted to travel to sites (see sample in Fig. 6-6). The form should list available transportation options and provide space for parents to identify any other transportation that meets with their approval (such as bicycle or motorcycle). The form should state explicitly any means of transportation that do not have school sanction and are undertaken at the student's own risk. Parental approval of a student's transportation options does not cause the school's liability to be waived but it does establish that the institution proceeded in a rational and reasonable manner in attempting to provide for student safety.

_____

*For experience-based learning this term means resource person or person responsible for committing a site to participate, because the student is not in an employer/ employee relationship.

```
┌─────────────────────────────────────────────────────────────────┐
│                   Student Transportation Agreement                │
│                                                                   │
│  It is our understanding that _____, given          │
│  our permission to participate in off-campus learning             │
│  activities, will be moving among various learning sites in       │
│  the community.  He/she has our permission to drive or to         │
│  travel only by the means of transportation checked below:        │
│                                                                   │
│   ☐  Metropolitan bus system      ☐  Volunteer adult driver       │
│                                                                   │
│   ☐  Personal or family auto      ☐  School district bus          │
│                                                                   │
│   ☐  Student car pool             ☐  Employer vehicle             │
│                                                                   │
│   ☐  Program vehicle              ☐  Other (specify)              │
│                                                      _____   │
│                                                                   │
│  Any other means of travel, such as hitchhiking, is without       │
│  our sanction.                                                    │
│                                                                   │
│  Date _____     Signed: _____    │
│                                      Parent or Guardian           │
│                                                                   │
│                              _____    │
│                                          Student                  │
└─────────────────────────────────────────────────────────────────┘
```

Figure 6-6. Sample parental agreement form for student transportation to community sites.

Your school may have budgeted funds to provide for student transportation to community sites. These may be available for several transportation options or may be limited to use of school-operated vehicles. It is worth checking into financial options.

Students may be limited to using the local public transit system. Some schools provide transit passes for students, and this should be explored as one option regardless of other transportation modes available to students.

You will have to answer certain questions regarding the time and money necessary to guarantee transportation flexibility for students as they move into the community. For example, how much staff and student learning time can you allow for travel to and from a site without compromising learning goals? Can you arrange longer student stays at distant sites to reduce frequency of time-consuming trips? Do some sites offer learning experiences unique and desirable enough to justify special transportation considerations? Will your transportation system accommodate the needs of all students, even for inconveniently located sites? All of these questions relate to how far geographically you can go to recruit sites without compromising your time, money and transportation system.

SHOULD STUDENTS BE PAID FOR ONSITE LEARNING?

The question of whether or not students should be paid for hands-on learning activities at community sites should be determined by your educational goals. Many districts with experience-based activities have chosen to provide nonpaid learning placements for reasons such as the following:

1. If students were considered employees, employer priorities rather than educational priorities could dictate student activities.
2. Paying students might unnecessarily limit the number and range of institutions willing to participate.
3. Organized labor, which has supported community involvement in offering educational experiences for youth, wants to keep the focus of such experiences clearly on learning and to ensure that workers are not displaced by students.

In clarifying their commitment to nonpaid learning placements, districts have carefully distinguished between what might be called educational productivity and financial productivity, as follows:

- **Educational productivity** occurs when students agree to tasks that have the prospect of resulting in meaningful learning experiences. Students may use equipment; handle materials; make, assemble, draw and paint things and perform services for the purpose of learning as much as possible about how these things are done and how it feels to do them. Students do a variety of tasks and remain in specific work areas only as long as those areas contribute to learning. The student's payoff is in terms of understandings acquired, skills learned, habits developed and experiences gained. Students might be very productive but the production serves specified educational purposes, and evaluation is based on how well the student work meets stated learning objectives.

- **Financial productivity** is distinctly different from educational productivity. It would occur if a student remained on one job with the intent of performing that job. Emphasis would be on the production of goods or services rather than development of skills, attitudes and values, and the student's work would be commercially productive for the employer. Evaluation would be based on quality and volume of productive work done.

It is important to note that existing federal statutes concerning work and employment do provide for students to be involved in extensive learning experiences in the community without pay. According to the U.S. Department of Labor Employment Standards Administration, the Fair Labor Standards Act includes provision for bona fide student nonpaid placements with employers.

If *all* of the following six criteria apply to the placement, the trainees or students are not employees within the meaning of the Act:

1. The training, even though it includes actual operation of the facilities of the employer, is similar to that which would be given in a vocational school.
2. The training is for the benefit of the trainees or students.
3. The trainees or students do not displace regular employees but work under their close observation.
4. The employer who provides the training derives no immediate advantages from the activities of the trainees or students; in fact, on occasion, operations may actually be impeded.
5. The trainees or students are not necessarily entitled to a job at the conclusion of the training period.
6. The employer and the trainees or students understand that the trainees or students are not entitled to wages for the time spent in training.

Districts offering nonpaid community-based experiences for students should consider adopting a policy statement on student learning and work for pay similar to the sample in Fig. 6-7.

HOW DO WE GIVE STUDENTS CREDIT?

As a professional educator, you will be required to certify specified student outcomes based on completed learning experiences. Many districts with experience-based learning activities are evaluating student progress on the basis of performance indicators other than grades. If you follow the same pattern, you will be asked to provide guidelines for determining how activities, experiences and performances can be translated from your reporting system to another, including recommendations for equivalent units of credit and grade translation when these are required by other institutions.

While some institutions have been reluctant in the past to accept credentials differing from the standard transcript format, this attitude is changing. For example, many forward-looking college admissions officers are recognizing the value of narrative performance records and the detailed student profile they offer. This change is inevitable in view of the variety of alternatives becoming available to students. More and more school programs are nongraded, a condition which may soon be commonplace.

The secret of successful translation of program activities into more traditional credentials is in the language. Credibility is less of an issue if the transmitter and receiver are speaking in similar or commonly understood terms.

Four guidelines will make your credentialing task easier:

1. Student credentials should be as brief as possible while at the same time including explicit information about skills and levels of proficiency the student has acquired.
2. Course completion requirements and student performance should be communicated in a visually clear way.

POLICY REGARDING STUDENT LEARNING AND WORK FOR PAY

It is the policy of ___(district)___ that students do not receive financial reimbursement for any experience-based learning activities at community sites.

The reasons for this policy are as follows:

1. Paying the student creates legal and financial barriers detrimental to experience-based learning (work permits, withholding requirements, tax reporting, union membership and so on).

2. Paying the student suggests productive work has been done. Students must not be commercially productive while on community sites for learning purposes. (Rule of thumb: the student should demand more of the community site in terms of time, attention, materials and so forth than the student is returning in the way of production or services.)

3. Employers would soon be classified as those willing and those not willing to pay students. This is not a valid determinant for establishing a community site network.

4. Students are reluctant to leave a site where they are receiving pay. The school staff must retain flexibility for new sites to be selected when the learning potential of the current one is exhausted.

5. When pay and learning are mixed the pay activities too often take precedence.

6. Students do earn a high school diploma for successful completion of experience-based activities. In addition they receive a reality-based education that gives them excellent preparation for assuming future adult citizen and worker roles.

The above policy does not suggest, however, that the district is in any way prejudiced against students working for pay. The opposite is true. Adequate pay for honest and productive work is central to career development.

Therefore:

1. We will encourage students to find gainful employment outside program hours.

2. We will permit employers to hire students from the program, but there is no expectation that they do so. Any such agreement is entirely between the employer and student.

3. Students will be placed on and moved from community sites according to the educational issues involved and no consideration will be given to the students' employment at that site.

4. Students may hold part-time jobs during the day as long as the hourly requirements of the program are met. Such employment may be by employers participating in the program. Jobs with employers where students are currently placed or have had an in-depth learning placement must be performed before 8:30 a.m. or after 5:00 p.m. weekdays or on weekends and vacations. In no case are work-for-pay hours at community sites participating in the program to be coincidental with program hours.

5. We will make information about job opportunities available to students as they come to our attention.

Figure 6-7. Example of a policy statement to clarify student nonpaid status.

3. The official records should always begin with one page that sets forth the major areas of experience-based learning, what the student has accomplished and how long the student has been in these activities.

4. Information in the credential should be easy to locate quickly.

One way to begin the credit translation process is to draw up a grid that relates experience-based learning to traditional school course work (see Fig. 6-8). Often, however, a far more specific correlation may be desirable or necessary, especially for required courses. In this case there are several ways you can plan a student's experience-based learning to ensure meeting the requirements and then communicate this completion to appropriate school people:

1. If your school has translated course work into basic minimum competency statements, you can prepare a grid that shows the match-up between the students' experience-based work and required graduation competencies. Minimum competencies not addressed by the experience-based work could then be satisfied in other ways. As the student completes activities you can use the standard format of your school to check on competency completion.

2. For required courses, your district may provide general curriculum guides from which classroom teachers adapt their individual class lesson plans. You could use those curriculum guides as a starting point and help your students meet the requirements in one of two ways:

   • With a subject like writing, students could meet the requirements through the accumulation of experience-based activities in journals, explorations, competencies and projects. Within these activities, students will experience a vast range of writing skills: personal, reflective, corresponding; business letters and memos; completion of forms and contracts; research papers; book reviews; interviews; questionnaires and so forth. You could record these writing activities on a simple cumulative form to be presented to appropriate school officials to justify writing credit.

   • For required subjects with more specific content, such as American history, one or more of the student's required projects could be addressed to the identified curriculum goals and objectives for American history used by your school. You could get prior approval of the project(s) as work equivalent to a given number of credit hours in classroom work.

Whatever method you use, it will be helpful to prepare a written credit equivalency statement that is acceptable to receiving institutions.

EXPERIENCE-BASED LEARNING STRATEGIES	Communications	Math	Science	Social Studies	P.E.	Health	Citizenship	Personal Finance	Career Education	Electives
Projects										
1. Critical Thinking	√	√							√	√
2. Creative Development	√	√		√					√	√
3. Functional Citizenship	√	√		√			√		√	√
4. Personal/Social Development	√	√			√	√			√	√
5. Scientific Investigation	√	√	√	√					√	√
Survival Skills for a Changing World										
1. Credit	√	√						√		√
2. Checking Account	√	√						√		√
3. Insurance	√	√						√		√
4. Taxes	√	√						√		√
5. Budget	√	√						√		√
6. Health/Leisure	√	√			√	√				√
7. Emergencies	√					√				√
8. Electoral Process	√			√			√			√
9. Government	√			√			√			√
10. Legal Rights	√			√			√			√
11. Public Agencies	√	√					√			√
12. Employment	√	√						√	√	√
13. Automobile	√	√						√		√
Community Explorations									√	√
Journals	√								√	√

Figure 6-8. Worksheet for correlating experience-based learning activities with school subjects.

WHOM DO WE NEED TO KEEP INFORMED?

Basically you have two groups to keep informed about your activities: in-school and community.

In-School Communications

You must help other school staff know how experience-based learning operates and why students are away from campus, especially if yours is a traditional school situation. Other teachers may be suspicious of off-campus learning activities; the more substantial the progress reports you circulate, the better received your activities will be.

Keep in close touch with other teachers in your school through informal meetings with staff members about students, written reports to individual staff members and regular progress reports at teachers' meetings. Items of particular interest to other school staff will include learning objectives or anticipated student outcomes, initial responses of the community, how student attendance and behavior are monitored at sites and what learning strategies are used.

Once you have set up a procedure for sharing information, evaluate it periodically by circulating a questionnaire among school staff. This may sound burdensome and unnecessary; it is important, however, to recognize that some school staff will be reluctant to accept community-based learning. By soliciting their questions and opinions you may ward off potential difficulties. An attitude of respect and consideration for the honest concerns of others will go a long way toward gaining support and cooperation.

Keeping the Community Informed

One of your primary tasks is to let people in the community know what experience-based activities have to offer young people—to convince taxpayers, parents and students that these activities have educational significance and are worthy of their support and participation. Experience-based learning simply cannot operate without active support from parents, business, labor and government agencies.

You and your students are your school's best advocates. Think about making presentations to key groups such as labor union locals and central committees, the local Chamber of Commerce, boards of trade, Rotary, Kiwanis, Lions and other business, government, professional, religious and service organizations. Groups concerned with general community development and educational opportunities for young people can be influential allies in establishing new programs and generating community support, and many of these groups maintain standing committees on education.

In addition, consider early contact with editors, publishers and managers of radio and television stations in the community to generate interest in your activities. As opinion leaders these individuals can lend valuable assistance to planning and implementation.

A Few Suggestions for Public Presentations

Keep the following points in mind when planning a presentation:

1. Consider ways to *involve the audience*, perhaps by separating large groups into smaller ones for informal discussion.
2. Have *supporting materials* in sufficient quantity for your anticipated audience.
3. Use *visuals* during the presentation to add interest and variety and help your audience understand the intent of experience-based learning and remember specific details.
4. *Panel discussions* and *role play* can be effective ways of conveying information. A panel of student, parent, staff person and resource person could field questions from the audience and amplify each other's answers—or a staff member, student and resource person could act out the kind of interaction and negotiation that takes place between them in the course of student activities.
5. The *type of meeting* and *time of day* will influence presentations. Mealtime meetings, for example, lend themselves to brief overviews and opportunities for students to speak about their experiences, but detailed discussion is better handled in meetings addressing themselves solely to that purpose.
6. Ask your audience to *evaluate the presentation* on forms or cards you provide. This can help you in planning future meetings. It also gives audience members an opportunity to let you know if and how they wish to be further involved.

Other Ways to Keep the Community Informed

Information about community-based activities can also be transmitted to community groups and individuals through channels other than presentations. These include printed materials (newsletters, brochures, reports); targeted mailings; news releases, interviews and feature stories in local media (newspapers, radio, television); articles in community publications (school newsletters, shoppers' guides, trade journals); displays; open houses and so forth. Local business and labor publications (the inhouse newsletters of potential learning sites and bulletins of labor locals, Chamber of Commerce and service clubs) can be valuable communication channels, too. Communications can also be targeted to particular segments of the community—senior citizens, for example, whose time and expertise might be an invaluable resource.

And don't overlook the value of personal contacts in the community—the personal involvement of school staff in civic groups, for example.

WHAT ABOUT STAFFING?

Time and Tasks

A big question mark in the minds of many educators assessing whether or not they should attempt expanding the walls of their classrooms to include the community is, "How much more time is it going to take for me to get the job done?" As mentioned earlier, one set of activities for which time will have to be provided is community site recruitment and monitoring of student activities. Effective use of counselors and aides can help staff provide community-based learning activities with a minimal amount of additional staff. You may even be lucky enough to win approval for a full-time co-ordinator for experience-based learning. This person can survey potential resources, be largely responsible for setting up a network of sites and visit the sites during student placements to see that everything is working well.

Staff Skills

To manage the varied activities of experience-based learning, staff will need commitments and skills in several major areas:
1. Recognition that education's major outcome should be an effective person and a responsible citizen
2. Willingness to make a commitment of as much time as the job takes
3. Recognition that education can be improved, coupled with ability to articulate needed improvements
4. Flexibility and openness to new ideas
5. Commitment to teaching
6. Willingness to undergo the necessary training to improve skills such as counseling, keeping records, communicating and community involvement
7. Supervisory and organizational ability
8. Tolerance of uncertainty and ambiguity
9. Knowledge of general educational goals and philosophies

This profile adds up to a good teacher in any system, but the attributes are paramount in experience-based learning where the individual does not have the ringing of a bell and the arrival of students as a "captive audience" every hour. Likewise this profile would apply where teachers are not just presenters or organizers of subject matter. The teacher's role in experience-based learning should encompass the dimensions of friend, guide, counselor, facilitator, adjuster, expediter, organizer and orchestrator of activities.

The administrator's profile should include all of the above, as well as knowledge about experimental education and the ability to spot problems in their initial stages and suggest solutions or encourage the staff to find solutions. The ideal administrator of experience-based learning will manage the decision-making process rather than being the decision maker, follow up on decisions that are made, see that people carry through on their commitments, be familiar with the policies and resources of the school district and its community, and encourage and develop the best in each staff member.

WHERE DO WE GO FROM HERE?

Districts like yours around the country are finding that experience-based learning is not only an effective way of giving students realistic educational experience but is stimulating for staff as well. Experience-based learning has also produced some noteworthy results in school-community cooperation and parent-student communication. Yet it would be misleading to imply that these ideas will work for *all* students who want to be involved. And there will be other trade-offs to be considered, like separating some young people from their peers. You can offset the isolation some students may feel by providing opportunities for the community-based students to continue to interact with their peers in some in-school experiences including extracurricular activities.

We believe alternatives are important and students should be able to choose options in learning. Despite the challenges of implementing experience-based learning, if you do try some of these activities with students you will probably observe some important student gains, as noted in the following anecdote from an existing experience-based learning program.

> We don't know exactly which thing did it for Margaret, but at the end of two years she was a completely different person from the one who entered the program. She liked herself better, her appearance improved dramatically, her attitude toward school completely reversed itself and she seemed much more in command of her own life.

Margaret herself said:

> I was walking down the street one night coming home from school and I was carrying a bunch of books. All of a sudden I said to myself, 'Wait a minute. This isn't me carrying all these books.' And I realized I had really changed a lot. I was actually reading and studying now and I didn't even mind homework, because it was stuff I was interested in.

That's the kind of feedback that makes experience-based learning worth pursuing.

FOOTNOTES

[1]Eliot Wigginton, *Moments: The Foxfire Experience* (Washington, D.C.: Institutional Development and Economic Affairs Service, Inc., 1975), p. 22.

[2]*A Guide to Child Labor Provisions of the Fair Labor Standards Act*, Child Labor Bulletin No. 101 (revised) (Washington, D.C.: U.S. Government Printing Office, 1971), "Hazardous Occupations," Exemption II, p. 9.

APPENDIX A

Twenty-Five Student Projects That Worked

The 25 sample projects presented in this appendix illustrate the wide range of approaches you can use when writing individualized learning projects for students using nonclassroom resources. The samples are real. They represent hundreds of student projects that were written and carried out in several different experience-based learning programs and, as such, reveal the workability of the project approach to learning. They were chosen not simply because they are "good" but because they reflect the varying abilities of students and the widely differing resources that can be utilized.

Student names have been changed to assure anonymity. The descriptions of activities have been standardized, although differences in staff style may still be evident. An asterisk (*) on each list of community resources denotes the kind of site for which the project was written; other sites were either supplementary or have been added to trigger your imagination concerning possible adaptations of projects to new settings.

Five projects are presented in each of the five life skills areas (see Chapter 3): critical thinking, functional citizenship, personal/social development, creative development and scientific investigation.

These samples have been condensed into single "idea sheets" rather than following the more detailed project format illustrated in Chapter 4. Each sample includes the following information:

1. **Subject area**—the life skill to which the project was generally addressed
2. **Topic**—the problem or theme around which the project was built
3. **Career focus**—careers being pursued by the individuals who were the student's resource people for the project
4. **Basic skills emphasis**—one or more basic skills in which the student would gain practice while completing project activities
5. **Community resources**—places in the community where the student could find information and experience relevant to the project
6. **Activities**—what the student and staff person agreed the student would do to complete the project

SUBJECT AREA   Critical Thinking   **BASIC SKILLS EMPHASIS**

TOPIC   Fiberglass Techniques   Reading x
CAREER FOCUS   Auto body work   Math x
    Fiberglass work   Writing x
    Fiberglass research   Speaking x
    Study___

COMMUNITY RESOURCES
*Auto body shop
Boat building company
Boat repair shop
Fiberglass development company
Fiberglass supply store

ACTIVITIES

1. To someone who is unfamiliar with the process, explain the principles of fiber-glass/heat transfer in relation to fiberglass application techniques. Research the history of fiberglass technology in auto body fabrication and repair. Cite examples from the past as well as present-day applications at your community site.
2. Demonstrate the following mathematical processes used in the application of fiberglass to the satisfaction of your resource person:
   a. Compute mixture ratios based on desired amounts. Explain how mixtures are ordinarily gauged by experience rather than exact measures.
   b. Compute surface areas and interpret diagrams necessary for applying fiberglass.
3. Demontrate to the satisfaction of your resource person that you can perform at least three tasks commonly involved in fiberglass work and explain the techniques involved:
   a. Sanding
   b. Filling pits and chips
   c. Feathering old finish to blend new paint
4. Prepare a videotape of the entire process of sectioning and fabrication of an auto body panel. Write a brief but clear narrative to accompany the videotape. Ask your resource person to certify that your presentation is accurate.
5. List and briefly describe at least ten different career possibilities for a person who knows how to use and apply fiberglass. Be sure all words are spelled correctly.

SUBJECT AREA	Critical Thinking	**BASIC SKILLS EMPHASIS**
TOPIC	Retail Lumbering	Reading___
CAREER FOCUS	Lumber sales	Math x
	Inventory control	Writing x
	Shipping	Speaking___
	Recordkeeping	Study___

COMMUNITY RESOURCES

*Lumberyard
Building supply store
Wood products wholesaler

ACTIVITIES

1. Prepare a descriptive report outlining this company's inventory procedures. Interview the manager and two salespeople who regularly call on your site to understand how these people regard the stock control and recordkeeping process. Be prepared to discuss the concept of "prediction" and identify at least four other life situations where it is necessary to make accurate predictions based on past experience.

2. Analyze the major types of customers at your site (e.g., do-it-yourselfers, contractors) and determine the percent of total volume of business done by each, the comparative discount offered to each and how these relationships affect the total operation of a lumberyard.

3. Compute the total retail value of plywood in a storage area designated by your resource person. First, define board feet, linear feet and square feet and explain how each is computed. Then, calculate the total board feet of each of three sizes of plywood. Next, calculate the total square feet of at least two thicknesses of plywood. Ask your resource person to certify your accuracy.

4. Figure the total value of merchandise in one square on each side of an aisle as specified by your resource person. Your computations should include retail value, wholesale value, dollar profit and percentage of profit. Your resource person will indicate the records you will need to keep.

5. Keep a daily log of all tasks you perform while at this site. Record your reactions to each. Analyze your skills to determine if there are areas in which you would need to improve if you decided to pursue a career in retail wood products.

SUBJECT AREA	Critical Thinking	**BASIC SKILLS EMPHASIS**
TOPIC	Rock Concerts and Social Services	Reading___ Math___
CAREER FOCUS	Sociology Psychology Law enforcement	Writing_x_ Speaking___ Study___

COMMUNITY RESOURCES

*Law enforcement agency
Mental health agency
Social welfare agency
Legal aid office
Public assistance agency

ACTIVITIES

1. Visit and obtain information about the social needs being met by at least five community agencies. Prepare a brief written statement of the mission of each agency, the number of people it serves, its funding base and related background.
2. Select one social problem of personal interest. Interview knowledgeable resource people and read relevant materials that will supplement your own opinions on this subject. Summarize these various views in an essay that will be evaluated on the basis of logical organization and technical accuracy.
3. Develop a questionnaire survey form that tries to assess unmet social needs in your community and gather information from at least ten persons. Based on your survey, prepare a report detailing the areas where there may be insufficient social services to meet expressed needs.
4. Using rock concerts as an example of an issue that can have either a positive or negative impact on a community, describe your feelings about this phenomenon and offer concrete examples that illustrate your opinions.
5. Prepare a written statement based on your attendance at a rock concert. Include an analysis of the age group attracted to the event and the activities and responses of the audience while the concert was proceeding.
6. Arrange an interview with a police officer who has worked at least two rock concerts and other large group events. In preparing for this interview, design at least ten questions that will elicit the kind of information you seek, remembering that certain kinds of questions will trigger certain kinds of responses.
7. Discuss the various ways that rock concerts can contribute to a community's well-being and how they may also necessitate increased social services (not just law enforcement).

SUBJECT AREA	**Critical Thinking**	BASIC SKILLS EMPHASIS
TOPIC	World Travel	Reading_x_
CAREER FOCUS	Travel agent	Math_x_
	Airline representative	Writing___
		Speaking___
		Study_x_

COMMUNITY RESOURCES

*Travel agency
Airlines
AMTRAK
Foreign consulates
International bank

ACTIVITIES

1. Plan two comparative "packaged" trips to Hawaii. Write up each as a descriptive brochure that advertises your offers. Include the following information: itemized and total costs, flight data, accommodations, sightseeing tours, meals, time period.
2. Plan a specific trip for two people to Rome, Italy. Research climatic conditions in Rome throughout the year and prepare charts that illustrate these conditions. Recommend a favorable time for travel. Prepare a one-page description of the geographical features of prime interest to clients of your travel agency site. Ask your resource person to certify the accuracy of your work.
3. Plan a detailed itinerary for the above trip based on the following customers' interests:
   a. They wish to see the well-known historical sights in Rome.
   b. The trip can be no more than ten days, including flight time.
   c. They desire average not luxurious accommodations and no kitchen facilities.
   d. They want an itemized and total cost estimate for the trip, including approximate costs for meals and other expenses.
   Submit your worksheets, itinerary forms and final trip plan to your resource person for approval.
4. Develop a conversion chart for monetary equivalents for the United States, Great Britain, France and Russia. Include examples of how a person can use the chart.
5. Determine a place in the world you would like to visit. Research that place and write a two-page paper that describes climate, geographical features, tourist attractions, economic status, cost of goods and services and other appropriate information. Ask your resource person to review how well you can use the skills and knowledge you have learned at this site.

SUBJECT AREA	Critical Thinking	**BASIC SKILLS EMPHASIS**
TOPIC	Television Production	Reading___
CAREER FOCUS	Television	Math___
	Film production	Writing___
	Photography	Speaking_x_
	Journalism	Study_x_

COMMUNITY RESOURCES

*Television studio
Radio station
Photographer

ACTIVITIES

1. While at this site prepare your own technical glossary of terms you encounter in the television production process. Define each one in words that anyone can understand. Ask your resource person to review your word list.
2. Research and explain the use of the following equipment used in television production to the satisfaction of someone unfamiliar with this technology: video-tape recorder, camera, transmitter, microwave transmitter.
3. Survey the Federal Communications Commission (FCC) regulations that affect the production department. Determine how these rules came into being and to what extent they are "felt" by the studio staff. Arrange to discuss this with the head of the production department.
4. Arrange to visit a communications class at a local community college. Describe the training that is required for TV production careers.
5. Observe and participate in the design, development and production of broadcast material by completing the following activities:
   a. Observe the dialogue between sales staff and client and produce your own tape recording of a simulated advertising plan.
   b. Describe in detail the processes involved in preparing and filing slides for broadcast.
   c. Assist studio staff in preparing art cards, supers and displays. Display samples of your work to other students.
6. Research a current news event in your community. After spending time with news staff, write a two-page essay that explains how a news event is covered on television, including how much information is necessary to present an accurate portrayal, what kind of information can "clutter" the presentation and how one evaluates the presentation of a news event.
7. Prepare a diagram or chart of the TV studio showing significant relationships among the various work units and how the processes of TV production are related. Use art production equipment at the studio to prepare your presentation.

SUBJECT AREA	Functional Citizenship	BASIC SKILLS EMPHASIS
TOPIC	Citizen and Consumer	Reading _x_
CAREER FOCUS	Law	Math ___
	Social work	Writing _x_
		Speaking _x_
		Study _x_

COMMUNITY RESOURCES

Better Business Bureau
Consumer protection groups
Common Cause
Congressional representatives
Legal Aid

ACTIVITIES

1. Research materials (U.S. Constitution, government texts, pamphlets on citizens' legal rights) and interview staff at local agencies (Public Defenders Office, Legal Aid, City Police Department) to determine what your legal rights and responsibilities are as a U.S. citizen. List these rights and responsibilities and discuss your findings with school staff.
2. Make up a hypothetical situation (such as being arrested for speeding) and explain your procedural rights to an official of the agency that would be involved.
3. Complete a voter registration form and present it to school staff.
4. Explain clearly to school staff the terms of a warranty included with some recent purchase.
5. Research local agencies (Better Business Bureau, Common Cause, consumer protection groups) to discover which ones could assist you if you had difficulties as a consumer. List the agencies and describe the kinds of consumer assistance they would provide. Discuss this list with school staff.
6. Write to legislators and consumer groups for information on state and federal laws protecting the rights of consumers. Explain to school staff which consumer rights are fully protected by laws and which are not.
7. Based on the preceding activities, choose a law you feel does not adequately protect your rights. Investigate the avenues you can take to try to change the law and initiate at least two activities to attempt this. Discuss your findings, the steps you are taking and any results with school staff.
8. Make a presentation to a group of your choice expressing your opinion about the power of individual citizens to influence legislation and government. Document your opinion with examples from your own experiences in Activity 7 and your research with various community resources (government agencies and consumer groups).

SUBJECT AREA	Functional Citizenship	**BASIC SKILLS EMPHASIS**
TOPIC	Abortion	Reading x
CAREER FOCUS	Prospective parenthood	Math___
	Counseling	Writing x
	Medicine	Speaking x
		Study x

COMMUNITY RESOURCES

Right to Life groups
Planned Parenthood
Doctors
Library
State laws
National Organization of Women
Religious leaders

ACTIVITIES

1. Think seriously about the word "law." Reflect on why societies make laws, how they change them and how you feel about obeying laws whether or not you agree with them. Write an entry in your journal or tape record a statement concerning what "law" means to you.
2. Research the legal history of abortion nationally and locally. Prepare a paper detailing your findings and addressing these questions: What year did legalization of abortion become a major issue in the U.S.? What were some other major national concerns at that time? Are there any reasons why legal abortion logically gained more acceptance at that particular time? Which people and groups have lined up for and against abortion? What are their basic arguments for and against? What has been the attitude toward abortion in your local community? What is the state law regarding abortion? When was it passed? What are the major points of the law? What is the most current Supreme Court position on abortion?
3. Explore the moral questions surrounding abortion. Describe arguments for and against abortion in terms of the rights of the mother, the fetus and the father. Then investigate the attitudes of your peers and adults toward the "right" and "wrong" of abortion by using a standard interview technique and questionnaire (explain your plans to school staff before conducting this interview). Tape record some of the interviews. Compile the information you have gathered into a short talk you then give to school staff and/or a group of students.
4. Review your reflections about "law" from Activity 1. If your views have changed, revise your statement. Consider the relationship between the climate of opinion and laws. Apply what you have said in your statement to recent events regarding legalization of abortion in the state and nation and discuss this with school staff.
5. Study the political impact of abortion and construct charts and graphs that depict how many abortions are occurring annually, in what age groups, and how this is affecting the birth rate/growth rate in the nation.
6. Study the various avenues of influence available to a citizen wishing to have some say in the directions of the abortion issue. Prepare a diagram portraying the various avenues and submit a short statement to staff estimating which method has the greatest influence and why.

SUBJECT AREA   Functional Citizenship   <u>**BASIC SKILLS EMPHASIS**</u>
TOPIC   <u>Newspaper Operation</u>   Reading<u> x </u>
CAREER FOCUS   Journalism   Math<u> x </u>
Small business management   Writing<u> x </u>
Speaking___
Study___

COMMUNITY RESOURCES
*Local newspaper
Legal Aid office
District attorney
Public defender
Local judges

ACTIVITIES

1. Prepare a research paper that traces the development of the free press in America. Pay particular attention to the designation of the press as the "fourth branch of government" and demonstrate an understanding of the laws that govern the ownership and operation of news media.

2. Describe in detail the jobs of managing editor, editorial editor and news editor indicating how each is crucial to the operation of a newspaper. Outline tasks you might perform to assist each. Participate in the following operations that make a newspaper functional: taking orders for subscriptions, estimating costs for ads of different sizes, preparing copy for press, proofreading, distribution system.

3. Discuss the free speech amendment to the Bill of Rights and its relationship to the public's right to know and an individual's right to privacy. Select a recent or current event (preferably local) where this controversy was the focal point and write a standard news article reporting the issue and an editorial that presents your carefully reasoned views on the event. Try to get your writing published.

4. Prepare a report that compares a weekly small-circulation newspaper with a larger daily newspaper along the following dimensions:
   a. How the editors view their role in society (to lead, report or challenge majority opinion, for example)
   b. Reporters' positions on the conflict you analyzed in Activity 3
   c. Budgets and balance sheets
   d. Costs per issue
   e. Staff salaries
   f. Legal status (if different)
   g. "Investigative" vs. "standard" journalism

SUBJECT AREA	Functional Citizenship	**BASIC SKILLS EMPHASIS**
TOPIC	The Mexican American	Reading___
CAREER FOCUS	Political science	Math___
	Social work	Writing___
		Speaking_x_
		Study_x_

COMMUNITY RESOURCES

Mexican American organizations
Other minority groups
Community action groups
Bureau of Labor
Migrant Council
Mexican American elders
Geography department, local college

ACTIVITIES

1. Define the following characteristics of Mexican Americans and trace the changes in meaning:
   a. Mexican American as defined in 1930
   b. Mexican American as defined in 1976
   c. La Raza
2. Research the three major waves of Mexican migrations to the U.S., occurring primarily in 1900, 1920 and during World War II. Prepare graphs, charts and maps depicting numbers, reasons, jobs obtained and areas settled, with a brief explanation of the data.
3. Research and write a report tracing the major historical events involving Mexican Americans:
   a. The effects of the Depression
   b. The repatriation of Mexicans
   c. Their involvement in the American farm movement
   d. The conflicts between Mexican Americans and Anglos
   Try to determine how much these conflicts were influenced by economic issues and how much they were influenced by language, customs, skin color and so forth. In your report, try to use examples from older members of the Mexican American community who personally observed and participated in these events.
4. Interview key leaders in local Mexican American organizations to determine the major issues of concern today. Prepare an interview outline and check this outline with school staff before you contact these people. Either take careful notes or tape record the interviews for later analysis.
5. Choose one of the issues identified in Activity 4 and research this issue carefully, looking for information such as history and causes, laws affecting this matter, what has been and is being done about the issue by public and private groups alike. Prepare an oral presentation about this issue and give it to a group of your choice (staff, students, community organizations).

SUBJECT AREA   Functional Citizenship   **BASIC SKILLS EMPHASIS**

TOPIC   Legal Aid   Reading___
CAREER FOCUS   Law   Math___
                             Legal assistance   Writing _x_
                             Court clerical work   Speaking___
                                                              Study _x_

COMMUNITY RESOURCES
                             *Legal Aid Bureau
                             Local, state, federal courts
                             Attorney

ACTIVITIES

1. Understand the purposes and function of Legal Aid services in a community by answering the following questions to the satisfaction of your resource person:
   a. Why was this program developed?
   b. Who are the clientele?
   c. In what legal areas are services provided?
   d. Why do people go to Legal Aid?
   e. Who pays the bills?
   f. How is it like and unlike a Public Defender's Office?
   g. How great is the need for this kind of program?
   h. What other groups are concerned with Legal Aid?
2. Develop a vocabulary list and definitions of the new words you encounter during this project. Use each term in an interview with school staff.
3. Write a brief description of each area of specialization handled by Legal Aid staff.
4. Under the supervision of resource people, familiarize yourself with the practical aspects of family and housing laws by doing the following:
   a. Research relevant statutes and discuss them with resource people.
   b. Assist in drafting pleadings and court papers.
   c. Gain experience in working directly with clients (phone, interview, letter).
5. Write a formal paper that demontrates your understanding of the concept of democracy by answering the following questions:
   a. How does democracy work in this setting?
   b. How does it work compared to the ideals set forth in the Constitution?
   c. What "evidence" of the Bill of Rights is apparent at this site?
   d. What is the role of a citizen in an operating democracy?
   e. What is a responsible and informed citizenry?
6. Discuss and evaluate this project with school staff and Legal Aid personnel.

SUBJECT AREA	Personal/Social Development	**BASIC SKILLS EMPHASIS**
TOPIC	Mental Retardation	Reading x
CAREER FOCUS	Special education	Math___
	Nursing	Writing x
		Speaking x
		Study x

COMMUNITY RESOURCES

*Mentally retarded training center
Special education department
Mental health clinics
Rehabilitation service
Goodwill Industries
Local doctors

ACTIVITIES

1. Survey library materials on mental retardation. Prepare your own definition of mental retardation that will also satisfy your community contact. Make sure your citation of materials is in proper bibliographic form.
2. Prepare a list of service agencies that work with mentally retarded and describe the clientele and services of each. Do a more complete analysis for the site where you spend the most time.
3. Become familiar with the teaching methods at a training center for the mentally retarded. If behavior modification is emphasized at your community site, research B.F. Skinner and his contribution to the field. Then write a short paper describing the philosophy and methods of Skinner's theories with special attention to how they are applied at your community site and what other treatment options are available.
4. Discuss your opinions about behavior modification with your community resource person. Be prepared to back up your opinions with information you have researched.
5. Prepare a chart that interprets the major types of mental retardation (e.g., Down's Syndrome) and discuss the causes and effects of each with your resource person. Factors to consider include symptoms and teachability.
6. As you observe and participate in a teaching situation with the mentally retarded, concentrate on how instructors teach functional words. Then prepare a lesson (including charts and/or other visual aids) that demonstrates your ability to devise an original method of teaching functional words. Discuss your plans with your resource person to check for teachability, then demonstrate your plan to school staff.
7. Prepare a statement summarizing your experience and how it has affected your long-range plans. Make a tape recording that demonstrates your ability to articulate important concepts and enunciate words clearly. Submit this tape to school staff.

SUBJECT AREA Personal/Social Development   **BASIC SKILLS EMPHASIS**
TOPIC   Librarianship   Reading_x_
CAREER FOCUS   Librarian   Math___
                           Clerk   Writing_x_
                           Research assistant   Speaking_x_
                                                          Study___

COMMUNITY RESOURCES
                           *Public library
                           School library
                           Corporate research library
                           Bookstore

ACTIVITIES

1. Keep a log of ten unfamiliar words encountered each week while conducting this project. Write each word legibly and use it in a sentence as it comes up in the course of library work. Find a synonym and antonym for each word and break all into syllables. Identify root, suffix and prefix if appropriate.
2. Work on communication skills that are essential in library work: eye contact with the customer, a pleasant greeting, offering to help. Keep a daily record of your communication skills and develop a graph that plots your progress with these skills.
3. Select a good novel to read and review. Pay particular attention to character development and plot. Write an essay that describes the plot and the main character and make a recommendation on the type of reader who might prefer this book. List your reasons for making the recommendation. Ask the chief librarian to approve your essay.
4. Become familiar with the Dewey Decimal or Library of Congress classification system. Show that you can use and apply a classification system by applying it to ten books ready for processing.
5. Demonstrate to the satisfaction of your resource person that you can handle at least five front desk tasks commonly performed by library staff (e.g., checking materials in and out, reference work, clerical tasks, collecting and reporting fines).
6. Evaluate the progress you have made in improving interpersonal skills by writing an essay that backs up each point with examples from your experiences at the resource site. Have the essay approved by your resource person and school staff.

SUBJECT AREA   Personal/Social Development   **BASIC SKILLS EMPHASIS**

TOPIC   Living Away from Home   Reading____

CAREER FOCUS   Taxpayer   Math _x_

                                      Renter   Writing _x_

                                      Homeowner   Speaking____

                                                                                       Study _x_

COMMUNITY RESOURCES

                                      Apartment managers   Public agencies

                                      Supermarket   Insurance agent

                                      Parents   Hospital

                                      Home economist   Public utilities

ACTIVITIES

1. Prepare a large chart on which you will tally the various living expenses revealed in the following activities (keep figures and computations on separate worksheets):
   a. Find out how much it costs to rent a one-bedroom apartment in your community, including deposits, first and last month's rent, utilities, etc. Collect the same information for a two-bedroom apartment. Compare the costs of living alone and living with another person.
   b. Prepare a two-week menu outlining three full, well-balanced yet inexpensive meals per day. Find ways to stretch food for more than one meal. Be creative. After planning three meals, do a cost estimate for at least one week's meals, forecasting what you will need to spend on a monthly basis.
   c. Determine what types of insurance you will need (medical, life, car, renter). For each type, contact at least two insurance agents and compare their costs for each policy. Add the costs to your chart.
   d. Pretend you have a sudden attack of appendicitis. Call a hospital to determine costs for this kind of surgery and care. Then determine how much you would have to pay beyond what is covered by the medical insurance plan you selected. Add this cost to your chart.
   e. Plan a clothing budget for a six-month period.
   f. Estimate the possible miscellaneous expenses you might encounter for gifts, vacations, entertainment, transportation, supplies, etc. Add these to your growing budget.
2. Add up these expected expenditures and estimate the amount you will have to earn. List the types of jobs you might be able to perform that normally pay what you will need. Check all available sources to determine if there are any jobs like that available in your community.
3. Determine the ways you can cut expenses (by taking a bus, for instance, instead of driving to and from work). How much can you save?
4. Ask a home economist to review your budget chart and worksheets and certify if your estimates are realistic.
5. Prepare a two-page essay that evaluates this project and the decisions you have made. List any remaining questions you may have.

SUBJECT AREA Personal/Social Development   **BASIC SKILLS EMPHASIS**

TOPIC   Creative Marriage   Reading _x_
CAREER FOCUS   Marriage counseling   Math___
                            Ministry   Writing _x_
                            Social work   Speaking___
                                                                     Study___

COMMUNITY RESOURCES
                            Married and unmarried adults
                            Clergy
                            Attorney
                            Licensing agency
                            Psychologist/marriage counselor
                            Financial planning service or credit union

ACTIVITIES

1. Prepare written answers to questions like these based on your current feelings about the institution of marriage:
   a. Why do most people get married?
   b. For what reasons would you get married?
   c. List some reasons for marriage that are common but misguided.
   d. How have reasons for marriage changed in the last half century or so?
2. Explore what others have said about marriage by selecting and reading at least three current magazine articles and one book on the topic. Prepare a critical review of each reading, including a summary of the main ideas. Include complete bibliographic references.
3. Prepare a tape recording of your feelings about love as an integral part of marriage. What is your own definition of love? Can love develop and be cultivated if a marriage is started without it? Is it possible for love and marriage to exist one without the other? What enhances the growth of love?
4. Chart statistics reflecting marriage/divorce rates for several decades in your community. Draw some conclusions based on these findings. Refer to both your readings and your personal opinions.
5. Brainstorm with someone else the roles and responsibilities present in a marriage. Are some of these shared while others are held by only one mate?
6. Describe the following procedures and costs in your state: obtaining a marriage license, obtaining a divorce, preparing a will, obtaining insurance (including the kinds of insurance that are critical to households and individuals and those that are not).
7. Assume that you want to marry. Prepare a household budget that estimates the kind of household needs you and your spouse will face in the first few months of marriage. Estimate the income you will need. Consider the effect children will have on these plans.
8. List the kinds of communications skills required for effective marriage. Suggest ways these can be learned and practiced.
9. Interview at least five married people to gather their insights and experiences, drawing questions from the above activities. Summarize their reactions in a written report.

SUBJECT AREA Personal/Social Development   **BASIC SKILLS EMPHASIS**

TOPIC — Survival in the Wild   Reading_x_
CAREER FOCUS — Recreation   Math_x_
Medicine   Writing_x_
Speaking___
Study___

COMMUNITY RESOURCES

*Survival school
Red Cross
Outdoor clubs
Youth organizations
Environmental groups

ACTIVITIES

1. Put together a complete survival kit for camping or hiking based on your reading and discussion with knowledgeable experts.
2. Read and review a book written on emergency survival situations based on actual incidents. Summarize what the crisis was and how the people responded and predict how you would have responded. Ask your resource person to approve your work.
3. Prepare and give a survival lesson for a group of people interested in the topic. After teaching the lesson, ask each person to evaluate your instruction and the skills acquired.
4. Prepare a chart that lists a variety of possible survival situations and what both individuals and groups should do if they find themselves in those predicaments.
5. Submit a planning diagram and scale model for a survival shelter. First, read about the various kinds that are possible, then construct a scale model. Keep an accurate record of all measurements and dimensions. Show your resource person your planning diagram and scale model and ask the resource person to evaluate and certify the effectiveness of your design.
6. Participate in a three-day survival school training session and keep a daily log of events, accomplishments and your feelings about the experience. Summarize what you have learned about yourself in the process. Discuss this with a school staff person and ask that person to evaluate your ability to express yourself confidently.

SUBJECT AREA   Creative Development   **BASIC SKILLS EMPHASIS**

TOPIC   Merchandising   Reading___
CAREER FOCUS   Retail sales   Math _x_
    Advertising   Writing___
    Speaking___
    Study _x_

COMMUNITY RESOURCES
    *Clothing store
    Advertising firm

ACTIVITIES

1. Show your resource person that you can competently perform the following job tasks related to the stockroom and inventory control:
   a. Verify packing slips for accuracy.
   b. Set pricing machine, stamp price tickets, ticket merchandise.
   c. Complete form SW-4 and attach to merchandise.
   d. Count merchandise on selling floor and in stockroom and prepare supply lists.
2. Demonstrate your ability to perform the following job tasks related to merchandise display to the satisfaction of your resource person:
   a. Iron clothes to be displayed.
   b. Straighten clothes, displays, racks and so forth.
3. Perform the following job tasks related to maintaining cleanliness, customer appeal, etc.:
   a. Care for plant displays.
   b. Clean windows.
   c. Dust shelves, ledges and so forth.
4. Perform the following creative functions related to the store's artistic decor:
   a. Arrange and care for needed floral decorations and design a new floral display.
   b. Discuss this plan with your resource person to make sure it is both creative and feasible.
5. Perform the following display activities related to the store's up-to-date look and customer appeal:
   a. Assist a store employee in planning and arranging a high ceiling merchandise display.
   b. As your own project, go through the whole process of creating a display with your resource person as a consultant, drawing up your plans on graph paper, complete with color keys. Submit plans to school staff.
6. Visit a clothing store that caters to different clientele than your community site. Compare the two stores in terms of atmosphere and creativity of merchandise displays. Communicate this comparison to the school staff on a taped monologue giving careful consideration to the following issues: clientele, price range of clothes, store overhead and staff involvement in displays.
7. Show school staff and students what you have learned about merchandising by creating a bulletin board display at school designed to ''sell'' an event or idea:
   a. Develop an evaluation form for staff and students to use in evaluating your bulletin board for color, visual clarity and creative communication. Have the evaluation form checked by a staff member before distributing it.
   b. Compile the results of the evaluation and turn in to school staff.

SUBJECT AREA	Creative Development	**BASIC SKILLS EMPHASIS**
TOPIC	Advanced Welding	Reading___
	Techniques____	Math_x_
CAREER FOCUS	Electrical engineering	Writing_x_
	Welding	Speaking___
		Study___

COMMUNITY RESOURCES

*Metalwork shop
Manufacturing company using welding
Auto body shop

ACTIVITIES

1. Become familiar with the principles of an electric arc welder:
   a. Diagram and explain to your resource person the relationship of electrical input to variable output.
   b. In a well-written report describe the electronic principles involved, paying special attention to accuracy of information and writing skills.
2. Learn the principles of oxygen acetylene welding and cutting:
   a. Draw an accurate diagram of an oxygen acetylene welding unit including gas source, flow mixture and flame. Describe your diagram to your resource person and discuss gauges, gas and its properties and the mixer head and tips.
   b. Learn to make horizontal join welds in mild steel. Show a three-inch sample of your joined materials to your resource person, demonstrating a smooth and strong weld.
   c. Braze any two materials using a gas welder and show a three-inch sample to your resource person, demonstrating efficient brazing techniques.
   d. Demonstrate your ability to cut mild steel by making a pattern cut using one angle and one curve plus a straight line in a ¼" piece of steel. Total material size need not be over 4" x 4."
3. Learn to use the hydroblaster. Take at least six pictures of the machine. Mount and provide a creatively written narrative for each photo. Learn and demonstrate how to use, adjust and maintain the equipment.
4. Learn to operate the heli arc to make welds in aluminum.
   a. Write a paper for your resource person and school staff comparing the different welding characteristics of steel and aluminum.
   b. Perform simple repair welds in aluminum to the satisfaction of your resource person.
5. Practice your welding skills to make them more salable:
   a. Practice a minimum of five joints (right angle, side by side veed and welded on both sides, T weld with material centered, round to flat stock, round to round butt weld).
   b. Practice five three- to five-inch welds from five different positions.
   c. Explain to school staff how these skills can be an expression of creative abilities.
6. Explore the opportunities for a welder in the field of art:
   a. Observe some exhibits of metal sculpture by local artists.
   b. Interview one metal sculptor (prepare questions in advance).
   c. Make a tape or write a paper for the school staff expressing your impressions of metal sculpture, both in terms of technical skill and artistic appeal.

SUBJECT AREA	Creative Development	**BASIC SKILLS EMPHASIS**

TOPIC   Teaching Preschool   Reading _x_
CAREER FOCUS   Teaching   Math___
                                                      Writing _x_
                                                      Speaking _x_
                                                      Study___

COMMUNITY RESOURCES
*Local preschool
Children's bookstores
Library

ACTIVITIES

1. Become familiar with math and reading readiness activities in a local preschool:
   a. Give an oral explanation of the programs to school staff.
   b. Create lesson plans in preparation for teaching classes in these areas and discuss your plans with preschool staff.
   c. Teach the students from your own lesson plans in both of these programs. Discuss your efforts with preschool staff.
2. Research existing curriculum files and other sources for examples of exercises which teach hand-eye coordination; discuss these ideas with a teacher. Make up a test or structured activity to determine whether a child has developed normal hand-eye motor coordination. If the test or activity identifies students as less advanced than others, create at least two activities to help them develop these skills. Either carry out your activities or write a clear description of them and discuss your efforts with preschool staff.
3. Create a bibliography of books that can be read to children, focusing on finding new books rather than familiar ones. Select and read one of these books to a small group of children, using visual aids. While reading, observe the children's behavior, noting especially their attention span and interest level. After reading the story, write a statement about your success in keeping the attention of the children. If any children were bored, write a plan for improving your reading performance and discuss this plan with preschool staff.
4. Draw a storybook without words. "Read" the story to a small group of students by involving them in the creation of the narrative. Give the storybook to school staff and discuss its effectiveness with them.
5. Create at least one art activity for the children. Write a lesson plan including the objective or goal, the process you will use to teach the activity and the necessary materials. Discuss the lesson plan with preschool staff before the activity is taught. Direct a class session using your lesson plan. Evaluate the session with preschool staff.
6. Write a short paper relating this experience to other job situations you have encountered in terms of personal satisfaction, creative use of your skills and opportunity for usefulness to others. Submit your paper to school staff.

SUBJECT AREA	Creative Development	BASIC SKILLS EMPHASIS
TOPIC	Videotaping a Mystery	Reading___
CAREER FOCUS	Multimedia production	Math___
	Journalism	Writing_x_
	Television production	Speaking___
		Study_x_

COMMUNITY RESOURCES

*Audiovisual supply company
Television studio
Filmmaking company
Multimedia production studio
Drama coach

ACTIVITIES

1. Research videotaping and filmmaking and produce an annotated bibliography of resources. Discuss these with your resource person, demonstrating your knowledge of the similarities and differences between the two media.
2. Plan your own videotape production:
   a. Brainstorm possible theme/plot ideas and select one for your story. Summarize theme and plot in writing.
   b. Consider various kinds of mysteries (Peter Sellers comedy, Alfred Hitchcock-style, Gothic, science fiction, etc.) to see which method of treatment best suits what you want to get across.
   c. Decide whether you want a script for the characters or just a plot with lots of ad libbing.
   d. Develop a shooting script or storybook that maps out the visual images you want to capture on tape to convey your story.
3. Prepare a complete cost analysis for the production you are planning. If funds are available to help you with the production, prepare a written request for your principal's consideration. Submit this request to a member of the staff before it goes to the principal.
4. Casting is the next step. Select your players carefully, then discuss each selection with your staff adviser.
5. For each scene, plan location, lighting, placement and movement of people and video camera. Begin taping when you feel confident and ready.
6. Consult with your resource person about editing and dubbing in other sound. Write a short paper summarizing what you learned about editing and the kinds of equipment you use.
7. Design an evaluation sheet for others to use as a way to judge the quality of your work. Discuss this form with your resource person.
8. After your videotape mystery is finished, view and critique it according to your evaluation form, then gather data from other sources:
   a. Ask at least five students not involved in the production to watch the tape and evaluate it according to the criteria you set.
   b. Try to get someone with film or videotape experience to evaluate and critique your work.
9. Summarize your evaluation results and synthesize recommendations for your future work in videotaping.

SUBJECT AREA   Creative Development   <u>**BASIC SKILLS EMPHASIS**</u>

TOPIC   <u>Graphic Design</u>   Reading___

CAREER FOCUS   <u>Graphic arts</u>   Math <u> x </u>

Advertising   Writing <u> x </u>

Speaking___

Study <u> x </u>

COMMUNITY RESOURCES

*School graphic arts department
Advertising artists
Graphic designers
School art classes

ACTIVITIES

1. Develop a comprehensive orientation to the field of graphics:
   a. Define the term "graphics" as it applies to this site. Write it clearly in your own words.
   b. Identify and describe various forms of graphics used on this site. Write descriptions of them and outline the processes involved in each. Discuss with your resource person.
   c. Develop a vocabulary list of at least 30 new terms you have heard used at the site. Write your own definitions and check with your resource person for accuracy.
2. Become familiar with learning and professional resources in the field of graphics and design. Develop an annotated bibliography noting resources and general contents. Discuss with school staff and your resource person.
3. Become thoroughly familiar with the use, care and cleaning of tools and equipment. Investigate the replacement cost for the most crucial pieces of equipment (i.e., the minimum you'd need to begin free-lance business).
4. If available, learn how to use lamination equipment. Demonstrate your competence to your resource person.
5. Work on developing communication skills (paraphrasing, summarizing, listening and questioning positively) to aid customers in clarifying their needs. Discuss your performance with your resource person, noting areas in which you may need to improve.
6. To gain an understanding of the steps involved in completing a graphics project, make a flow chart that includes all steps in the process.
7. After your flow chart has been evaluated and certified by your resource person, demonstrate that you can complete a graphics assignment from beginning to end. Share your finished project and samples of your work with school staff in a small, informal group discussion.
8. Write an essay assessing and reflecting on your performance at this site in terms of personal growth, creative ability and career possibilities.

SUBJECT AREA	Scientific Investigation	**BASIC SKILLS EMPHASIS**
TOPIC	Fisheries Resources	Reading___
CAREER FOCUS	Fish and game management	Math _x_
	Biology	Writing _x_
	Commercial fishing	Speaking___
		Study___

COMMUNITY RESOURCES

*Fish hatchery
Game warden
Commercial fishing
Sports fishing charter service

ACTIVITIES

1. Gain an understanding of the biological explanation for the term "species" by developing a diagram and presentation that classifies five species of salmon. Use pictures and drawings to illustrate the differences. Demonstrate your understanding of terms like families, genus and so forth. This work will be certified by your resource person.
2. Keep a daily diary of your activities at the fish hatchery to be evaluated on its completeness, clarity of content, grammar, punctuation and style.
3. Assist in the actual identification of salmon fry and be able to tell the differences in species to the satisfaction of your resource person.
4. Participate in the marking of salmon and describe the various methods of marking the fry. Prepare a pictorial essay on this process to be evaluated on neatness, composition and clarity.
5. Interview your resource person and other fish hatchery personnel about what happens to the fry once they leave the hatchery:
   a. What bodies of water are the fry put in and how are these selected?
   b. How are the fish identified later?
   c. What is done with this information?
6. Develop a math "story problem" around the fish and game commission's computation of commercial fishing season dates based on escapement information. Solve the problem and have your answer approved by your resource person. Ask a math teacher to review and certify your step-by-step mathematical computations.

SUBJECT AREA	Scientific Investigation	BASIC SKILLS EMPHASIS
TOPIC	Scuba Diving	Reading___
CAREER FOCUS	Professional diving	Math _x_
	Recreational diving	Writing___
	Swimming instruction	Speaking___
		Study _x_

COMMUNITY RESOURCES

    *Scuba diving school
    Scuba gear shop
    Swimming pool, lake, ocean

ACTIVITIES

1. Investigate the level of swimming proficiency required for learning scuba diving.
2. List the various types of gear required for scuba diving. Describe each, both in words and with drawings. Do some comparison shopping for this gear, contacting at least two scuba diving equipment outlets and comparing each item in terms of price, quality and practicality. Ask your resource person to review and approve your work.
3. Find out all you can about how water density and buoyancy affect scuba diving and the techniques a diver must learn. Prepare a written report which includes computations of these phenomena that will satisfy your resource person.
4. Present an oral explanation (perhaps on a tape recording) that describes underwater breathing methods and the principles involved in each. This presentation should be designed for someone relatively unfamiliar with scuba diving. Then, demonstrate to the satisfaction of your resource person that you know how these methods work.
5. Prepare yourself in various first aid techniques necessary for responding to diving accidents. Demonstrate each to the satisfaction of your resource person, telling when each procedure is necessary.
6. Plan for and complete one successful scuba dive and present certification that you followed all procedures correctly.

SUBJECT AREA   Scientific Investigation   **BASIC SKILLS EMPHASIS**

TOPIC   Physiology of Running   Reading___
CAREER FOCUS   Medicine   Math_x_
Physical education   Writing___
Recreation   Speaking___
Study_x_

COMMUNITY RESOURCES
*YWCA
PE teacher
Coach
Recreation center
Physician
Physical therapist
Veterinarian

ACTIVITIES

1. Diagram and describe the differences in muscle structure and muscular inter-dependence for both a human being and any four-legged animal. Ask your resource person to verify the accuracy of your findings.
2. Now apply what you have learned about the physiology of muscular development to the physical activity of running. Diagram and explain which human muscles are used in running and how they relate to each other. Using a video or movie camera, visually record someone sprinting or running. View the film or tape in slow motion and analyze muscle use and body movement with your resource person.
3. Research and explain the reasons for speed limitations of running animals, specifically humans. Find out what factors including physical build contribute to greater speed. Have your written list of factors and explanation approved by your resource person.
4. Determine the factors contributing to endurance in running. List these variables and discuss with your resource person the combination that produces the greatest endurance.
5. Investigate how the lungs work to provide an interchange of air. Find out what type of breathing is best while running—and why. Prepare a short paper on this subject that will be evaluated on idea development and good journalistic style. Think of your audience for this paper as young people interested in sports and physical fitness.
6. Prepare a brief history and description of the four-minute mile. Why is this record now being broken repeatedly? Can you predict how long runners can continue to better this time? Is there a limit?
7. Design a running exercise that will test the effect of the variables you have learned over a period of several weeks. Conduct the test on yourself and keep accurate records on each activity. Summarize and graph the results in terms of daily time, rates of increase and so forth. Estimate when you would be able to break the four-minute mile if you continued to improve at the same rate as in your test period.

SUBJECT AREA	Scientific Investigation	BASIC SKILLS EMPHASIS
TOPIC	Dental Health	Reading___
CAREER FOCUS	Dentistry	Math___
	Dental hygiene	Writing___
	Medicine	Speaking___
	Nutrition	Study _x_

COMMUNITY RESOURCES
*Dental office
Dental school

ACTIVITIES

1. Find out all the information you can about the role of a dental hygienist. Summarize that information and explain it to your resource person, asking if it reflects what a dental hygienist actually does.
2. Build a vocabulary list of all the terms you encounter during the course of this project. Submit accurate definitions and make sure each word is properly spelled. Write a sentence using each word to illustrate that you understand what the term means. Ask your resource person to certify your understanding of the terms.
3. Answer the following questions to the satisfaction of your resource person:
   a. What is preventive dentistry?
   b. Is it a new concept?
   c. What needs caused its evolution?
   d. What are some recent developments?
   e. Would most dentists want to hire a person skilled in preventive dentistry?
   f. Does preventive medicine take business away from a doctor?
4. To become familiar with common patient needs, conditions and complaints, assist in general office tasks for at least three hours—answering the phone, scheduling patients, filing charts and so forth. Keep a log of the reasons people give for making appointments and the number of times each reason is given. Develop a hypothesis about the need for and current success of preventive dentistry and discuss this with your resource person.
5. Using materials available from your resource person, become informed about the causes of tooth decay and gum disease. Discuss these with your resource person.
6. Analyze the role that nutrition plays in both dental and general health. Keep a record of everything you eat for seven days including junk foods. Compute the amounts of carbohydrates, fat, protein and sugar consumed to determine if you are maintaining a healthy diet. Analyze the effects of your diet on oral health and discuss your records and your analysis with your resource person.

SUBJECT AREA   Scientific Investigation   **BASIC SKILLS EMPHASIS**

TOPIC   Auto Emissions and   Reading___
                     Environmental Quality   Math_x_

CAREER FOCUS   Auto mechanics   Writing___
                     Environmental quality control   Speaking___
                     Chemistry   Study_x_

COMMUNITY RESOURCES

    *Auto repair shop
    Environmental quality agency
    Auto inspection center

ACTIVITIES

1. Develop and define a list of key terms used to describe how a gasoline engine works. Demonstrate your understanding of how a gasoline engine works by drawing a chart or making a model of a gasoline engine and explaining the principles involved to the satisfaction of your resource person.

2. List and define the vocabulary associated with auto tune-ups. Observe and assist an auto mechanic in the process of tuning up an engine, following the process from writing the customer order to testing the completed work. Participate in the diagnosis and offer your own observations. Prepare a written summary of everything that occurs to demontrate you understand all procedures. Have your resource person certify your report.

3. Apply a scientific method of inquiry to an actual auto tune-up. Select a car that needs an engine tune-up and pose a hypothesis about the problem. Complete a work order estimating the parts to be replaced and listing parts numbers, parts costs, labor charges and total charges. Then, tune up the car keeping careful records of what you do. Your resource person will review and approve all steps, including the necessary math computations and how well you performed the actual tune-up based on your original hypothesis.

4. Analyze the relation of automobile tune-up to our general environment:
   a. What is the primary economic reason for tuning an auto engine?
   b. Why do environmentalists favor this procedure?
   c. How does the government encourage automobile owners to participate in cleaning up auto emissions?

APPENDIX B

APPENDIX 3

WHERE TO TURN FOR MORE INFORMATION

The literature on experience-based learning seems to grow with each passing month. Our bibliography is arranged in two sections:

- The following **annotated section** offers you brief descriptions of publications we find ourselves using when talking about various forms of experience-based learning.
- A concluding **alphabetical listing** provides a comprehensive yet selective overview of available literature on experience-based learning plus some additional alternative education options. These are in standard reference form and include complete citations for all the resources listed in the annotated part of the appendix.

THE NEED FOR EXPERIENCE-BASED LEARNING

Momentum for offering options to students grows almost daily. Woven into the report of almost every study commission, consultant or critic is a plea for student and community interaction—both in initial program design and actual learning activities. The following are some of the many prestigious groups or agencies calling for changes in how we prepare young people for complex life tasks:

Gibbons, Maurice, *The New Secondary Education: A Phi Delta Kappa Task Force Report*.
One of the most forceful statements supporting experience-based learning, this volume should be on the bookshelf of anyone who believes that valuable learning experiences in the community must supplement and extend traditional school curricula.

Panel on Youth of the President's Science Advisory Committee, *Youth: Transition to Adulthood*.
This little volume packs a lot of weight and is "must" reading if you need a look at what some important educational thinkers have said about education in the future.

National Commission on the Reform of Secondary Education, *The Reform of Secondary Education*.
This Kettering Foundation-sponsored report encourages learning options in junior and senior high schooling. The influential Commission looked at many trends and programs in the compilation of its recommendations.

National Committee on Secondary Education, *American Youth in the Mid-Seventies*.
This is one of the earliest endorsements of experiential learning by the National Association of Secondary School Principals.

Faure, Edgar, *et al.* (for the International Commission on the Development of Education), *Learning to Be: The World of Education Today and Tomorrow*.
This study, financed by UNESCO, expresses concern for people, their relationships to other people, their culture, their society and their world at large.

National Association of Secondary School Principals, *This We Believe: Secondary Schools in a Changing Society*.
Another report of a task force of secondary school administrators focusing on educational programs and based on "reflective experience," these proposals for action are practical and workable. They carry the influence of the key decision makers in the schools: principals.

National Panel on High School and Adolescent Education, *The Education of Adolescents: Final Report and Recommendations*.
This publication is the culmination of a long study headed by Dr. John Henry Martin that was seen as the sequel to James Conant's work. It gives a strong endorsement to experience-based learning.

Organisation for Economic Co-Operation and Development, *Education and Working Life in Modern Society*.
Here is international support for a new alliance between education and work prepared by the U.N. Secretary-General's Ad Hoc Group on the Relations Between Education and Employment. (The committee was chaired by Clark Kerr.)

U.S. Office of Education and National Association of Secondary School Principals, *New Dimensions for Educating Youth: A Report on America's Secondary Schools*.
This is a summary of a bicentennial conference on secondary education held in Denver, Colorado in April 1976. Nearly 800 participants heard proposals for change that often embodied the concepts of experiential learning.

Wirtz, Willard, *The Boundless Resource*.
Former Labor Secretary Wirtz, now affiliated with the National Manpower Institute, makes a strong plea for more school-community linkages (Education and Work Councils) to pave the way for experience-based learning.

There are also full-length "popular" books that deal at least in part with the need for experiential learning using community resources:
Arms, Myron and Denman, David, *Touching the World: Adolescents, Adults and Action Learning*.
Weinstock, Ruth, ed., *The Greening of the High School*.
Saxe, Richard W., ed., *Opening the Schools*.

Then there are briefer statements that deserve attention. Look for Brison's "Out-of-School Education in the Social Service Sector," Gibbons' "Walkabout: Searching for the Right Passage from Childhood and School" and Coleman's "How Do the Young Become Adults?" in various issues of the *Phi Delta Kappan*. See also Coleman's "The Children Have Outgrown the Schools" in *Psychology Today* (complete citations are in the alphabetical section of this appendix).

One of the oft-cited studies of work itself emerged as career education was becoming a national priority. It is called *Work in America* and was a special task force report for then-Secretary of Health, Education and Welfare Elliot Richardson. One chapter deals with education and work and endorses experienced-based learning with the words, "Every worker is a teacher and every workplace is a school..." (p. 144).

SUPPORT FOR NONTRADITIONAL APPROACHES TO EDUCATION

People are looking for alternatives to the lock-stepped scope and sequence of most formal educational systems. They are seeking immediate help with problems facing them now and during the process of lifelong learning that will carry them through adulthood. Nonformal education is certainly not a new idea. An excellent scholarly look at how developing countries have begun to turn toward nontraditional learning is Brembeck and Thompson's *New Strategies for Educational Development*. At the postsecondary level a number of experiments are underway that illustrate changing attitudes on the part of consumers and educational institutions alike. Books like *Planning Nontraditional Programs* by Cross *et al*. are aimed at adult learning alternatives, but there are implications for secondary education as well. One network —called The Union for Experimenting Colleges and Universities—has led the way in opening up higher education to ideas like "universities without walls."

THE ALTERNATIVE SCHOOLS MOVEMENT

Some alternatives are part-day, others are full-time; some are on campus, others are housed elsewhere. Mario Fantini, whose *Public Schools of Choice* drew considerable attention in 1973, has provided a helpful background for alternatives in education in his 1976 *Alternative Education: A Source Book for Parents, Teachers, Students and Administrators*. For an earlier look at the alternative schools movement, see the National School Public Relations Association's *Alternative Schools: Pioneering Districts Create Options for Students*. A good summary of one school district's approach with a nice bibliography is the Oregon School Study Council's Bulletin titled "Alternative Education: An Introduction, Special Report on Pasadena, California and a Bibliography." How the National School Boards Association is preparing its members for the need to offer options for students is contained in a 1976 interview survey titled *Research Report: Alternative Schools*. This paperback notes that one quarter of America's school systems were operating alternative schools and programs in 1975–76.

An extensive annotated bibliography on critiques of alternative schools and solutions that have been proposed through 1975 is contained in an article by Harvey Allen in the May 1975 issue of *Phi Delta Kappan*. Smith, Barr and Burke's *Alternatives in Education: Freedom to Choose* is also a Phi Delta Kappa publication.

There are some specialized resources available now, too. The Center for Law and Education at Harvard published a guidebook titled *Alternative Schools: A Practical Manual* and Chernow and Genkin's *Teaching and Administering the High School Alternative Education Program*.

For newsletters that deal exclusively with experience-based learning approaches contact the Northwest Regional Educational Laboratory for *EBCE Update* and look into *Walkabout*, available through Phi Delta Kappa, Box 729, Bloomington, Indiana 47401 and *Exchange*, the Foxfire concept quarterly bulletin available from IDEAS, 1785 Massachusetts Ave., N.W., Washington, D.C. 20036.

There are at least two other organizations that may be able to share additional information: National Consortium on Educational Alternatives, School of Education 32 B, Indiana University, Bloomington, Indiana 47401 and National Alternative Schools Program, University of Massachusetts School of Education, Amherst, Massachusetts 01002.

FULL-TIME COMMUNITY-ORIENTED ALTERNATIVE HIGH SCHOOL PROGRAMS

The most publicized model is Philadelphia's Parkway Program, which is oriented to the liberal arts but closely akin to many of the concepts in this book. Cox's *The City As a Schoolhouse* describes the early years of Parkway and some of the successes it enjoyed and problems it encountered. An earlier account by Parkway's founder, John Bremer, titled *The School Without Walls: Philadelphia's Parkway Program*, gives an insider's view. The "school without walls" idea has now spread throughout the country, in addition to other areas of Philadelphia.

Two examples of Parkway spin-offs are "City-as-School" in New York City and Chicago's Metro High School. In these programs, participating students visit sites for the content that will be "taught" there (in contrast to experience-based learning's approach that weaves a number of academic objectives into the career-related activities naturally found there). For example, in most schools-without-walls programs, a student might visit a TV studio (picked from an approved catalog of resources) and receive English credit for certain activities completed, whereas using the project approach described in this book, the student might also be asked to acquire a general understanding of broadcasting theory, practice interpersonal skills and apply some methods of critical thinking as part of the individualized project written for each particular student and site.

The internship idea for high school age young people also places students in the community. A private school operation in Worcester, Massachusetts offers community experiences to students who can pay the fee or obtain a scholarship. (Contact "Dynamy: Learning Through Internships," 850 Main St., Worcester, Massachusetts 01610.) Longer than the typical action-learning experience but less than a full-year program is "Executive High School Internships of America." (Contact Sharlene P. Hirsch, 680 Fifth Avenue, Ninth Floor, New York, New York 10019.) Students in this program typically spend a semester on sabbatical working on community sites for academic credit.

Last but certainly not least in our lexicon is Experience-Based Career Education (EBCE), developed by four regional educational laboratories—Appalachia Educational Laboratory, Far West Laboratory for Educational Research and Development, Northwest Regional Educational Laboratory and Research for Better Schools—with support from the National Institute of Education. With the additional support of the U.S. Office of Education, this full-scale experience-based learning program is now being operated in some form or other in almost every state in the Union. For a summary of the four original models, see the National Institute of Education's booklet, *A Comparison of Four Experience-Based Career Education Programs*. Additional information about EBCE can be obtained from any one of the four laboratories or your state department of education.

ACTION LEARNING PROGRAMS

Here's another example of programs that break through traditional molds and make it possible for students to become actively involved in their learning by using community resources. There are literally hundreds of ways this is happening—sometimes for one class period a day, sometimes for a semester, sometimes as regular work experience, but most often as nonpaid volunteer work in government, health and social service agencies. Several good publications are available on action-learning programs. An up-to-date review and bibliography of what's happening is the National Association of Secondary School Principals' *25 Action Learning Schools*. Aronstein and Olsen compiled a similar monograph for the Association for Supervision and Curriculum Development titled *Action Learning: Student Community Service Projects*. The group which has been promoting action-learning programs the longest is the National Commission on Resources for Youth, which offers a newsletter, films and numerous publications such as *What Kids Can Do* and a book titled *New Roles for Youth in the School and Community*.

APPRENTICESHIP PROGRAMS

Apprenticeship has been around for a very long time as the most effective method of preparing skilled craftspeople. It involves labor, employers and public educators in the delivery of unique, highly specialized skills to young people who are ready to make a training commitment to a specific job area. Apprentices earn a paycheck while acquiring related "academic" skills according to a structured training plan. Contact your state departments of labor or education or local labor councils for information about programs in your area.

COMMUNITY EDUCATION

Here's a popular concept that complements experience-based learning while not resembling it in the least. Community education received national visibility through the Mott Foundation, which used its highly successful demonstration center in Flint, Michigan for dissemination and training. In its simplest form, community education is an effort to open up school facilities at night, on weekends and in summers for more extensive educational usage by individuals and organizations.

A number of publications are available that describe this trend in lifelong learning. For a look at the sequential steps that have worked in planning and implementing community education, see Berridge's *The Community Education Handbook*. For the basic concepts behind community education, how it grew and how citizens in experimental communities are benefiting, examine Seay, *et al., Community Education: A Developing Concept*.

If a strong community education program operates in your town, you have a base for offering experience-based learning because of the alliance already built between schools and citizens-at-large. The next step is to ask for resources in the *other* direction—placing students in *community* facilities.

THE LEARNING OPPORTUNITIES OF COMMUNITY SITES

The best eye-opener you'll find is *Yellow Pages of Learning Resources* by Richard Wurman, which invites readers to explore 71 different types of people, places and career roles that are common in most medium-sized towns. However, you should also read John Bremer's "ABC's of City Learning" in the August 1972 *Saturday Review* for an analysis of the book pointing to some of the dangers of oversimplifying the use of community resources.

For an exciting look at how community resources can be used in one subject matter area, examine any of the three Foxfire books. Foxfire's cultural journalism approach is not far removed from the project method in experience-based learning. A founder's eye view of this successful concept is Wigginton's *Moments: The Foxfire Experience*.

COOPERATIVE EDUCATION

Cooperative education is designed to let students enjoy the benefits of formal school course work in tandem with on-the-job paid training under the direction of a cooperating employer-sponsor. This contrasts with the community exploration process we advocate which puts students in touch with *several* careers on a *nonpaid* basis.

Co-op programs are a recognized option in many high schools, and some of the problems vocational educators have wrestled with in providing cooperative work experience and cooperative education are the same ones you may face. Consequently, it might be useful to study this particular kind of linkage between school and community.

A quick look at what cooperative education can be is a short article by Hruska in the November 1973 *Clearinghouse*. Since cooperative education is more widespread at the two- and four-year college level, several of the basic resources that treat this alternative in its purest sense are Knowles, *et al.*, *Handbook of Cooperative Education* and Heerman's *Cooperative Education in Community Colleges*. If you want to see aids developed for students and cooperative employers, try Chapman's *Work Experience Survival Kit*.

CERTIFYING EXPERIENCE-BASED LEARNING

There are several good references to guide you in creating a whole new approach to credentialing or reporting student accomplishments. The most comprehensive resource (actually a study of what a large number of colleges and universities think about nontraditional transcripts) is Bellanca and Kirschenbaum's *A College Guide for Experimenting High Schools*. The National Association of Secondary School Principals' *Curriculum Report* titled "Guidelines for School-to-College Transcript Content" is also useful. Educational Testing Service, Princeton, New Jersey is conducting research on an "educational passport" that resembles the student portfolio developed in NWREL's EBCE program. A chapter titled "Awarding Credit" in *Planning Nontraditional Programs* by Cross, *et al.* is also interesting reading. The Commission on Schools of the North Central Association has issued *Policies and Standards for the Approval of Optional Schools and Special Function Schools, 1976–77*, which could be useful in your planning, too.

WHY ALTERNATIVES SOMETIMES FAIL

If there is any one thing experience-based learning program planners should read about the challenges they face, it's Deal's "An Organizational Explanation of the Failure of Alternative Secondary Schools" in *Educational Researcher*. A short, concise set of reminders is McCarthy's "Critical Factors in Alternative Education" in the April 1975 NASSP *Bulletin*. A book by Arms and Denman titled *Touching the World: Adolescents, Adults and Action Learning* also covers these kinds of problems.

Fantini, in *Public Schools of Choice*, raises some issues about alternatives within the regular school system and suggests some considerations in planning for options. Paskal and Miller describe twelve characteristics of effective optional programs in their article "Managing Controversy About Optional and Alternative Programs" in *Educational Leadership*.

ALPHABETICAL LISTING

Allen, Harvey A. "Alternatives in Education: A Bibliography," *Clearing-house*, April 1974: 491-96. (Updated version appears in *Phi Delta Kappan*, May 1975: 632-34.)

Aronstein, Laurence W., and Olsen, Edward. *Action Learning: Student Community Service Projects*. Washington, D.C.: Association for Supervision and Curriculum Development, 1974.

Arms, Myron, and Denman, David. *Touching the World: Adolescents, Adults and Action Learning*. New York: Charles Scribner's Sons, 1975.

Bellanca, James, and Kirschenbaum, Howard. *A College Guide for Experimenting High Schools*. Upper Jay, New York: Adirondack Mountain Humanistic Education Center, 1973.

Berridge, R.I. *The Community Education Handbook*. Midland, Michigan: Pendell Publishing Company, 1973.

Brembeck, Cole S., and Thompson, Timothy J. *New Strategies for Educational Development: The Cross-Cultural Search for Nonformal Alternatives*. Lexington, Mass.: Lexington Books, D.C. Heath and Company, 1973.

Bremer, John. "The ABC's of City Learning," *Saturday Review* 55, No. 34 (August 1972): 34-38.

Bremer, John and von Moschzisker, Michal. *The School Without Walls: Philadelphia's Parkway Program*. New York: Holt, Rinehart and Winston, 1972.

Brison, David W. "Out-of-School Education in the Social Service Sector," *Phi Delta Kappan*, December 1973: 237-39.

Center for Law and Education. *Alternative Schools: A Practical Manual*. Cambridge, Massachusetts: Harvard University Press, 1973.

Chamberlain, Neil W. *The Limits of Corporate Responsibility*. New York: Basic Books, Inc., 1973.

Chapman, Elwood N. *Work Experience Survival Kit*. Pacific Palisades, California: Goodyear Publishing Co., Inc., 1973.

Chernow, Fred B., and Genkin, Harold. *Teaching and Administering the High School Alternative Education Program*. West Nyack, New York: Prentice-Hall, 1975.

Coleman, James S. "How Do the Young Become Adults?" *Phi Delta Kappan*, December 1972: 227-30.

_____. "The Children Have Outgrown the Schools," *Psychology Today*, February 1972: 72-82.

Commission on Schools, *Policies and Standards for the Approval of Optional Schools and Special Function Schools, 1976–77*. Boulder, Colorado: North Central Association, 1976.

Cox, Donald W. *The City As a Schoolhouse: The Story of the Parkway Program*. Valley Forge, Pennsylvania: Judson Press, 1972.

Cross, K. Patricia, *et al*. *Planning Non-Traditional Programs*. San Francisco: Jossey-Bass Publishers, 1974.

Deal, Terrence E. "An Organizational Explanation of the Failure of Alternative Secondary Schools," *Educational Researcher*, April 1975: 10-16.

Executive High School Internships of America. *The Executive High School Internships Kit*. New York: Executive High School Internships of America, 1976.

Fantini, Mario D. *Alternative Education: A Source Book for Parents, Teachers, Students and Administrators*. New York: Doubleday, 1976.

_____. *Public Schools of Choice*. New York: Simon & Schuster, 1973.

Faure, Edgar, *et al*. *Learning To Be: The World of Education Today and Tomorrow* (Report of the International Commission on the Development of Education). Paris: UNESCO, 1972.

Finley, G.J. *Business and Education: A Fragile Partnership*. New York: The Conference Board, 1973.

Gibbons, Maurice. *The New Secondary Education: A Phi Delta Kappa Task Force Report*. Bloomington, Indiana: Phi Delta Kappa, Inc., 1976.

_____. "Walkabout: Searching for the Right Passage from Childhood and School," *Phi Delta Kappan*, May 1974: 596-602.

Glatthorn, Allan. *Alternatives in Education: Schools and Programs*. New York: Dodd, Mead, 1975.

Heerman, Barry. *Cooperative Education in Community Colleges: A Sourcebook for Occupational and General Education*. San Francisco: Jossey-Bass Publishers, 1973.

Hruska, Jack. "Cooperative Education: Not for Some, But for All," *Clearing-house*, November 1973: 154-58.

Keeton, Morris T. and Associates. *Experiential Learning: Rationale, Characteristics and Assessment*. San Francisco: Jossey-Bass Publishers, 1976.

Knowles, Asa S., *et al. Handbook of Cooperative Education*. San Francisco: Jossey-Bass Publishers, 1971.

McCarthy, Robert B. "Critical Factors in Alternative Education," National Association of Secondary School Principals *Bulletin*, April 1975: 23-24.

National Association of Secondary School Principals. "Guidelines for School-to-College Transcript Content," *Curriculum Report* 3, No. 5 (April 1974).

_____. *This We Believe: Secondary Schools in a Changing Society* (Report of Task Force on Secondary Schools in a Changing Society). Reston, Virginia: National Association of Secondary School Principals, 1975.

_____. *25 Action Learning Schools*. Reston, Virginia: National Association of Secondary School Principals, 1974.

National Commission on the Reform of Secondary Education. *The Reform of Secondary Education*. New York: McGraw–Hill, 1973.

National Commission on Resources for Youth. *New Roles for Youth in the School and Community*. New York: Citation Press, 1974.

_____. *What Kids Can Do*. New York: National Commission on Resources for Youth, Inc., 1973.

National Committee on Employment of Youth. "Youth in Transition from School to Work," *New Generation* 55, Nos. 2 and 3, 1973.

National Committee on Secondary Education. *American Youth in the Mid-Seventies*. Reston, Virginia: National Association of Secondary School Principals, 1973.

National Institute of Education. *A Comparison of Four Experience-Based Career Education Programs*. Washington, D.C.: National Institute of Education, Department of Health, Education and Welfare, 1976.

_____. *The Community Is the Teacher*. Washington, D.C.: National Institute of Education, Department of Health, Education and Welfare, 1975.

National Panel on High School and Adolescent Education. *The Education of Adolescents: Final Report and Recommendations.* Washington, D.C.: Office of Education, U.S. Department of Health, Education and Welfare, 1976.

National School Boards Association. *Research Report: Alternative Schools.* Evanston, Illinois: National School Boards Association, 1976.

National School Public Relations Association. *Alternative Schools: Pioneering Districts Create Options for Students.* Arlington, Virginia: National School Public Relations Association, 1972.

Oregon School Study Council. "Alternative Education: An Introduction, Special Report on Pasadena, California and a Bibliography," *OSSC Bulletin* 17, No. 10 (June 1974).

Organisation for Economic Co-Operation and Development. *Education and Working Life in Modern Society.* Paris: Organisation for Economic Co-Operation and Development, 1975.

Panel on Youth of the President's Science Advisory Committee, James S. Coleman, Chairman. *Youth: Transition to Adulthood.* Chicago: University of Chicago Press, 1974.

Paskal, Dolores, and Miller, William C. "Managing Controversy About Optional and Alternative Programs," *Educational Leadership*, October 1975: 14-16.

Passow, A. Harry. "Reforming America's High Schools," *Phi Delta Kappan*, May 1975: 587-90.

Saxe, Richard W., ed. *Opening the Schools.* Berkeley, California: McCutchan Publishing Corp., 1972.

Seay, Maurice F., *et al. Community Education: A Developing Concept.* Midland, Michigan: Pendell Publishing Company, 1974.

Smith, Vernon, *et al. Alternatives in Education: Freedom to Choose.* Bloomington, Indiana: Phi Delta Kappa, Inc., 1976.

Special Task Force to the Secretary of Health, Education and Welfare. *Work in America.* Cambridge, Massachusetts: M.I.T. Press, 1973.

U.S. Office of Education and the National Association of Secondary School Principals. *New Dimensions for Educating Youth: A Report on America's Secondary Schools.* Denver: U.S. Office of Education, 1976.

Weinstock, Ruth, ed. *The Greening of the High School*. New York: Educational Facilities Laboratories and I/D/E/A, 1973.

Wigginton, Eliot, ed. *Foxfire 1*. Garden City, New York: Anchor Books, Anchor/Doubleday, 1971.

_____. *Foxfire 2*. Garden City, New York: Anchor Books, Anchor/Doubleday, 1973.

_____. *Foxfire 3*. Garden City, New York: Anchor Books, Anchor/Doubleday, 1975.

_____. *Moments: The Foxfire Experience*. Washington, D.C.: Institutional Development and Economic Affairs Service, Inc.—I/D/E/A, 1975.

Williams, Catherine. *The Community as Textbook*. Bloomington, Indiana: Phi Delta Kappa, Inc., 1975.

Wirtz, Willard, and the National Manpower Institute. *The Boundless Resource: A Prospectus for an Education/Work Policy*. Washington, D.C.: The New Republic Book Company, Inc., 1975.

Wurman, Richard S. *Yellow Pages of Learning Resources*, Cambridge, Massachusetts: The MIT Press, 1972.

APPENDIX C

Supplementary Materials and Services For Experience-Based Learning

The Northwest Regional Educational Laboratory (NWREL) is offering three separate booklets to help school staff organize community-based activities into systematic learning experiences for students. These materials are 8½ x 11," three-hole punched, consumable guides to help students work through three of the experience-based learning components described in Chapter 2 of this book:

- *Student Guide to Writing a Journal*, 16 pp.
- *Student Competencies Guide: Survival Skills for a Changing World. 44 pp.*
- *Student Record of Community Exploration.* 24 pp.

In addition, NWREL is offering *The Community Resource Person's Guide for Experience-Based Learning*, designed especially for resource people to help them create effective learning opportunities for students. 24 pp.

All of these materials are based on more than six years of development and evaluation in NWREL's Education and Work Program.

For price and order information, contact the Office of Marketing and Dissemination, Northwest Regional Educational Laboratory, 710 S.W. Second Avenue, Portland, Oregon 97204.

Training and Technical Assistance

The NWREL staff who developed and tested these unique learning materials can also provide training and technical assistance to programs interested in implementing experience-based learning. These information services include awareness sessions and slide/tape presentations to introduce the newcomer to experience-based education strategies and goals. Further interest can lead to planning and staff training sessions to implement new programs or modify existing ones. NWREL's experienced, skilled staff can provide seasoned advice in designing local program adaptations. Contact Education and Work Program, Northwest Regional Educational Laboratory, 710 S.W. Second Avenue, Portland, Oregon 97204; (503) 248-6822 for additional information on services and costs.

INDEX

237